# Mapping, Connectivity and the Making of European Empires

# Global Epistemics
## In partnership with the Centre for Global Knowledge Studies (*gloknos*)

*Founding Editor:*

Inanna Hamati-Ataya (University of Cambridge)

*Editorial Assistants:*

Felix Anderl and Matthew Holmes (University of Cambridge)

*Editorial Review Board:*

Rigas Arvanitis (Institut de Recherche pour le Développement) | Jana Bacevic (University of Cambridge) | Patrick Baert (University of Cambridge) | Shadi Bartsch-Zimmer (University of Chicago) | Maria Birnbaum (University of Bern) | Avital Bloch (Universidad de Colima) | Jenny Boulboullé (Utrecht University) | Jordan Branch (Brown University) | Sonja Brentjes (Max Planck Institute for the History of Science) | Karine Chemla (Centre National de la Recherche Scientifique & Université de Paris) | David Christian (Macquarie University) | James H. Collier (Virginia Tech) | Steven Connor (University of Cambridge) | Helen Anne Curry (University of Cambridge) | Shinjini Das (University of East Anglia) | Sven Dupré (Utrecht University) | David Edgerton (King's College London) | Juan Manuel Garrido Wainer (Universidad Alberto Hurtado) | Simon Goldhill (University of Cambridge) | Anna Grasskamp (Hong Kong Baptist University) | Clare Griffin (Nazarbayev University) | Marieke Hendriksen (Utrecht University) | Dag Herbjørnsrud (Senter for global og komparativ idéhistorie) | Noboru Ishikawa (Kyoto University) | Christian Jacob (Ecole des Hautes Etudes en Sciences Sociales) | Martin Jones (University of Cambridge) | Katarzyna Kaczmarska (University of Edinburgh) | Isaac A. Kamola (Trinity College, Connecticut) | Alexandre Klein (Université Laval) | Tuba Kocaturk (Deakin University) | Pablo Kreimer (Universidad Nacional de Quilmes) | Michèle Lamont (Harvard University) | Helen Lauer (University of Dar es Salaam) | G.E.R. Lloyd (University of Cambridge) | Carlos López-Beltrán (National Autonomous University of Mexico) | Eric Lybeck (University of Manchester) | Christos Lynteris (University of St Andrews) | Amanda Machin

(Witten-Herdecke University) | Tara Mahfoud (King's College London) | Maximilian Mayer (University of Nottingham Ningbo) | Willard McCarty (King's College London) | Atsuro Morita (Osaka University) | Iwan Morus (Aberystwyth University) | David Nally (University of Cambridge) | John Naughton (University of Cambridge) | Helga Nowotny (ETH Zurich) | Johan Östling (Lund University) | Ingrid Paoletti (Politecnico di Milano) | V. Spike Peterson (University of Arizona) | Helle Porsdam (University of Copenhagen) | David Pretel (The College of Mexico) | Dhruv Raina (Jawaharlal Nehru University) | Amanda Rees (University of York) | Hans-Jörg Rheinberger (Max Planck Institute for the History of Science) | Sarah de Rijcke (Leiden University) | Francesca Rochberg (University of California at Berkeley) | Alexander Ruser (University of Agder) | Anne Salmond (University of Auckland) | Karen Sayer (Leeds Trinity University) | James C. Scott (Yale University) | Elisabeth Simbürger (Universidad de Valparaíso) | Daniel Lord Smail (Harvard University) | Fred Spier (University of Amsterdam) | Swen Steinberg (Queen's University) | Tereza Stöckelová (Czech Academy of Sciences) | Jomo Sundaram (Khazanah Research Institute) | Liba Taub (University of Cambridge) | Daniel Trambaiolo (University of Hong Kong) | Corinna Unger (European University Institute) | Matteo Valleriani (Max Planck Institute for the History of Science) | Stéphane Van Damme (European University Institute) | Andrés Vélez Posada (Universidad EAFIT) | Aparecida Vilaça (National Museum, Brazil) | Simon Werrett (University College London) | Helen Yitah (University of Ghana) | Longxi Zhang (City University of Hong Kong)

tinyurl.com/GlobalEpistemics | tinyurl.com/RLIgloknos

**Titles in the Series:**

*Imaginaries of Connectivity: The Creation of Novel Spaces of Governance*
Edited by Luis Lobo-Guerrero, Suvi Alt and Maarten Meijer

*Mapping, Connectivity and the Making of European Empires*
Edited by Luis Lobo-Guerrero, Laura Lo Presti and Filipe dos Reis

# Mapping, Connectivity and the Making of European Empires

Edited by Luis Lobo-Guerrero,
Laura Lo Presti and Filipe dos Reis

ROWMAN & LITTLEFIELD
*Lanham • Boulder • New York • London*

Rowman & Littlefield
Bloomsbury Publishing Inc, 1359 Broadway, New York, NY 10018, USA
Bloomsbury Publishing Plc, 50 Bedford Square, London, WC1B 3DP, UK
Bloomsbury Publishing Ireland, 29 Earlsfort Terrace, Dublin 2, D02 AY28, Ireland
www.bloomsbury.com

An imprint of The Rowman & Littlefield Publishing Group, Inc.
4501 Forbes Boulevard, Suite 200, Lanham, Maryland 20706
www.rowman.com
Copyright © 2021 by The Rowman & Littlefield Publishing Group, Inc.

*All rights reserved.* No part of this publication may be: i) reproduced or transmitted in any form, electronic or mechanical, including photocopying, recording or by means of any information storage or retrieval system without prior permission in writing from the publishers; or ii) used or reproduced in any way for the training, development or operation of artificial intelligence (AI) technologies, including generative AI technologies. The rights holders expressly reserve this publication from the text and data mining exception as per Article 4(3) of the Digital Single Market Directive (EU) 2019/790.

British Library Cataloguing in Publication Information available

**Library of Congress Cataloging-in-Publication Data**
ISBN: 978-1-5381-4639-2 (cloth)
ISBN: 978-1-5381-4641-5 (electronic)

# Contents

List of Figures ix

Series Editor's Note xiii

Preface: Poseidonians and the Tragedy of Mapping
European Empires xv
*Luis Lobo-Guerrero*

1 Mapping and the Making of Imperial European Connectivity 1
 *Luis Lobo-Guerrero, Laura Lo Presti and Filipe dos Reis*

2 Mapping the Invention of the Early 'Spanish' Empire 19
 *Luis Lobo-Guerrero*

3 Freezing Cartographic Imaginaries: Mapping the Rediscovery
 of Greenland and the Restoring of the Danish Monarchy 51
 *Jeppe Strandsbjerg*

4 Surveying in British North America: A Homology of Property
 and Territory 77
 *Kerry Goettlich*

5 Empires of Science, Science of Empires: Mapping, Centres
 of Calculation and the Making of Imperial Spaces
 in Nineteenth-Century Germany 105
 *Filipe dos Reis*

6 Representing France's Syrian 'Colony without a Flag': Imperial
 Cartographic Strategies at the Margin of the Peace Conference 139
 *Louis Le Douarin*

7   The Cartographic Lives of the Italian Fascist Empire                    175
    *Laura Lo Presti*

Index                                                                        201

About the Editors and Contributors                                           213

# Figures

| | | |
|---|---|---|
| 1.1 | René Magritte, *La Condition Humaine*, 1933, c/o Pictoright Amsterdam 2020. | 4 |
| 2.1 | *Carta de Juan de la Cosa*, 1500. Original at the Museo Naval de Madrid. Courtesy of the Centro Virtual Cervantes, Museo Naval de Madrid. | 27 |
| 2.2 | World Map by Diego Ribeiro, 1529 (The Second Borgian Map). From a facsimile by W. Griggs, 1886. Original in the Museum of Propaganda in Rome. | 37 |
| 2.3 | America's Map by Diego Gutiérrez, Antwerp, 1562 (Americae Sive Qvatae Orbis Partis Nova et Exatissima Descritptio). Courtesy of Library of Congress, Geography and Map Division. | 41 |
| 3.1 | 'The Kinge Christianus His Forde: Names of rodestes, havens, and soundes within this ford'. With permission by Hakluyt Society. | 53 |
| 3.2 | 'The Coast of Groineland: With the lattitudes of the havens and harbors as I fovnde them'. With permission by Hakluyt Society. | 54 |
| 3.3 | Swart's first map – the older one – adding Northern Scandinavia and Greenland to the Ptolemaic Map. The original from ca. 1424 is unknown but a copy from 1427 exists in a later edition. Bibliotheque municipale Nancy Manuscrit 441. By courtesy of the Danish Royal Library. | 63 |
| 3.4 | Section of Mercator's 1606 map of the Arctic. Image in Public Domain. | 64 |
| 4.1 | A Map of Pensilvania, New-Jersey, New-York, and the Three Delaware Counties (Evans and Hebert, 1749) | 78 |

| | | |
|---|---|---|
| 4.2 | Illustration in John Love (1768, 83), *Geodaesia: Or, the Art of Surveying and Measuring Land Made Easy*. Image in Public Domain. | 88 |
| 4.3 | Plat of the Seven Ranges of Townships (Hutchins, Barker, and Carey 1796) | 91 |
| 4.4 | Illustration in Clarence Bowen (1882, 75), *The Boundary Disputes of Connecticut*. Image in Public Domain. | 96 |
| 4.5 | A plan of the west line or parallel of latitude, which is the boundary between the provinces of Maryland and Pensylvania (Mason, Dixon, Smither, and Kennedy 1768). | 101 |
| 5.1 | Map of Africa including itineraries for the 'German Expedition to Inner Africa', Justus Perthes Gotha 1861. | 122 |
| 5.2 | Map of 'Four Martyrs of German Science in Inner-Africa' in *Petermanns Geographische Mitteilungen*, Justus Perthes Gotha 1864. | 125 |
| 5.3 | Map of Africa in register volume of *Petermanns Geographische Mitteilungen*, Justus Perthes Gotha 1865. | 126 |
| 5.4 | The History of the Discovery of the Artic and Antarctic regions in supplementary volume to *Petermanns Geographische Mitteilungen*, Justus Perthes Gotha 1865. | 128 |
| 5.5 | World Map with the North Pole in its centre in supplementary volume to *Petermanns Geographische Mitteilungen*, Justus Perthes Gotha 1865. | 129 |
| 5.6 | The ship *Germania* during the German North Pole Expedition in supplementary volume to *Petermanns Geographische Mitteilungen*, Justus Perthes Gotha 1868. | 131 |
| 6.1 | Bolzé, René. 1920. «Carte des intérêts français au Liban». Published in Congrès français de la Syrie, Congrès français de la syrie et Chambre de commerce de Marseille, 1919. Fascicule 2. Paris; Marseille: E. Champion. Courtesy of the Bibliothèque nationale de France. | 146 |
| 6.2 | 'Syrie. Œuvres françaises' in Comité central syrien. La Syrie devant la Conférence. Paris, 1919. Courtesy of the Bibliothèque nationale de France. | 150 |
| 6.3 | Bernard, Augustin, "Populations de la Syrie" in Comité d'études. 1919. Travaux du comité d'études. Tome 2. Questions européennes. Atlas. Paris: Service géographique de l'Armée. | 153 |
| 6.4 | Sketch of Syria and Mesopotamia attached to the Note on the economic value of Syria sent to the Ministry of Foreign affairs by the Chamber of commerce of Marseilles in July 1915, Archives of the Chamber of Commerce of | |

*Figures* xi

|     | | |
|---|---|---|
| | Marseilles, MQ 5435. Courtesy of the Chambre de commerce de Marseille. | 158 |
| 6.5 | Bolzé, René. 1920. 'Carte des intérêts français au Liban'. Published in Congrès français de la Syrie, Congrès français de la syrie et Chambre de commerce de Marseille, 1919. Fascicule 2. Paris; Marseille: E. Champion. Courtesy of the Bibliothèque nationale de France. | 160 |
| 6.6 | Map of the populations and religions of Syria, in Froidevaux, Henri. 'Les difficultés de la France en Syrie. Leurs causes' *L'Asie Française* 20, no. 179 (février 1920): 43–47. Courtesy of the Bibliothèque nationale de France. | 166 |
| 7.1 | A map of the Italian Fascism's Empire still displayed in Piazza delle Erbe, Padova (Italy). Photograph taken by Giada Peterle. | 184 |
| 7.2 | School report-card showing the progressive imperial conquests of Fascism on the front and the back of the document. Year 1939–1940. Manieri Collection. Courtesy of Enrico Manieri. | 188 |
| 7.3 | Examples of colonial postcards with cartographic representations of the empire. Author's photograph. | 189 |
| 7.4 | Video still from 'Sulle orme dei nostri pionieri' (De Feo, 1936). Copyrights: Istituto Luce. The documentary represents several transformations and uses of the map in the cinematographic narrative of the empire. | 192 |

# Series Editor's Note

*Mapping, Connectivity and the Making of European Empires* is the second volume of a trilogy that explores how particular imaginaries and practices of connectivity bring new historical spaces into existence and infuse them with political meaning and efficacy. As a companion to *Imaginaries of Connectivity and the Creation of Novel Spaces of Governance* already published in this series, this volume investigates the connectivity effects of mapping and map-making on the constitution, materialization and deployment of imperial power in different configurations and stages of Europe's imperial history.

Empire is here never assumed as the all-knowing, almighty, almost inevitable force the knowledge-power lens often makes it to be. Empires in the making are revealed as unpredictable networks of potential agencies, where the knowledge, ignorance and imagination of makers, mediators and consumers conspire to turn blank or fanciful spaces into real and desirable territories carrying new connections, resources, partitions and performative worldviews.

In carefully decentring the site of imperial knowledge from seats of power to multiple loci of epistemic praxis, this volume offers us illuminating snapshots of historical connections established in mind, matter and space being translated into unpredictable pathways of expansion, rule and control. In doing so they enjoin us to reflect on the sources of the worldviews and relations we are about to create or lose, as we engage with our own spaces of global connectivity.

Inanna Hamati-Ataya<br>
(Cambridge, 21 December 2020)

# Preface

## *Poseidonians and the Tragedy of Mapping European Empires*

### Luis Lobo-Guerrero

*Mapping, Connectivity and the Making of European Empires* is a collective reflection on the connectivities and spatial imaginaries immanent to maps, map-making, map-using and map interpretation from a specific Western (epistemological) perspective. Such reflection betrays a continuous tragedy which results from re-discovering and coming to terms with the idea that an allegedly secular and scientific approach to mapping the world relies intensely on sedimented cosmological imaginaries of space and power and their multiple ways of life. These, in turn, challenge a Western pretension of uniform spatial objectivity and factualness. In such tragedy, the space of the world's others becomes evident in the process of making explicit the practices, beliefs, conducts, principles and economic considerations upon which European ways of mapping imperial acts, aspirations and failures have operated.

Perhaps nobody has better described this tragedy as Constantine Cavafy unknowingly did in his poem *Poseidonians*.

> The Poseidonians forgot the Greek language
> after so many centuries of mingling
> with Tyrrhenians, Latins, and other foreigners.
> The only thing surviving from their ancestors
> was a Greek festival, with beautiful rites,
> with lyres and flutes, contests and garlands.
> And it was their habit towards the festival's end
> to tell each other about their ancient customs
> and once again to speak Greek names
> that hardly any of them still recognized.
> And so their festival always had a melancholy ending
> because they remembered that they too were Greeks,
> they too once upon a time were citizens of Magna Graecia.

> But how they'd fallen now, how they'd changed,
> living and speaking like barbarians,
> cut off so disastrously from the Greek way of life.
>
> (Cavafy 1998)

In Greek mythology, Poseidon, god of the sea, storms, earthquakes and horses, was known for his bad temper, greediness and moodiness. His ways prevailed, and insult would be answered with vengeance. His was the Truth. When Odysseus, on his voyage from Troy back to Ithaka, blinded the god's son, Poseidon sent him storms, made him shipwreck and caused on him a ten-year delay (Homer 2006). On the other hand, Tyrrhenians, Latins and other barbarians represented alternative ways of life which, in Cavafy's poem, slowly changed that of Poseidonians and made them live and speak like barbarians, showing them that there is always the possibility of being otherwise, and simultaneously so, even if in their memory lived an ideal past, an ideal truth.

As explored by the various authors in this book, the 'beautiful rites, with lyres and flutes, contests and garlands' of the various practices of mapping European empires, become sites of interrogation where the knowledges underlying lines, symbols, monsters, monuments, voids, colours and styles in maps can be politically historicized in their contextual complexity. In doing so, it is possible to reconstruct the stratified conditions of possibility (cf. Hacking 2006, 136) of specific spatial (imperial) imaginaries and their attempt to connect ideas, people, places, values and interests into (coherent) political aspirations and projects. It is possible to observe that the very terms under which these elements are connected, or attempted to be so, can be explored to reveal the creativity and resourcefulness involved in making them possible. In this respect, *Mapping, Connectivity and the Making of European Empires* is an attempt to approach maps and mapping practices as experimental sites from which to make strange what has become invisible over time and through normalized mapping practices. The imaginaries and processes behind the making, consciously or not, of spatial orders, leave their traces in maps and mapping.

As good barbarians, map-makers, map-users and map interpreters are the result of diverse experiences and interactions with cultures, contexts and power relations over time. The life that creates, uses and interprets maps is always more than the knowledge and the ideas through which individuals are educated, trained and normalized. It exceeds their role of workers, citizens, market players, religious believers, sensual beings and political subjects. Such life reveals the experience of being in particular moments and places, in specific worlds. The imaginary of map barbarians always exceeds the frames upon which they seek to know the world through what Foucault referred to as the 'already encoded eye' and 'reflexive knowledge'(Foucault 2002, xxii).

The tragedy of mapping European empires, where the alleged objectivity of the map reveals the life excess of those involved in it, is therefore a wonderful opportunity for us, to cease being Poseidonians, to reflect on our perceived Greekness and embrace our barbarism by assuming an attitude of wondering about how, and why, we see the world through maps in the ways we do. The tragedy opens for us a space in which to identify markers that can help us understand the sedimented cosmological imaginaries of space and power that seem to have been forgotten when the ink of the maps dried out. Our role as barbarians is therefore to think with maps, rather than through them, about the lives, forms of life and relationships of power that the map is anxiously wanting to reveal. In doing so, we come to realize that the alleged empires depicted by maps were never more than an aspiration which mapmakers never truly realized. The tragedy of mapping reveals the brittleness of the very idea of an empire as a projection of spatialized power.

## A WONDERING EPISTEMIC COMMUNITY

The origin of this book responds to acts of curiosity imbued by an attitude of wondering about how cartography could be 'domesticated' as an empirical space from which to interrogate relationships of power and of empire-making from the situated perspective of modern Europe. The use of the term *domestication* reveals, of course, an attempt to relate cartography with our intellectual 'home', normally, if not innocently, understood as a disciplinary ground. Coming from the wider discipline of International Relations, at first, but with a broad understanding of it as the study of order, power and governance unconstrained by (political) borders and temporalizations, it came as a surprise, through initial discussions, that not much work had been produced from 'within' International Relations on this problem (see chapter 1). With at first skeletal knowledge of the serious contributions made by scholars engaged with critical cartographic studies, I initially posed the idea of constituting a small research group with the aim of exploring the epistemological conditions underlying the role of maps as instruments of power, and of supporting each other on learning about this topic. The idea was that this would allow us to produce an edited volume to inspire others in joining us in these reflections.

The book project thus began in the context of a visit I made to the University of Erfurt in December 2017 under an Erasmus teaching mobility grant. Widely inspired by a tour of some of the collections and globes kept at the University's research library at Schloss Friedenstein in Gotha, organized by Filipe dos Reis who was one of my hosts, the focus of exploring how mapping and cartographic imaginaries related, started to be developed. Filipe was then exploring together with Zeynep Gülşah Çapan some maps at the Justus Perthes publishing house at Gotha and had a particular interest in understanding how the idea of Germandom and Germanness figured in those maps. This initial enthusiasm led us to brainstorm further about the possible contents of an edited volume during a workshop held two months later at La Sage, in the Swiss Alps, as part of a consortium we had created between colleagues at universities of Groningen, Lausanne, Oslo, Brussels and Erfurt (the GLOBE consortium). The workshop sponsored a broad discussion on epistemologies of order, power and governance and allowed us to engage with some complex literature on cartography and the creation of space.

Months later, within the context of a call launched by the European International Studies Association (EISA) for proposals on exploratory symposia to be held at Rapallo, Italy, in September 2018, Filipe and I decided to take it as an opportunity to give shape to a small research team. To broaden the scope, we invited a cultural geographer, Laura Lo Presti, whom I had met in April 2017 at a workshop in Duisburg on 'Mapping, Mercator and Modernity'. Laura had published a very inspiring piece in an edited volume that came out of that event on the problem of how to reframe cartographic exhaustion at a time of mapping excess. She would bring an erudite insight on critical cartography and a fresh cultural geography angle to the group, as well as a solid southern European perspective. We also invited Jeppe Strandsbjerg whom I had to find a way to contact since he had left a fancy associate professorship at the Copenhagen Business School some years before to work with an academic publisher in Denmark. Jeppe, who had published his doctoral thesis as one of the two existing books on cartography and International Relations, enthusiastically embraced our invitation and brought a mature angle to the wider problem of space and power as well as a perspective from a Nordic life experience. To complete the group, we invited Kerry Goettlich who was then working on his doctoral thesis at the London School of Economics on the problem of boundaries and linear borders in International Relations and was engaging with the details of practices of surveyance in the British colonies. He would bring his knowledge of surveying together with an Anglo-Saxon experience to the group. I would contribute through my work on the epistemologies of mapping, my reflections on historical epistemology and the politics of global connectivity, and I would provide the institutional support of my chair at Groningen, and would facilitate leadership and coordination to the team. We were ready to apply for an exploratory symposium grant . . . and we got it.

At Rapallo, with the energizing Italian riviera as frame, we took the opportunity to learn from each other's work and from what we had found particularly interesting in the course of exploring this topic. Hoping for the inspiration that Nietzsche had derived from the mountains and sea at that location when writing his *Thus Spoke Zarathustra*, we worked on a programme where everyone contributed to through their own writing on maps, three pieces of scholarship that had influenced our thoughts on the topic, as well as a 2,000-word reflection on what we all thought maps, as empirical spaces for analysis, had to offer to a critical understanding of empire. This all prepared us for very fruitful conversations. We learned enormously from each other, enjoyed our walk-and-talk sessions, and on the basis of our individual reflections, began to focus the project. As a result, we chose to continue with the problem of mapping and the making of empire privileging epistemological elements without falling into nationalist narratives or disciplinary angles. We agreed to start working on some draft pieces for a subsequent workshop in the spring of 2019 which Jeppe kindly offered to host and sponsor.

By now, we were operating as a research group with five different, if overlapping, small research projects. To facilitate interaction and work, we all contributed to, and shared, a digital library and an online archive. Jeppe and Laura were offered visiting research fellowships at the University of Groningen to facilitate access to further academic resources. During the course of the project, it was very reassuring to see how we were all advancing in our endeavours. In August 2019, Filipe had just completed his PhD and left Erfurt to join us at the University of Groningen as assistant professor. Laura remained associate researcher at the University of Padova, and her visiting fellowship at Groningen was extended for another period. Jeppe has continued with his exciting projects as senior editor at the Danish publishing house Djøf Forlag and has now partially returned to the academic world with the Danish Institute for International Studies. Kerry completed his PhD in 2019 and moved onto a lectureship at the University of Reading.

As the group consolidated, and as a way to reach out to other students and colleagues working on this topic, we launched a call for papers for a panel on Epistemologies of Mapping and the Making of Empire at the Pan-European International Studies Conference in Sofia, September 2019. The result was very positive, and we constituted a panel that attracted an engaged audience. The conference also coincided with the launch of the Global Epistemics Book Series with Rowman & Littlefield International edited by Inanna Hamati-Ataya and the presentation of its first book, *Imaginaries of Connectivity and the Creation of Novel Spaces of Governance*, more on which will be said in the following.

Our second meeting was a workshop entitled 'Mapping and the Making of Empire' which took place at Snekkersten, Denmark, on 1–3 May 2019. Jeppe, as host, took us first on a guided tour of the map collection of the Royal Library of Denmark in Copenhagen where we had the opportunity to enjoy, among others, a large map of Christian VI of Denmark and Norway's visit to Norway in 1733, a beautiful example of itinerary maps used to display territorial possession. We then made our way to Snekkersten, on the northeast of the island of Zealand, north of Copenhagen. Our objective was to have extensive discussions on how to interrogate maps as empirical objects to reveal the historical rationalities of power involved in the making, projection and reading of spatial imaginaries in given moments. The workshop was aimed to help us understand not only the effects but also the production and translation involved in imperial map-making. To spice up our work, Jeppe took us on a second tour, this time to the nearby Kronborg, a XVI C castle (Elsinore in Shakespeare's play *Hamlet*) from where the famous Sound Dues (or Sound Tolls) were collected. These were a tax charged by the king on foreign ships crossing the Danish Sound connecting the North Sea with the Baltic between 1497 and 1857.[1] During our walk to the castle we could also see the island of Hven where Tycho Brahe had established in 1576, under the patronage of Frederick II of Denmark, the observatory castle of Uraniborg – after Urania, the muse of astronomy. Urania is famous for being the first custom-built observatory of modern Europe, the last built before the invention of the telescope. Observing the monumentalization of the history of a site of state revenue at a key geopolitical chokepoint for North European maritime connectivity, together with the location and story of a state-sponsored astronomical observatory, and having enjoyed the wonderful maps of the Royal Library's collection, was inspiration enough for us to proceed with our individual study of particular cases as chapters for the book.

Following the second workshop, we constituted an editorial team with Laura Lo Presti and Filipe dos Reis, and myself, to provide some clear markers that would allow us to produce a book. At this stage we invited Louis Le Dourain to contribute a chapter drawing on his work on mapping parts of the French (post)colonial space. With all the authors in place, and after the EISA Sofia conference in September, we had planned to hold a third workshop in Groningen in the spring of 2020 to share advanced drafts and enable cross-fertilization. By late February that year, however, the Covid-19 pandemic resulted in restricted travel in Europe and the partial closure of universities. Due to the extra workload that resulted from performing our academic duties online, we decided to cancel the final workshop, continue to work individually on the chapters, provide detailed editorial reviews and support to our authors and collaborate amongst the editorial team remotely toward the completion of the book.

## BOOK TRILOGY ON CONNECTIVITY AND THE (IM)MATERIAL CREATION OF SPACES

*Mapping, Connectivity and the Making of European Empires* is the second volume of a trilogy of edited books devoted to exploring how the problem of connectivity relates to the (im)material creation of spaces in time. The general problematic of the trilogy addresses connectivity as a quasi-transcendental category of thought that enables particular forms of political orders, reveals the exercise of specific relationships of power and materializes in regimes of governance in given times and spaces (see Lobo-Guerrero,

Alt, and Meijer 2019, 1–3). Connectivity is usually invoked but normally not thought of and reflected upon. It is difficult to think of it in the abstract, although it becomes visible when approached in relation to any political and spatial practice. It allows deep reflections on the complex conditions of possibility of the terms under which something is made to connect and disconnect, or remain connected. An apparently banal problem, it enshrines the very practice of politics and the production of space(s), and allows for, as Michael Shapiro put it in his review of the first volume, a creative indisciplinarity. Seeking to explore the developing of an original approach to ontopolitical connectivity, as Larry George nicely stated in his review, the trilogy aims to firmly locate connectivity as a central problem in the analysis of order, power and governance in time and space.

The first volume, *Imaginaries of Connectivity and the Creation of Novel Spaces of Governance*, addressed the problem of how the creation of novel spaces of governance relates to imaginaries of connectivity in particular historical and geographical settings. This second volume explores the problem of connectivity in relation to the use of maps and mapping practices in the attempt to make modern European empires. The third volume, currently at a stage of conception, will explore the problem of navigation and connectivity in relation to the invention of spatial orders. Common to all three volumes are the active practices of creation, making and invention, which betray political agency. Focusing on imaginaries, mapping and navigation as complex empirical sites of investigation, the books seek to 'ground' the analysis of connectivity on specific fields of power relations. Analysing novel spaces of governance, European empires and spatial orders as connectivity effects, the volumes aim to make a distinct contribution to the study of connectivity as productive of specific spatial-political formations.

## ACKNOWLEDGEMENTS

As in any collaborative project, many institutions and people intervene in making it possible. We wish to express our gratitude to the University of Groningen, its Research Institute for the Study of Culture (ICOG), and the members of the Chair Group on History and Theory of International Relations for institutional support and active encouragement. We also want to thank the European International Studies Association for funding our exploratory workshop, the Copenhagen Business School as well as Jeppe Strandsbjerg and Leonard Seabrook for facilitating the second workshop, Oliver Kessler and members of his Chair on International Relations at Erfurt, as well as the GLOBE consortium and participants of the doctoral training schools organized by Jean-Christophe Graz in Leysin in February 2018 and 2019 where parts of some of the chapters of the book were presented. Naturally, we want to thank our authors Louis Le Douarin, Kerry Goettlich, Jeppe Strandsbjerg, Laura Lo Presti, Filipe dos Reis and Luis Lobo-Guerrero for their enthusiastic commitment and patience. Through their engagement and energy this book is more than the sum of its chapters, it is the result of an intensive and engaged collaboration: a connectivity effect!

Last but not least, we want to thank the editor of the Global Epistemics book series, Inanna Hamati-Ataya, for her enthusiastic support and confidence, and our editor at Rowman & Littlefield International, Dhara Snowden, for her commitment to our project. We hope this current book will continue with the tradition of frontier scholarship established by the series.

Luis Lobo-Guerrero

## NOTE

1. The Sound Toll Registers, the historical register of the Sound Dues, remains one of the most accessible sources for maritime and seaborne trade history in the early modern period in Northern Europe. Access to the registers and research about it has been made available by the project Sound Toll Registers Online, led by Dr. Jan Willem Veluwenkamp, University of Groningen: http://www.soundtoll.nl/index.php/en/over-het-project/str-online, accessed 29 October 2020.

## REFERENCES

Cavafy, Constantine P. 1998. The Poseidonians. In *Collected Poems*, translated by Edmund Keelye and Philip Sheered, 141. London: Chatto and Windus.
Foucault, Michel. 2002. *The Order of Things: An archaeology of the human sciences*. London: Routledge.
Hacking, Ian. 2006. *The Emergence of Probability*. Cambridge: Cambridge University Press.
Homer. 2006. *The Odyssey*, tranlsated by Robert Fagles, London: Penguin.
Lobo-Guerrero, Luis, Suvi Alt, and Maarten Meijer. 2019. 'Introduction'. In *Imaginaries of Connectivity: The Creation of Novel Spaces of Governance*, edited by Luis Lobo-Guerrero, Suvi Alt, and Maarten Meijer, 1–11. London: Rowman & Littlefield.

*Chapter 1*

# Mapping and the Making of Imperial European Connectivity

Luis Lobo-Guerrero, Laura Lo Presti
and Filipe dos Reis

> In that Empire, the Art of Cartography attained such Perfection that the map of a single Province occupied the entirety of a City, and the map of the Empire, the entirety of a Province. In time, those Unconscionable Maps no longer satisfied, and the Cartographers' Guilds struck a Map of the Empire whose size was that of the Empire, and which coincided point for point with it. The following Generations, who were not so fond of the Study of Cartography as their Forebears had been, saw that that vast Map was Useless, and not without some Pitilessness was it, that they delivered it up to the Inclemencies of Sun and Winters. In the Deserts of the West, still today, there are Tattered Ruins of that Map, inhabited by Animals and Beggars; in all the Land there is no other Relic of the Disciplines of Geography.
>
> (Borges 1999)

Jorge Luis Borges's very short story *On Exactitude in Science*, quoted as epigraph to this introduction, poses the problem of politics in relation to issues of accuracy and precision in spatial representation. The politics of spatiality he depicts is not simply a technical matter of scale, but one of representing the meaning of the experience of power in time and space. The problem is not simple. It invites reflections on the very idea of representation, on its objects, subjects, practices and epistemologies. It also demands careful thought with regard to the relationship between the depiction of the expected materialization of power in space (the map), the knowledge through which this is done (cartography and geography), and its effects on the observer (and the mapmaker). Taken as a whole, Borges's map highlights the fallacy of an empire attempting to represent itself through maps.

Maps have been assumed by many, at different times, as authoritative and valid sources from which historical facts can be ascertained, which are in turn used to legitimate nationalist, economic and legalistic narratives of all kinds. Moreover, maps have been used as devices for the representation and dissemination of spatial ideas, as objective and incontestable facts. Cartography has been used to legitimize the rights of property over land (e.g. cadastral maps and plans), to debate jurisdictional and territorial boundaries (e.g. Weissberg 1963, Ford 1999, Rajkovic 2018), and to validate claims to discovery and sovereignty (cf. MacMillan 2003), to name but some. However arguable those ideas are, as they will be discussed in the following, they *represent* a particular way of understanding maps and cartography and relate strongly with established orders, power relations and forms of governance. Such form of representation assumes a highly debatable stable correspondence between the depicted and the real. Multiple elements play a role in dequalifying the map as an authoritative image, many of which are explored in this volume through particular cases of how mapping contributed to the creation of imaginaries of empire.

In a recent book, Matthew Edney defined cartography as 'at once a practice found in all socially complex cultures and a particular historical formation associated with Western imperialism' (2019, 5). To argue for the problematic relationship between the use (and abuse) of maps in creating and reasserting European imperial narrative is not, in fact, a new idea. For example, Mark Neocleous noted that cartography has a 'predisposition towards colonialism and imperialism' (2003, 419), and Brian Harley famously claimed that maps served as 'weapons of imperialism' as 'maps anticipate empire' (1988, 282). Maps are expected to create spaces for further expansion and might turn them in the end into administrative units for colonization. This aspect was also stressed by Matthew Edney's essay on the 'irony of imperial mapping' (2009), which was part of the Kenneth Nebenzahl Jr. Lectures, and printed in an edited volume on *The Imperial Map* (Akerman 2009), and where Edney contrasted the cartographic discourse around the 'state' with the one around 'empire'. While the former was mainly driven by the idea that its 'participants inhabit, or at least own, the lands being mapped', the latter, in turn, is 'constructed through cartographic discourse that represent a territory for the benefit of one group but that exclude the inhabitants of the territories represented' (Edney 2009, 13). The idea of 'imperial mapping' is thus an ironic act, Edney continued: 'Postulating as it does a double audience: the population in the mapped territories remains ignorant while another population is actively enabled and empowered to know the mapped territory' (Edney 2009, 13). This idea was further developed by a follow-up of the collection, based on another Kenneth Nebenzahl Jr. Lectures discussing *Decolonizing the Map* (Akerman 2017).

Contributing to contemporary debates on mappings and empires in the history and theory of international relations, human geography and in the critical history of cartography, this volume seeks to collectively explore how maps can be approached, experimentally, to understand the making of European empires through the forms of connectivity they seek to portray. Rehearsing mapping's past and its multifarious relations with European imperial orders is not merely a historical exercise to contribute to a global history of cartography, which would sound quite redundant in the light of the already many contributions to the topic. What binds the several interventions in this volume is rather the awareness that looking at a particular moment of the past with composite methodologies and interdisciplinary gazes may harbour potential observations on the context-embedded relations between mapping, connectivity and European empire to which we are not yet attuned.

While cartography, historically, is a privileged instrument of thought, imagination, research and production of geography, within the academic field of International Relations, maps and cartography have only begun to be studied. Jordan Branch says that mapping 'shapes the conditions of possibility of how actors conceive space, territory, and political authority' (2014, 41). As such, 'maps, like theories, shape our understanding of the world by highlighting – and obscuring – particular spatial and social features' (Branch 2014, 36). This approach focuses mainly on the governance effects of cartography. An alternative position reconstructs instead how transformations in European cartography between the fifteenth and seventeenth century created new imaginaries of space – and the idea of territory itself (Strandsbjerg 2010; see also Elden 2013). This book continues on that tradition and focuses on the processes of production and translation of maps, and the epistemological analysis of the imaginaries of connectivity they depict, in an attempt to reveal their contribution to the making of empire.

## PROBLEMATIZING REPRESENTATION IN MAPPING

What characterizes traditional scholarship on map studies is a direct challenge to the previously mentioned representational approach. Their critique is not new. In line with Borges's story, originally written in 1945, other artists and thinkers were puzzled by the wider problem of representation throughout the early twentieth century. René Magritte, for example, formulated a critique which was later developed in different ways and registers in, amongst others, Jacques Derrida's idea of deconstruction (Derrida 1997), Michel Foucault's role of problematization (Foucault 1984) and Gilles Deleuze and Félix Guattari's approach to the assemblage (Deleuze and Guattari 2004). In his two paintings from 1933 and 1935 entitled *The Human Condition,* Magritte offered a critique of the objectivity of the image and the subjectivity of the viewer, as well as the flawed logics of representation that support these perspectives. His first painting illustrates the point nicely (see figure 1.1.). In it, as described by the Magritte Organisation, he

> displays an easel placed inside a room and in front of a window. The easel holds an unframed painting of a landscape that seems in every detail contiguous with the landscape seen outside the window. At first, one automatically assumes that the painting on the easel depicts the portion of the landscape outside the window that it hides from view. After a moment's consideration, however, one realizes that this assumption is based upon a false premise: that is, that the imagery of Magritte's painting is real, while the painting on the easel is a representation of that reality. In fact, there is no difference between them. Both are part of the same painting, the same artistic fabrication. It is perhaps to this repeating cycle, in which the viewer, even against his will, sees the one as real and the other as representation, that Magritte's title makes reference.
>
> (Magritte Organisation 2020)

**Figure 1.1.** René Magritte, *La Condition Humaine*, 1933. © Rene Magritte La Condition Humaine 1933 c/o Pictoright Amsterdam 2020.

By placing the viewer 'both inside the room within the painting and outside in the real landscape' (as Magritte was quoted in Gablik 1973, 87), whilst recognizing the externality of the viewer with regard to the painting, Magritte advanced what in critical map studies has been recently labelled as a *post-representational* approach to mapping (Dodge, Kitchin, and Perkins 2009, 10–23). Such an approach recognizes the performative character of the viewer, the map-maker and the publisher – as well as the market in which it circulates – the cartographic elements involved (e.g. lines, scale, projection, symbols, materials) and, as we argue collectively throughout the chapters in this book, the knowledge formations involved in contributing the possibility of each of these elements. Whilst the disciplinary apparatus of cartography has been variously unpacked with its own historical legacy and system of belief, the post-representational approach has challenged and integrated with new insights the field of map studies. Considering maps as always mappings, scholars have brought attention to the processes, practices and performances through which 'maps emerge into the world to do their work' (Dodge, Perkins, and Kitchin 2009, 231). Such work, whether governmental or subaltern, practical or imaginative, logistic or communicative, majestic or banal, suggests that not only are there different graphic modes of mapping to be explored but also different performative practices of mapping. This performativity should be traced back to the uses, feelings, debates and actions that are generated when interacting with the cartographic sensorium. This means that even if a map is inherently an abstract representation, the process through which it is created, used and perceived is certainly not. What the various chapters of this volume attempt to achieve is thus to situate the reader in the position of not believing in what he or she sees at first glance: that is, not confusing the immobile representation (the map) with the unstable process from which it derives (mapping).

The term *map-making* should already intuitively suggest that cartography is always a process, the process of making, creating or better, as Luis Lobo-Guerrero argues in the second chapter of this book, *inventing* space through symbolic and inscriptive patterns that change, although slowly, over time. In contrast to origins, invention emphasizes novelty, fabrication, contingency and politics of origins. The cartographer Denis Wood, however, distinguishes between mapping as a cognitive process aimed at tracing and mediating relationships with the environment, and cartography (or map-making), as requiring the inscription of such spatial relations into a stable object – the map – which adheres to specific and political projects (Wood 1993). In this volume, Lobo-Guerrero furthermore problematizes the tension between mapping and cartography, considering mapping a rational process of spatial actualization that transcends the materiality of the cartographic object, though requiring the visual and perceptual apparatus of the map to move from a state of latency to one of external efficacy.

Thinking within the context of post-representational mapping, the urgency to read the map as an open process concerns the act of creating, circulating and interpreting maps. Oscillating from debates over the material and symbolic space depicted by maps of empire to the epistemological, social and political processes that precede, accompany and follow their materialization (i.e. cartographic acts), the chapters of this book differently unfold the sense of the map and mapping as the result of a series of always emerging political, relational and contextual practices. Practices that may not even have, at their embryonic stage, any relation with a Eurocentric and modern conception of cartography, as the ones analysed by Jeppe Strandsbjerg in the third chapter of this book illustrate the point.

In this volume, we sympathize with the need of going beyond the monolithic readings of cartography, approaching instead the formation and use of map-making in its plurality, movements, contingencies and differences. In this respect, Kerry Goettlich avers in his chapter that the significance of maps may go beyond mere representations of rhetorical power, and they can have effects which appear unrelated or even contrary to their aims. Within the concerns of post-representational cartography, the work on representation requires in fact to understand also what happens when a map is put into circulation. Once published, maps begin an autonomous life, often conflicting with the initial intentions of their creators, and activate various exponential circuits and dynamics: departing from various 'centres of calculations' (Latour 1987), they circulate either within epistemic communities or quotidian places. Different levels of post-representational analysis of maps and mapping are brought effectively together by Louis Le Dourain (chapter 4): the networks of map-makers, colonial circles and diplomats; the performativity of maps and how these maps create imperial spaces; and the use of specific genres of thematic maps (population, economy, transport). Filipe dos Reis also foregrounds a 'process-focused understanding of mapping' that helps to reconstruct those epistemological traces that become unseen once the map has been produced and normalized as a social vehicle within the horizon of the modern empire. Blank spaces, in his case, are not accounted 'as "passive" spaces of non-knowledge but rather seen as actively produced by incorporating certain sources (or "authorities") and silencing others' (p. 108).

In line with the efforts of a post-representational analysis and contrasting the traditional tendency of critical historical cartography to deconstruct the hidden agenda of map-makers, Laura Lo Presti proposes to shift attention from the moment of production of maps to that of their consumption. Once incorporated into objects of everyday life, maps become part of our 'material culture' (Cosgrove 1999), and their messages need to be deconstructed at the crossroad of intention and expectation, and between production and reception.

In short, cartography and practices of mapping explored by the contributors of this book show that the history of mapping is a multifaceted history of the unstable politics of representation underlying any map. The idea of fact in a map, and of a map as a fact, requires a careful epistemological engagement with the details around which knowledge formations give rise to specific cartographic objects. The interpretation of the rhetoric in a map, as J. B. Harley put it, is an interrogation of objects such as lines, scale, projection, empty spaces. Those are in turn mediated by the imaginary of the map-maker and the knowledge supporting his creations, the always historically located imaginary of the map observer and user, and the anachronistic character of current knowledge (Harley 1989).

## CONNECTIVITY EFFECTS AND SPATIAL IMAGINARIES

Whereas it is by now well known that cartography is a practice of space-making, it is yet to be understood how the knowledge practices involved in map-making relate to the making of European empires as connectivity effects. Moving beyond the challenging relationships between the use of maps in creating and reasserting European imperial narratives, and drawing on the post-representational approach to maps and cartography, this volume takes the debate on the usefulness of maps as sites for the study of the relationality of power a step forward by focusing on *the forms of connectivity* the different maps and mapping experiences studied by our authors, created, attempted and/or challenged. As the second volume of a trilogy of books aimed at exploring the problem of connectivity in relation to the making of spaces of governance, it follows *Imaginaries of Connectivity: The Creation of Novel Spaces of Governance* (Lobo-Guerrero, Alt, and Meijer 2019). This argues, in particular, that the relationality of power must not simply be described and analysed in relation to hierarchies and forms of domination, but also with regard to the connectivity effects it creates. Such effects are not automatic processes or result from linear causal logics, they are the outcome of complex strategizations, conscious or not, through which disparate elements get connected with each other in such a way that a novel effect is produced (Lobo-Guerrero 2012). This is illustrated in this volume, for example, in how Kerry Goettlich approaches the notion of connectivity by borrowing the concept of 'homology' from Patricia Owens (2015), to show how ideas, protocols and practices at the basis of property mapping were transferred from the making of property boundaries to that of *imperial* boundaries. Filipe dos Reis provides another example when he approaches connectivity as a symbolical and graphic space represented *in* maps, that corresponds to the 'back-and-forth' work of accumulation and circulation of ideas, tools, maps that continuously invented and fabricated the idea of empire.

More broadly, *Mapping, Connectivity and the Making of European Empires* poses questions on how to explore the 'configuration' of such mapping experiences that, as the term suggests, results from a particular way of *connecting* parts or components. Such connections do not just happen but do so under specific terms, which are worthy of investigation since they give away the operation of very specific practices of power. Engaging with the terms under which something is made to connect, or disconnect, and the connectivity effects this creates, involves a careful analysis of the epistemological conditions under which the representation of space, in time, materializes in maps. Rather than conceiving connectivity as a rational impulse of establishing a new imperial order in Greenland, Strandsbjerg advances, for instance, a temporal understanding of connectivity, and considers that 'Danish-Norwegian mappings of Greenland, and the route to the island, were driven by a desire to re-establish contact, ensure sovereignties and thus secure dominion over these far away and mythical lands' (p. 52).

An approach to connectivity also requires composite methodologies that explore the construction of an empire emerging through the action, interaction, circulation and collision of different mapping's representational practices and interests. In this sense, Louis Le Dourain traces different levels of connectivity, focusing not only on representations of networks and transport systems in maps but also on the circuits and venues (e.g. congresses) where they were produced and presented to a broader audience made of political leaders and geographers. Connectivity effects are thus unfolded throughout the chapters in very different ways; on the one hand, by seeing their visual materialization on maps and, on the other hand, by discussing their emergence through maps as maps circulate in networks (and thereby create and stabilize these networks). Maps, in this respect, are better conceived as either 'immutable mobiles' (Latour 1987) or 'mutable mobiles' (Edney 2019). While, on the one hand, the notion of immutable mobiles highlights the relative stability of maps as material objects and their role in stabilizing networks and imaginaries of space (necessity), to speak of mutable mobiles, on the other hand, emphasizes the instability of maps, how they are permanently reinscribed and translated and how maps transform spatial imaginaries (contingency). By approaching maps and cartography in such a way, we are able to highlight the complex negotiations and contestations of imaginaries of the world of which empire is but one manifestation. To argue that connectivity effects, deployed in maps and and enacted though maps, can be approached to interrogate space-making, requires an engagement with the idea of imaginary, which as argued in the first volume of the trilogy, 'is more mundane as it appears' (Lobo-Guerrero, Alt, and Meijer 2019, 3). Instead of assuming connectivity as a given,

> imaginaries can be approached as empirical spaces from which to observe the creative processes productive of connectivity. In turn, these processes can

be interrogated through the ideas, practices, beliefs and material objects and conditions that combined in specific ways . . . give rise to novel specifications of orders interpreted as constituting reality. In other words, imaginaries can be used to reveal the novel terms that are to constitute the ground for political decision and action.

(Lobo-Guerrero, Alt, and Meijer 2019, 4)

As such, Lobo-Guerrero's chapter reconstructs how maps outline novel imaginaries of connectivity in the XVI C 'Spanish' empire. Following Pagden's provocative claim that there never was a 'Spanish' empire (Pagden 1998, 3), Lobo-Guerrero identifies different imperial modes and manifestations, all of them connecting space and power differently.

Highlighting the visual and material dynamic performances of maps in many contexts of everyday life during the Italian Fascism's Empire, Lo Presti stresses the idea that connectivity to the empire can be experienced at the level of imaginary: by focusing on the map as a multisensorial experience – a touchable, observable, audible medium – connectivity becomes 'a multisensorial ritual', where the imaginal empire of fascism becomes understandable by larger strata of the population. Further, by addressing the temporal narrative plotted in the granite of large maps or in the celluloid of newsreels, connectivity emerges as a chronomobile frame, overlapping the glories of the Old Roman Empire to the fascist present in order to manipulate imperial future claims in a manner similar to the one addressed by Strandsbjerg in this book. As an output of heterogeneous movements and a further solicitor of global mobilities, mapping practices cannot be easily disentangled from imaginaries of connectivity, circulations and networks they contribute to enact.

## MAPPING IMPERIAL ASPIRATIONS

By exploring the imaginaries of the world in the mapping of Western modern empires, the book also links to the burgeoning literature on the history of international relations and empire (Barkawi and Laffey 2002; Long and Schmidt 2005; Bader 2015; Bayly 2016; Phillips and Sharman 2020; for international law, see Koskenniemi, Rech, and Jiménez Fonseca 2017). The emphasis on empires serves here as an important corrigendum within the academic field of International Relations, but also the broader social sciences and humanities, to overcome 'methodological nationalism' (also, state centrism) and Eurocentrism, as it contributes to further erode the myth of Westphalia. Studying empires promises, inter alia, to rethink the 'international' as a rather '"thick" set of social relations' compared with the "thin" space of strategic interaction, populated by diplomats, soldiers, and capitalists' (Barkawi and Laffey 2002, 100) of an international order composed by sovereign states in the 'Westphalian' tradition. Moreover, politics in the Westphalian tradition is mainly conceptualized as interaction between European great powers and located within Europe.

Paying greater attention to the imperial dimension of European politics highlights, in turn, the influence of the non-European world on Europe itself. The sharp distinction between the European and the non-European world as separated spheres of analysis becomes untenable as the idea that European empires only radiated out and diffused into the rest of the world. This helps to overcome Eurocentric conceptualizations of the international. It challenges as well various forms of 'methodological nationalism'. In studies of world politics this comes often in the form of the 'territorial trap', where states are taken as containers with impermeable boundaries and where progress and change occur only within these boundaries (Agnew 1994). In this regard, the individual chapters of this volume understand empires not just as a different form of political aggregates, which are closed entities in themselves, but highlight various modes of interconnectedness within world politics, and the effects of circulation and connectivity. Related to this, chapters problematize some core dichotomies and distinctions of studies of the international and social theory in general, such as the ones between the European and the non-European world, the domestic and the international, the private and the public or empire and nation/state.

Much valuable work has been produced from imperial, colonial, de-colonial and post-colonial perspectives which focus on different elements and processes of identity creation and destruction; cultural syncretism; relations of oppression and plunder; speciations of life in the form of race, gender, class and culture; and civilizationalist aspirations (e.g. Todorov 1984; Legg 2007; Mignolo 2011; Shilliam 2012; Anievas, Manchanda, and Shilliam 2014; Çapan 2017; Mignolo and Walsh 2018; Zondi 2018). Ideas of empire and imperialism are sometimes taken as ready-made categories for political analysis, as monolithic practices of power immutable over time, and as relations of explicit or implicit domination, which succeed one another, inevitably, from empire to empire (cf. Eisenstadt 1993; Muldoon 1999; Abernethy 2000). However, the general approach of this book toward European empires resembles the processual and post-representational take on mapping. Understanding empires as processual highlights the *making* of European empires. Yet, as the chapters of this volume show, empires are never made, they are always empires in the making – tied to processes of dynamic stabilization, hierarchization and ordering. To paraphrase Latour (2005), 'empire' does not explain but needs explanation; on the other hand, it is impossible to fix 'empire' completely on conceptual grounds. Attempts to find a core of empire (be it as successor of the Roman empire or reading

European empires backwards from the British empire of the nineteenth century) do not succeed because empires do not fully mirror each other. There is no transhistorically valid notion of empire. Therefore, as Luis Lobo-Guerrero puts it in his chapter 'In fact, it could be argued, there never were European empires' (p. 42). Thus, to attempt to map imperial aspirations goes beyond the idea of denouncing empire and imperialism as a 'European' creation exported and imposed around the globe.

When the idea of European empire was located by critics in the early modern period with the so-called trips of European discovery and the first wave of globalization, it is refreshing to think, for example, as Fisher and O'Hara among others have proposed, that early modern colonialisms were 'coterminous with the initial processes of European state-making' (Fisher and O'Hara 2009, ix). As they put it, 'the sixteenth and seventeenth centuries, witnessing profound transformations in political and economic life, spawned nothing less than a cultural revolution – or better said, a revolution in the possible ways of being human' (Fisher and O'Hara 2009, ix). To assume an imperial entity as pre-forming an imperial practice ignores the idea that power is a practice with a history. An example is the reflection that, assumed-to-be ready-made Europeans did not find 'indigenous' people in the Americas but people with their own identity (Langebaek 1995, 2008). These histories invite us to reflect on why and how are new and old worlds, past and present, recognized around the markers of the imaginaries that think of them, and what do critiques of imperial thinking have to tell us of how we reason about order, power and governance, in time.

So, how should the idea of empire be approached in order not to fall into false presuppositions or clichés which foreclose the possibility of interrogating the empirical richness of imperial practices and the connectivities they portray through maps? Imperialism is, in the words of Burbank and Cooper, 'the extension of power across space' (2010, 293). More precisely, as Ballantyne and Burton (2012, 29) emphasize 'grafting one space upon another, whether cartographically or imaginatively or both . . . is perhaps one of the signature moves of would-be imperial spaces'. In this respect, the idea of European empire, as explored in this book, relates mostly to a political understanding of the production of space, which, although it cannot be dissociated from a classical imperial imaginary emerging from Rome, needs to be understood in relation to its situated historical epistemologies. David Armitage argued that all European empires and their post-colonial successors looked back to Rome as its inspiration and aspiration: 'All roads lead to Rome, and from Rome, to Troy' (1998, xv). However, as Carlo Galli argued, whilst using a phrase from Rutilius Nanatianus in his *De Reditu Suo* from the beginning of the fifth century, empire is a space with 'an inborn founding authority, more *centering* than *central*'. In this respect, the idea of empire emerging out of Rome is one of 'a universal space of the world of civilised men' that, 'rather than excluding barbarians, . . . attracts them, exhorting them to cross the threshold of humanity' (Galli 2010, 12). Such an approach, putting aside the civilizational issues involved and the specificities of the Roman model, presents an idea of empire as a permeable space, where power relations operate both ways and mutually constitute the objects and subjects of empire as unstable, and as continuously emerging entities. This is not to deny the relationships of oppression and violence that result from imperial practices. It is to assume empire as an empirical object of mutually constituted relationships of power worth exploring in its empirical manifestations, such as maps, and analysed paying careful attention to its epistemological details. In this vein, chapters of this volume explore maps as crucial in the creation of European colonial spaces. Whether it is, for example, the creation of an imaginary of empty and therefore colonizable land through 'blank spaces' on maps (Filipe dos Reis), the partitioning of far-distant non-European territories in the European imperial centres (Louis Le Douarin) or the use of surveying techniques by European settlers on the ground (Kerry Goettlich), maps were crucial in the creation and stabilization of hierarchies of knowledge between the European and non-European world.

Reasoning within the *spaceness* of the empire relates also to the understanding of empire as a relational and mutable entity, an approach that chimes closely with the poststructuralist sense of space understood as the product of interrelations, the sphere of coexisting heterogeneity, and engulfing processuality (Massey 2005). Such an understanding followed the spatial turn in the social sciences and the humanities (Warf and Arias 2008). For long conceived as a prison, the container where power unfolds, or a matter of scaling and distance, space has been implicitly considered a theatrical scenery or an attribute of power but not its co-constitutive force. Such an approach has been countered by a position, as expressed in Foucault's *Eye of Power*, where space is presented as emerging as a catalyst of power relations (Foucault 1980, 149), which follows Lefebvre (1992) in analysing space as a constellation of 'moments', revelatory experiences, epiphanies of power fabrications or failures. As argued in the chapters of this book, relating issues of micro- and macro-politics, and revealing cultural and political struggles over territories, the spaceness of empire produces the conditions where to unfold its emergence as a historic-political problem. By taking the idea of empire as revealing an experience of governance, contributions to this volume complicate the analysis of the construct of the empire by approaching maps and mapping practices as sites of epistemological experimentation. It follows that the imaginaries of connectivity revealed through maps can be used to understand the making of empire.

## ON EMPIRES AND THEIR CARTOGRAPHIC MOORINGS: A ROAD MAP

Considering the epistemological richness and intricacies of both the constructs of empire and cartography, it should come as no surprise that there is a growing concern with how the two relate to each other. Chapters in this book deal with a wide range of cases that help us learn about the making of European empires and mapping in various non-traditional ways. They include narratives of first waves of imperialism in the modern age, as well as 'Enlightened' imperialism, and early twentieth-century late-state imperialisms.

Focusing on the making of the Early 'Spanish' Empire, or better, the ways that different imaginaries of a 'Spanish' Empire were made concrete and operative, Lobo-Guerrero discusses in chapter 2 the 'foundational' maps like the *Carta de Juan de la Cosa* (1500), the *Padrón Real* with the map of Diego Ribeiro (1529) and the map of America by Diego Gutierrez (1562). His speculative journey starts from the emerging global space shaped by each cartographic artefact to then reconstruct the broader epistemic and administrative practices that made the assemblage of colours, lines, human and geometric symbols a coherent and governed spatial order. The problem of knowing and knowledge is central in this early phase of European expansion as Europeans were confronted with the question of how to deal with the novelty of the encountered territories and people of the New World. The author develops the idea of maps 'as constituting sites for experimentation, from which to explore experiments of power, and in which to interrogate the conditions of possibility of such experiments' (p. 23). His reading of a global Christian space into the map of Juan de la Cosa, the consolidating role of cosmography as a legitimizing knowledge that authorizes a global imperial power in the map of Diego Ribeiro and his interpretation of the Gutierrez map as portraying the partitioning of Atlantic ocean space as a legitimate site of imperial confrontation in the late XVIC are examples of experimental reading of contending imperial imaginaries of connectivity.

Referring to the 'mapless empire' originally shaped by Viking explorers' oral mapping and empirical navigation during the tenth and eleventh centuries, in chapter 3 Jeppe Strandsbjerg examines how the space of Greenland was conceived and connected at a distance without any formal and political understanding of modern maps. It was only when the English explorer James Hall drafted four sketch maps of the Greenlandic coast in 1605–1612 that a process of epistemological translation from contingent and sensorial forms of mapping the environment to modern, rational and abstract cartography occurred. In particular, Strandsbjerg intersects two levels of connectivity effects. One is played in a political, economic and legal sphere and follows the metamorphosis of the Danish empire from a system of mutual benefit and exchange to a more hierarchical obligation toward the Kingdom. On a cartographic level, Strandsbjerg notices how the sovereignty over Greenland, and hence the politics of re-connecting the old lands conquered by Vikings, passed through the inscription and translation on modern forms of cartography: 'The mapping of Greenland not only connected Greenland to the king it also connected Greenland to a wider European cartographic theatre occupied with imperial rivalry alongside a territorialisation of sovereignty' (p. 71). In this sense, Strandsbjerg deals with a rather unusual case of European imperialism, namely the aspiration of Denmark to create an empire in the North Atlantic during the late-sixteenth and seventeenth century.

In examining property boundaries and intercolonial boundaries in the English colonies of North America, Kerry Goettlich focuses in chapter 4 on a distinct cartographic mode of imperial space-making, discussing maps resulting from technologies and practices of surveying. The author refers to maps produced through surveying as solidifications and incrustations of newly invented property claims that did have rhetorical power and were embedded in particular contexts and struggles. Surveying became crucial for settler colonial activities as it delegitimized native territorial claims and helped to convert the land of Native Americans into settler property. Practices of surveying were however not fully controlled by colonial authorities but organized by private landowners. The relationship between both groups was highly 'ambitious' and resulted in various struggles about the extent of land-claiming. Moreover, the author pays attention to the unintended consequences of survey mapping in British North America as a result of problems to govern at a distance.

Focussing on the work of the famous German cartographer August Petermann and the function played by *Justus Perthes* press in the provincial town of Gotha, Filipe dos Reis sheds light in chapter 5 to the complex, adventurous and 'precursory' cartographic enterprise that made possible the German imperial and colonial discourse in the nineteenth century. Considering the city of Gotha, the *Justus Perthes* press and the cartographic discoveries of Petermann as three different 'centres of calculations' (Latour 1987) or, as dos Reis also puts it, 'empires of science' where maps and their imaginaries were made active and mobile, dos Reis reflects on the performative functions of blank spaces on maps as catalysts for the hunger of explorations and colonization that the young *Deutschland* would have strongly manifested a few decades later.

In chapter 6, Louis Le Dourain studies the role of a large private colonial network in France. This epistemic community, which includes merchants, diplomats, army officers and scholars, developed in the context of the dissolution of the Ottoman Empire after World War I an opportunity to start a campaign for a French Syria in the Middle East. The campaign was supported by an important shift in how French imperial ambitions in that region were justified, namely not on grounds of glory and a civilizing mission but by economic interests and rather indirect rule. Such an economic empire was also an empire of metrics and statistics – technologies of governance that played a pivotal role in the peace negotiations after the Great War in general. The use of metrics and statistics, as in thematic maps, was not restricted to measure economic indicators but also to the governance of populations. As such, French imperial circles began to draw ethnographic maps, which were influenced by the way populations were mapped in Eastern Europe in the context of the simultaneous dissolution of the Austro-Hungarian Empire. Le Dourain's chapter, in particular, explores the contested cartographic imageries and practices or, as the author puts it, 'the cartographic combat' that surrounded and shaped the French imperial interests on the Levant before and after World War I.

In chapter 7, Laura Lo Presti introduces a multi-sensory approach to maps, mapping and the making of empire, advancing the idea that empire-making is part of a complex process that involves propagandistic consumption. As she puts it, 'The empire transforms from a concept into a practice only at the moment of its consumption' (p. 178). Lo Presti analyses maps produced and circulated within the understudied Italian Fascism's empire as part of 'a persuasive, communicative, and performative media apparatus' (p. 176) where popular maps and map-like objects reveal complex and interrelated epistemological formations through their materiality, for instance: the sensorial experience of the viewer, the propagandistic strategy of the mapmaker and the power it supported, as well as what could be called, 'a political sensorial economy of space'. Maps, in her case, operate as media for a Fascist imaginary of space, drilled into the audience through mundane practices such as radio broadcasts at school (asking students to engage with the Fascist maps almost as subliminal messages), in games and postcards, and in cinematic ways that combine aesthetic with politics.

## REFERENCES

Abernethy, David B. 2000. *The Dynamics of Global Dominance: European Overseas Empires, 1415–1980*. New Haven, CT: Yale University Press.

Agnew, John. 1994. 'The Territorial Trap: The Geographical Assumptions of International Relations Theory'. *Review of International Political Economy* 1 (1): 53–80.

Akerman, James R., ed. 2009. *The Imperial Map: Cartography and the Mastery of Empire*. Kenneth Nebenzahl, Jr., Lectures in the History of Cartography. Chicago: The University of Chicago Press.

———, ed. 2017. *Decolonizing the Map: Cartography from Colony to Nation*. Kenneth Nebenzahl, Jr., Lectures in the History of Cartography. Chicago: The University of Chicago Press.

Anievas, Alexander, Nivi Manchanda, and Robbie Shilliam, eds. 2014. *Race and Racism in International Relations: Confronting the Global Colour Line*. London: Routledge.

Armitage, David, ed. 1998. 'Introduction'. In *Theories of Empire, 1450–1800*, edited by David Armitage, xv–xxxiii. Aldershot: Ashgate.

Bader, Alexander D. 2015. *Empire Within: International Hierarchy and Its Imperial Laboratories of Governance*. Abingdon: Routledge.

Ballantyne, Tony, and Antoinette M. Burton. 2012. *Empires and the Reach of the Global, 1870–1945*. Cambridge, MA: Harvard University Press.

Barkawi, Tarak, and Mark Laffey. 2002. 'Retrieving the Imperial: Empire and International Relations'. *Millennium – Journal of International Studies* 31 (1): 109–127.

Bayly, Martin J. 2016. *Taming the Imperial Imagination: Colonial Knowledge, International Relations, and the Anglo-Afghan Encounter, 1808–1878*. Cambridge: Cambridge University Press.

Borges, Jorge Luis. 1999. 'On Exactitude in Science'. In *From Jorge Luis Borges, Collected Fictions*, translated and edited by Andrew Hurley. London: Penguin.

Branch, Jordan. 2014. *The Cartographic State: Maps, Territory and the Origins of Sovereignty*. Cambridge: Cambridge University Press.

Burbank, Jane, and Frederick Cooper. 2010. *Empires in World History: Power and the Politics of Difference*. Princeton, NJ: Princeton University Press.

Çapan, Zeynep Gülşah. 2017. 'Decolonising International Relations?' *Third World Quarterly* 38 (1): 1–15.

Cosgrove, Denis. 1999. 'Introduction: Mapping Meaning'. In *Mappings*, edited by Denis Cosgrove, 1–23. London: Reaktion Books.

Deleuze, Gilles, and Felix Guattari. 2004. *A Thousand Plateaus: Capitalism and Schizophrenia*, translated by Brian Massumi. London: Continuum.

Derrida, Jacques. 1997. *Of Grammatology*, translated by Gayatri Chakravorty Spivak. Second edition. Baltimore, MD: Johns Hopkins University Press.

Dodge, Martin, Rob Kitchin, and Chris Perkins, eds. 2009. *Rethinking Maps: New Frontiers in Cartographic Theory*. London: Routledge.

Dodge, Martin, Chris Perkins, and Rob Kitchin. 2009. 'Mapping Modes, Methods and Moments'. In *Rethinking Maps*, edited by Martin Dodge, Chris Perkins, and Rob Kitchin, 220–243. London: Routledge.

Edney, Matthew H. 2009. 'The Irony of Imperial Mapping'. In *The Imperial Map*, edited by James R. Akerman, 11–45. Chicago: The University of Chicago Press.

———. 2019. *Cartography: The Ideal and Its History*. Chicago: The University of Chicago Press.

Eisenstadt, Shmuel Noah. 1993. *The Political Systems of Empires*. Piscataway, NJ: Transaction Publishers.

Elden, Stuart. 2013. *The Birth of Territory*. Chicago: The University of Chicago Press.

Fisher, Andrew, and Matthew O'Hara. 2009. *Imperial Subjects: Race and Identity in Colonial Latin America*. Durham: Duke University Press.

Ford, Richard T. 1999. 'Law's Territory (A History of Jurisdiction)'. *Michigan Law Review* 97 (4): 843–930.

Foucault, Michel. 1980. *Power/Knowledge: Selected Interviews and Other Writings, 1972–1977*. Brighton: Harvester.
Foucault, Michel. 1984. 'Polemics, Politics, and Problematizations: An Interview with Michel Foucault'. Interview by Paul Rabinow. In *The Foucault Reader*, edited by Paul Rabinow, 381–90. New York: Pantheon Books.
Gablik, Suzi. 1973. *Magritte*. New York: New York Graphic Society.
Galli, Carlo. 2010. *Political Spaces and Global War*, edited by Adam Sitze, translated by Elisabeth Fay. Minneapolis: Minnesota University Press.
Harley, John Brian. 1988. 'Maps, Knowledge and Power'. In *The Iconography of Landscapes*, edited by Denis Cosgrove and Stephen Daniels, 277–312. Cambridge: Cambridge University Press.
———. 1989. 'Deconstructing the Map'. *Cartographica: The International Journal for Geographic Information and Geovisualization* 26 (2): 1–20.
Koskenniemi, Martti, Walter Rech, and Manuel Jiménez Fonseca, eds. 2017. *International Law and Empire: Historical Explorations*. Oxford: Oxford University Press.
Langebaek, Carl Henrik. 1995. 'De Cómo Convertir a Los Indios y de Porqué No Lo Han Sido: Juan de Valcarcel y La Idolatría En El Altiplano Cundiboyacense a Finales Del Siglo XVII'. *Revista de Antropología y Arqueología* 3 (11): 187–214.
———. 2008. *Herederos Del Pasado. Tomo I: Indígenas y Pensamiento Criollo En Colombia y Venezuela*. Colombia: Universidad de los Andes.
Latour, Bruno. 1987. *Science in Action: How to Follow Scientists and Engineers through Society*. Cambridge, MA: Harvard University Press.
———. 2005. *Reassembling the Social an Introduction to Actor-Network-Theory*. Oxford: Oxford University Press.
Lefebvre, Henri. 1992. *The Production of Space*, translated by Donald Nicholson-Smith. Oxford: Wiley-Blackwell.
Legg, Stephen. 2007. 'Beyond the European Province: Foucault and Postcolonialism'. In *Space, Knowledge and Power: Foucault and Geography*, edited by Jeremy Crampton and Stuart Elden, 265–289. Aldershot: Ashgate.
Lobo-Guerrero, Luis. 2012. 'Connectivity as the Strategization of Space – the Case of the Port of Hamburg'. *Distinktion: Scandinavian Journal of Social Theory* 13 (3): 310–21.
Lobo-Guerrero, Luis, Suvi Alt, and Maarten Meijer. 2019. 'Introduction'. In *Imaginaries of Connectivity: The Creation of Novel Spaces of Governance*, edited by Luis Lobo-Guerrero, Suvi Alt, and Maarten Meijer, 1–11. London: Rowman & Littlefield International.
Long, David, and Brian C. Schmidt, eds. 2005. *Imperialism and Internationalism in the Discipline of International Relations*. Albany: State University of New York Press.
MacMillan, Ken. 2003. 'Sovereignty "More Plainly Described": Early English Maps of North America, 1580–1625'. *Journal of British Studies* 42 (4): 413–47.
Magritte Organisation. 2020. 'The Human Condition'. *Rene Magritte* (blog). 2020. www.renemagritte.org/the-human-condition.jsp.
Massey, Doreen. 2005. *For Space*. London: Sage.
Mignolo, Walter D. 2011. *The Darker Side of Western Modernity: Global Futures, Decolonial Options*. Durham: Duke University Press.

Mignolo, Walter D., and Catherine Walsh. 2018. *Decoloniality: Concepts, Analysis and Praxis*. Durham: Duke University Press.

Muldoon, James. 1999. *Empire and Order: The Concept of Empire, 800–1800*. London: Palgrave Macmillan.

Neocleous, Mark. 2003. 'Off the Map: On Violence and Cartography'. *European Journal of Social Theory* 6 (4): 409–425.

Owens, Patricia. 2015. *Economy of Force: Counterinsurgency and the Historical Rise of the Social*. Cambridge: Cambridge University Press.

Pagden, Anthony. 1998. *Spanish Imperialism and the Political Imagination: Studies in European and Spanish-American Social and Political Theory 1513–1830*. New Haven, CT: Yale University Press.

Phillips, Andrew, and Jason C. Sharman. 2020. *Outsourcing Empire: How Company-States Made the Modern World*. Princeton: Princeton University Press.

Rajkovic, Nikolas M. 2018. The Visual Conquest of International Law: Brute Boundaries, the Map, and the Legacy of Cartogenesies. *Leiden Journal of International Law* 31 (2): 267–288.

Shilliam, Robbie, ed. 2012. *International Relations and Non-Western Thought: Imperialism, Colonialism and Investigations of Global Modernity*. London: Routledge.

Strandsbjerg, Jeppe. 2010. *Territory, Globalization and International Relations: The Cartographic Reality of Space*. Houndmills: Palgrave Macmillan.

Todorov, Tzvetan. 1984. *The Conquest of America: The Question of the Other*. New York: Harper & Row.

Warf, Barney and Santa Arias, eds. 2008. *The Spatial Turn: Interdisciplinary Perspectives*. London: Routledge.

Weissberg, Guenter. 1963. 'Maps as Evidence in International Boundary Disputes: A Reappraisal'. *The American Journal of International Law* 57 (4): 781–803.

Wood, Denis. 1993. 'The Fine Line between Mapping and Map-Making'. *Cartographica* 30 (4): 50–60.

Zondi, Siphamandla. 2018. 'Decolonising International Relations and Its Theory: A Critical Conceptual Meditation'. *Politikon* 45 (1): 16–31.

*Chapter 2*

# Mapping the Invention of the Early 'Spanish'[1] Empire

Luis Lobo-Guerrero[2]

In a letter from 1503, allegedly written by Americo Vespucci to his patron Lorenzo Pietro di Medici, he stated that,

> on a former occasion I wrote to you at some length concerning my return from those new regions which we found and explored with the fleet, at the cost, and by the command of this Most Serene King of Portugal. And these we may rightly call a new world. Because our ancestors had no knowledge of them, and it will be a matter wholly new to all those who hear about them. For this transcends the view held by our ancients, inasmuch as most of them hold that there is no continent to the south beyond the equator, but only the sea which they named the Atlantic; and if some of them did aver that a continent there was, they denied with abundant argument that it was a habitable land. But that this their opinion is false and utterly opposed to the truth, this my last voyage has made manifest; for in those southern parts I have found a continent more densely peopled and abounding in animals than our Europe or Asia or Africa, and, in addition, a climate milder and more delightful than in any other region known to us, as you shall learn in the following account wherein we shall set succinctly down only capital matters and the things more worthy of comment and memory seen or heard by me in this new world, as will appear below.
> 
> (Vespucci 1503, 1)

Vespucci's statement, or whoever the rightful author of this text was,[3] illustrates two closely interrelated issues at stake when exploring the problem of empire and the mapping of the New World. The first relates to *claims to epistemological novelty* with regard to how the Ancients knew the world and how Aristotle regarded its inhabitability. The second relates to *an imaginary of discovery* where European explorers *found* new continents and the marvels contained in them. Both issues, which will be used as analytical instruments throughout this chapter, are complexly interrelated. The first provides licence for the creation of knowledge on unprecedented grounds (see Maravall 1966; North 2013; Lobo-Guerrero 2019a), whereas the second projects an order of the real into newly found spaces (Lobo-Guerrero 2019b). This interaction, with its tensions, gives rise to early modern discourses of (Iberian) science (e.g. Cañizares-Esguerra 2002, 2006; Padrón 2004; Barrera-Osorio 2006, Portuondo 2009) as well as to narratives of discovery and conquest which support imperial historiographies.

By 1958, however, Mexican historian Edmundo O'Gorman challenged such imaginary of discovery by stating, controversially, that America had been invented (O'Gorman 1961). The discovery approach, he reasoned, only reinforced an idea that America was a natural object knowable through exploration, a position that presupposed a knowing subject and stable ways of knowing and forms of knowledge. What made sense for him was to approach America as an invention, as something that was crafted. As Ricardo Padrón puts it, 'as something produced historically, through the complex interaction of culturally contingent expectations and interests with observed geographical phenomena' (Padrón 2004, 19). If America was indeed invented, what constituted the invention?

O'Gorman's thesis, of great influence upon historians, cultural and (post/de)colonial thinkers, invites careful epistemological reflections on the relationships between imperial practices of power, the politics of subjectivity and the politics of space, with regard to knowledge. It fosters questions on what it means to discover, to conquer and to invent (cf. Naipaul 1988), in relation to who claims to know the world (e.g. Todorov 1984), how does it know it (e.g. Maravall 1966) and for what purpose. For, to presuppose America as an object of knowledge limits the possibility of learning about the subjects that sought and claimed to know, of how they were constituted and of how they constituted others through processes of knowing. It veils the epistemic struggles that characterized the formulation of ideas that would then stabilize the meaning and understanding of what is called America. Most importantly, it prevents learning about the forms of experience involved in knowing, in making it knowable and, as will be elaborated in this chapter, in transforming it into an object of governance. So, what was it that was invented?

To write about the mapping of the New World as part of a nascent 'Spanish' Empire as a purely natural object, as a fact of history which can be traced in its origins and developments, implies a stable understanding of an idea of empire, the objectivity of sources of knowledge and an established understanding of mapping and what it means to map. In practice, we have nothing of the kind. The idea of empire is yet to find a stable conceptual meaning away from ideologized intellectual and nationalist perspectives (cf. Muldoon 1999; Hardt and Negri 2001), and even if we ever had such a stable concept, we must remember that concepts have a history and a becoming (Deleuze and Guattari 1994, 17–19).

Maps, as critical cartography scholars keep on demonstrating, and as stated in chapter 1 of this volume, are not stable objects either. They can be actively deconstructed to reveal epistemic formations (e.g. Harley 1989), experiences of power (Turnbull 1996), imperial and commercial aspirations (e.g. Akerman 2009), as well as gendered and racial subjectivities (cf. Craib 2000). To write about the mapping of the New World in the making of the 'Spanish' Empire requires then, a similar approach to that suggested by O'Gorman. The 'Spanish' Empire has to be analysed as an invention which demands careful attention to the specificities of the power relations out of which it emerged, and the historic-epistemological contexts that made it possible. So, what was it that invented a 'Spanish' Empire?

An invention, as idea, requires some discussion given that there is no innocence in its invocation. Jacques Derrida argued some time ago that a true invention would have to emerge from a different episteme (Derrida 2007). An *episteme*, as Michel Foucault discussed, refers to the set of rules of formation that give rise to diverse and heterogeneous discourses at a given time and that mostly escape the consciousness of those who employ them. It is characterized by particular rules of validation/validity and truth-saying. Synthetically put, an *episteme* refers to the conditions of possibility of thought and action in time (Foucault 1989, xxiii–xxiv). In this respect, an invention is tightly allied with the operation of a new episteme, to a shift, if even slight, in the rules of formation of thought and action which enable something to be claimed as novel (cf. Maravall 1966; North 2013; Lobo-Guerrero 2019a).

Invention, consequently, is not devoid of power relations. Gaurav Desai, for example, whilst reflecting on Mudimbe's book *The Invention of Africa*, highlights the relationship between oppression, as in processes of colonization, and ideas of invention. For Mudimbe, the word 'colonization' comes from the Latin *colere*, meaning to cultivate, design and organize (Mudimbe 1988, 1). Desai reflects on the role of designing and organizing 'other worlds through corollary processes of sociopolitical/economic reorganisation and epistemological rearticulations' (Desai 1993, 122). He shows how invention and colonization work together to 'introduce, to bring into use formally [and] by authority, to found, establish, institute the empire' (Desai 1993, 122). As he further notes, this relationship is tightly related to the very essence of discourse, and he quotes Foucault as reminding us that discourse 'is at once controlled, selected, organized and redistributed according to a certain number of procedures, whose role it is to avert its powers and its dangers, to cope with chance events, to evade its ponderous, awesome materiality' (Foucault 1972, 216). So, how was it that a 'Spanish' Empire was invented?

Reflecting on the relationship between invention and episteme allows us to advance on an understanding of empire, and the making of empire, as a process deeply involved, if not determined, by the creation and imposition of knowledge(s), forms of knowing and processes of authorization and legitimation of knowledge(s). The emergence of an empire is deeply related to processes of invention which introduce the conditions of possibility for new orders of being, and imaginaries of being, which will regulate the generalities and the minutiae of individual and collective interaction. To reflect on the emergence of an empire is therefore a practice of exploring the detailed *empirical* manifestations of creating new terms and spheres of interaction. The creation of new languages and narratives of order and of controlling order (e.g. the imposition of Castilian as a 'Spanish' language, the establishment of a 'Spanish' inquisition as a form of political police), of new physical and political spaces of interaction (e.g. the 'Atlantic' as a new sea, the Pacific as a new Ocean, the Indies and its viceroyalties), the invention of new cultural genres (e.g. the modern novel and Don Quixote), of new terms of understanding trade and exchange (e.g. mercantilism), of new artistic forms of expressing being (e.g. the 'Spanish' and 'Portuguese' Baroque), of depicting places and spaces (e.g. evolution of and from Portolan cartographies) to name but some. The relationship between invention and episteme allows us to advance an answers to the questions of what was invented and what invented it, questions that, given the relationship, imply a who and a how. This chapter is concerned with the how, through the exploration of three particular maps which are constituted as an empirical space, not as a historical narrative, but rather, as a site of epistemological experimentation.

Mapping is one of many empirical sites for investigating the relationship between the making of empire and invention. As approached in this chapter, mapping is understood in its widest post-representational dimension (Dodge, Kitchin, and Perkins 2009). It assumes a processual rather than a representational knowledge character (science). Maps, from this perspective, do not represent space, they contribute to creating it (cf. Casey 1998). They constitute relational sites of power in the sense that they link particular ways of being in, and conceiving of, the world with the creation of spatial imaginaries (Lobo-Guerrero 2019b). The map, in this respect, never relates to a fixed ontology that can be historically located. Its ontology, its nature of being, is an emergent one, that can of course be historically explored but within its epistemic context. The mapping of an empire is therefore not a process of tracking the ontological origins and factual events and ideas constitutive of an entity labelled, or interpreted, as empire. It is an engagement with the epistemological processes involved in constituting the spatial imaginaries at play in a map. That said, maps, and mapping processes, although having a strong visual component, are not limited to cartographic objects. *Mapping* refers to the processes through which something is defined, which of course involves actors and the interaction of complex subjectivities. In consequence, for understanding the relationship between invention and empire, maps need to be approached as constituting sites for experimentation, from which to explore experiments of power, and in which to interrogate the conditions of possibility of such experiments.

Mapping the invention of the early 'Spanish' Empire is therefore not a task but a problematization (cf. Foucault 1994; Bacchi 2012). What is problematized here is the relationship between practices of power and the crafting of spatial conceptions which would render space(s) as governable. In other words, this chapter problematizes the processes through which spaces of governance are created whilst mapping out a 'Spanish' imperial idea. Building on this problematization, the chapter advances the thesis that what was invented in the early years of the 'Spanish' Empire was not America, as an object, *but an empirical space which was called America*. This distinction between an object of study and an empirical space is important. It does not presuppose a ready-made object of knowledge (an epistemic object), or knowing actors (an epistemic actor). It assumes, instead, that both epistemic objects and epistemic actors are constituted through empirical practices of power. The problem of empiricism has a lot to reveal in these regards. Suffice it to say for now that such a problematization has methodological implications which might not fall within standard methodologies of a scientific method that assume an object of analysis, a method and findings. For example, it cannot assume a 'Spanish' Empire as an object of study given that such an entity, if it is to be called such, was actually an emerging phenomenon constituted through knowledges and practices of power. It cannot assume either a body of empirical sources given that material explored in the chapter is approached as sites of experimentation, more on which will be said later. The findings of the chapter will come in the form of an empirical space of power relations of imperial practices, analysed through an engagement with a selection of mapping endeavours.

In what follows, the chapter sets up the problematic character of the term 'Spanish' Empire and presents three conceptions of this idea based on the realms of the Catholic empire of the Catholic Kings, the composite empire of Charles I (Charles V as the Holy Roman Emperor) and the individual empire of Philip II. It then continues with an engagement of each conception followed by a problematization based on a critical reading of a mapping practice to demonstrate three distinct geopolitical imaginaries, each based on different epistemological claims. The *Carta de Juan de la Cosa* from 1500 is critically, if speculatively, analysed for the first case depicting a Catholic global realm; the *Padrón Real* with the map of Diego Ribeiro from 1529 is explored for the second case to show the scientific and empirical base upon which the composite empire of Charles I relied; and for the third case the map of America by Diego Gutierrez from 1562 is explored as already depicting a contested Atlantic ocean-space that was to characterize European imperial spatial rivalry until the twentieth century. The chapter concludes by reflecting on the relationship between epistemological claims to novelty and imaginaries of discovery in relation to the three maps, and how an understanding of empire can be based on epistemological analysis rather than classifications of authority. It also reflects on the opportunities that approaching maps as sites of experimentation opens for the writing of a political theory that transcends written text.

## EMPIRE AND IMPERIAL SPACE-MAKING IN XVIC SPAIN

Was there ever a 'Spanish' Empire? Was there ever actually an empire after Rome? It really depends on how an empire is defined and conceived. Anthony Pagden, for example, once argued, that

> there never was, of course, a Spanish Empire. Although contemporaries sometimes referred to the territories over which first the Habsburgs and then the Bourbons ruled as an empire, and although in many respects the administration of those territories was an imperial one, they were always, in theory and generally in legal practice, a confederation of principalities held together in the person of a single king.
>
> (Pagden 1998a, 3)

On the other hand, he also argued in subsequent work that empires can be approached as an effect of the exercise of sovereign power. He stated that

> all empires, no matter how distinct they may be in the size or type – and there is a bewildering variety – share is that they involve the exercise of a sovereign authority that has usually been acquired, at least in the first instance, by force. Since the occupation of lands to which the occupier could make no prior claim on grounds of autochthony, spurious or no, necessarily involved some kind of violation, empires were inescapably lands of conquest. Moreover, in view of the fact that most European peoples did generally hold that that domination is – or at least should be – a spontaneous expression of the nature of society, conquest presented a considerable challenge to most notions of sovereign authority.
>
> (Pagden 2005, 30)

Whereas Pagden's positions remain influential, they assume an empire as an empirical object of study tightly linked to political authority, legal, practical or both. Even if such an approach was to be followed, ideas of empire in relation to XVIC 'Spain' demonstrate the empirical complexity of the very problem of authority. During the early years of the 'Spanish' Empire, approached here not as a territorial entity but as the discourses and practices through which spaces of governance were created in the process of mapping out a 'Spanish' imperial idea, such complexity becomes evident and constitutive of an empirical space for investigation. From the 1490s until the end of the XVIC, three powerful monarchies displayed different conceptions and practices of the Empire: (i) the reign of the Catholic queen and king Isabel and Ferdinand (1479–1504), and of Ferdinand alone (1504–1516); (ii) the reign of Charles I (1516–1556); and (iii) that of Philip II (1556–1598). All three monarchies undertook mapping practices that can be used to explore, if experimentally, what those ideas of empire were about.

## THE CATHOLIC EMPIRE AND THE *CARTA DE JUAN DE LA COSA*

A first conception, that of a Catholic empire, is tightly linked to the title of Catholic King given in recognition of the royal support for championing the Catholic faith in the Peninsula. It was given for the first time by the bishops at the Council of Toledo to Visigoth King Vicarred of Hispania (reigned A.D. 586–601) – who converted from Arianism to Catholicism, 'because he was the first to protect inviolate the Catholic faith, and because he freed the whole of Spain from the Arian heresy' (Muldoon 2015, 156; quoting from Solórzano Pereira 1629, 2.25.27; c.f. Hispalensis 2014). It was then used by Alfonso VIII of Castile (reigned A.D. 1158–1214) who led the union of all Iberian kingdoms and foreign Crusaders against the Almohads at the Battle of Navas de Tolosa under the banner of the Reconquista (Muldoon 2015, 156; quoting from Solórzano Pereira 1629, 2.25.27; c.f. Hispalensis 2014). It was finally granted by Pope Alexander VI through the 1496 Bull *Si Convenit*, to Isabel and Ferdinand for the pacification of the kingdoms of Spain, the conquest of Granada, the expulsion of Jews, the defence of Pontifical interests in Naples and Sicily, as well as campaigns in the North of Africa. Interestingly, New World ventures were not mentioned in the Bull (see Rey 1952).

This conception of *empire*, although it does not expressly use the term, operated as legitimization of practices of conquest against non-Christian people under the authority of the Church. In the case of Isabel and Ferdinand, however, the title operated both to recognize the legitimacy of their claims over conquered kingdoms and very importantly, as Papal legitimation of a process of 'Spanish' nation-building amongst the 'Spanish' kingdoms. Maravall referred to this process as the 'federal character of the crown of the Catholic Kings' (Maravall 1972, 109). It relates to the atomized nature of Castilian nobility at the time of Isabel's coronation, which was in turn a highly disputed issue (cf. Ladero-Quesada 2004; Del Val-Valdivieso 2004).

The banner of Isabel's realm was from the start a Catholic one which she put at the service of a secular form of government as an instrument for unification. This strategy was followed by the creation of core state institutions, for example, the Spanish Inquisition established in 1478, only four years after the union of Castile and Aragon, and which operated under the direct control of the monarchy in a way that it has been interpreted as a form of political police (cf. Pérez 2005; Kamen 2014). Another example was the appointment of bishops, which remained a prerogative of the Crown and not of the Pope (cf. Oro 1971).

Some particularities of this conception of imperial imaginary can in part be explored in the *Carta de Juan de la Cosa* (figure 2.1). In 1500, de la Cosa, owner and master of the *Santa Maria*, one of the three ships that sailed with Columbus in 1492, produced a mappamundi where the New World was depicted, visually, as a landmass. The map seems to have been commissioned by Archbishop Jua Rodriguez de Fonseca, royal chaplain to Isabel, who was in charge of organizing the trips to the Indies, and might have used it to impress courtiers and diplomats (Martin-Meras 2000, 80). To start with, the map makes a grand epistemological claim. It is the first map ever to speculate about the depiction of the New World as a separate landmass, at a time when the Pacific coast had not yet been 'discovered'. The new landmass is highlighted in colour green, when all other continents remain uncoloured, and no political detail other than banners on the coasts are included to signify possession, compared with the rich graphical information offered for other continents. The claim, which can be taken as the first visual invention of what was later to be known as America, is supported by an imaginary and practices of discovery in which the cartographer, Juan de la Cosa, was instrumental.

De la Cosa was an experienced navigator and cartographer with as much sailing experience to the New World as could be found at the time. Having spent time at the Portuguese court in 1488, he was familiar with the Portuguese explorations of Bartolomeu Diaz and was well versed in diplomatic and political circles. The practices of discovery contributing to this invention of a continent, however, were not only his or 'Spanish'. His map was partly the result of situated experience where he collected information for charting the coasts of the Caribbean region, but also relied on information collected from other navigators, including the Portuguese and the English, and speculation as to the contours of landmasses not yet explored by Europeans (most of the American coasts, the African West coast and great parts of the Indian Ocean). De la Cosa charted only part of the Antilles, the coasts of what is today Venezuela, and most likely relied on information provided by Portuguese sources on the coasts of today's Brazil probably obtained from the trip of Pedro Álvarez Cabral and from the 'Spanish' trip of Vicente Yanez Pinzón (Sáenz-López 2006, 16). For the north of the Americas, he probably used

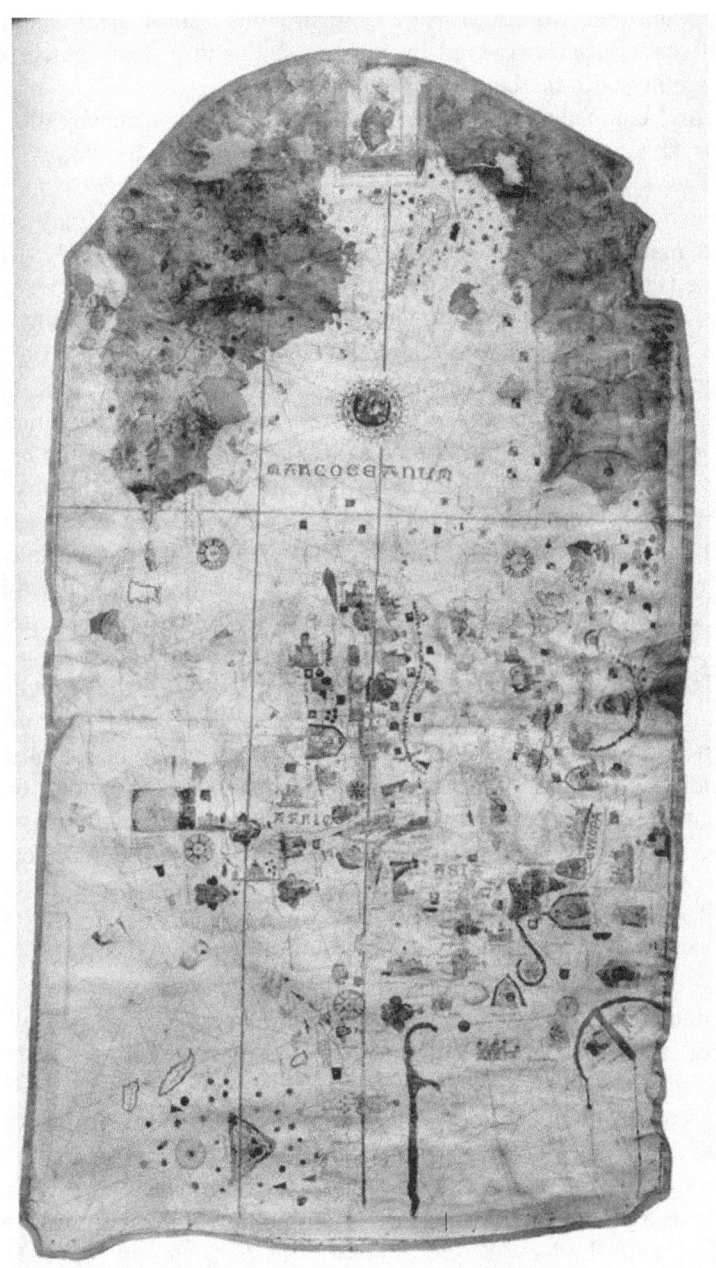

**Figure 2.1.** *Carta de Juan de la Cosa*, 1500. Original at the Museo Naval de Madrid. Courtesy of the Centro Virtual Cervantes, Museo Naval de Madrid.

information from the 1497 explorations of John Cabot – an Italian sailor and cosmographer then working for the English King – since there is an inscription that reads 'sea discovered by the English' and a name place 'English Cape' together with the banner of Henry VII.

A second claim that can be read into the map is the demarcation of the ocean as space (cf. Lefebvre 1991). At its core lies the *Mar Oceanum* depicted as a large sea contained between Europe and Africa on the east and the New World on the west. Two particular elements play a central role in demarcating the space it constitutes. The first is a highly decorated wind rose right in the middle of the ocean (of which more will be said in a moment) from which thirty-two wind lines, used to indicate sailing courses, emanate toward all directions of the two worlds. This wind rose plays a prominent role in the spatial imaginary portrayed by the map, as it centres the geographical imagination of the viewer beyond the oikoumenical space of the Mediterranean. Its importance is highlighted by its size, the biggest in the map, the most decorated, and helps focus the attention of the observer on the *Mar Oceanum* and the New World as occupied ocean-space, never a void, as Steinberg noted years ago (Steinberg 2001, 75–109). A second element is played by the very notorious meridian line demarcating the upper third part of the map which has been the subject of endless discussion. Some argue that it corresponds to the 'Spanish' interpretation, or politic-diplomatic portrayal, of the Tordesillas Line that divided the world between the 'Spanish' and the Portuguese (Martín-Merás 1993, 80; 2000). The Treaty of Tordesillas, based on Pope Alexander VI's Bull *Inter Coetera* of 1493, established the line as being 370 leagues west of Cape Verde islands off the coast of Africa (Goodman 2002). The problem was that nobody knew how to measure such distance, never mind how to demarcate it on water, and consequently, the location of the actual line was notably unknown. Others have argued that the line on the map corresponds to places where there was no magnetic declination (cf. Martínez 1993; Martín-Merás 2000; Alvarez 2003; Robles Macias 2010). In its place or not, the line here divides the new world space in two parts which are clearly demarcated. Waters and lands in the hands of Castile and Portugal, as well as England, are depicted through banners on land and onboard ships.

Related to this demarcation of ocean-space it is possible to make a third claim, which, if speculative, has a profound geographical meaning for the spatial imaginary the map could have portrayed. It relates to the depiction of the world as a global Catholic space. When looking at the map in its original orientation, with the New World at the top (as presented in figure 2.1), it is possible to observe that the space it created was structured by a giant Christian cross. Two features need to be highlighted in order to present the case. The first is a vignette with a portrait of St. Christopher, patron saint of all travellers, that was pasted on the map where the Panama isthmus is located. Its inclusion in the map has been the subject of diverse interpretations. Some argue that it was customary to include such saints in Christian maps. Others argue that, given the size and location of the portrait, it was simply used to cover a gap of unknown space in the landmass making it appear as a continuum from north to south. Its size, theme and location, however, are too prominent to be accidental. St. Christopher was recognized as the carrier of Christ following the legend that he had carried a child across a river who then revealed himself to him as Christ, his Lord. The use of the name Christopher, as in Columbus's name, can be interpreted allegorically as representing an idea of evangelization, one of the stated aims of the Catholic Kings-sponsored trips and explorations. The vignette is located on the western-most part of the line indicating the Tropic of Cancer, at the very top of the map where the sign of INRI in a Christian crucifix would normally be.

The second feature is the inclusion in the middle of the large wind rose mentioned before, of a Madonna and Child surrounded by angels. The image was cut from a codex, pasted on the parchment and later coloured in accordance to the other elements of the chart (Sáenz-López 2006, 13). Whereas the inclusion of a Madonna and Child was not uncommon in other portolan maps of the time, its location on the geographical centre of the chart should not be taken lightly. Its inclusion might be related to the revival of Mariology at this time, partly due to the agency of Pope Sixtus IV – from the Franciscan order which, since 1263, observed the feast of the Immaculate Conception. Sixtus IV was the first to refer to Mary as spiritual mother, as 'Mother of Grace' in 1477 (Miravalle 2006, 86), and her inclusion in the wind rose was perhaps intended to signify the benevolence of a crusading imperial venture. Possibly representing incarnation, the figure is located just above the Tordesillas Line, which constitutes the cross-bar of the giant cross, just where the head of a crucified Jesus would be located. The location of the Madonna and Child toward the west of the line, and the vignette of St. Christopher in the west, could be interpreted as signifying the investment of salvation history with westward movement, in accordance to the mediaeval mappamundi tradition of locating Eden in the east and Jerusalem in the centre.

Regardless of the precise meaning of these elements, the role of a cross in depicting the world as a global Catholic space relates to a long-standing medieval tradition which depicted mappamundi as a world created by God. T-O mappamundi, such as that of Isidore of Seville – originally sketched in his book from 623 and printed for the first time in 1472, making it the first ever printed map in the West – is a case in point. Medieval mappamundi focused on a world centred in Jerusalem with the pillars of Hercules to the west and paradise at the east, and included Europe, Africa and Asia, as continents divided and surrounded by water. They were intended to depict a world as revealed by God. De la Cosa's map portrays a global space, beyond the pillars of Hercules, where the new frontier is in the process of Christianization through the agency and work of those at the service of the Catholic Kings. The imaginary of discovery at play here is one of yet-to-be-discovered spaces coloured in green, the biblical colour for resurrection and growth, as making a promise of redemption of the new-found lands and the souls they 'contained'. The conception of Catholic empire performed here is one where the old meets the new world and creates a Christian imaginary of global space.

Beyond speculation, what is particularly interesting about this map for understanding the invention of the New World in an emerging empire is its experimental character. Most diplomatic and political observers of this map would have had no idea about the validity of its claims. They would have judged its legitimacy based on its decoration; the cultural elements they could recognize, such as the Christian ones; the inclusion of technical elements such as the wind roses and rhumb lines as well as a scale on its edges; and the resemblance in shape of landmasses they were familiar with, such as Europe and perhaps parts of Africa and Asia. They would have focused on the banners and some of the navigational details, but any information or claim with regard to precision, accuracy or technical validity would escape them, perhaps completely. Therein lay the value of de la Cosa's map as a diplomatic instrument. While offering a visual image of an emerging global space based on the Christian Tordesillas legal order, it legitimized the Spanish claim over the new-found lands and seas and stated its authority to govern them. The claims were deceptive and discreet through the forms in which they were made. The map was drawn on two parchments stitched together, it followed conventions and traditions widely used in Portolan maps, and did not stand out, in form, compared to maps of similar age. In doing so, while presenting the map in terms intelligible to an epistemic community, it was likely to be tolerated or at least not immediately rejected by observers. It sought to colonize the imaginary of the viewer as presenting a spatial fact.

## THE COMPOSITE EMPIRE OF CHARLES I, THE PADRÓN REAL, AND THE RIBEIRO WORLD MAP

A second conception is that of a composite empire in relation to the realm of Charles I (see Yun-Casalilla 2019). In this case, an explicit language of empire was used to relate to his various roles of Emperor of the Holy Roman Empire, Archduke of Austria, King of Spain (Castile and Aragon), Lord of the Netherlands and Duke of Burgundy, and of all the territories dependent on these entities. His is the typical case that exemplifies the debate between an idea of particular and limited empire, which allows for the juxtaposition of various empires on a single monarch, and an idea of an empire of universal character, such as that of the Holy Roman Empire (Frankl 1963; Pagden 1998b). The case of Spain under Charles I combined both ideas on the same person, but the Spain of his son, Philip II, was allegedly focused on the idea of personal empire, as will be elaborated on later.

There is, in Charles I, an interesting conundrum which betrays the role of the term *empire* in the old Europe, vis-à-vis the New World. As noted by Armitage, the two realms of Charles 'remained legally distinct' and 'the [legal] existence of the Holy Roman Empire debarred the "Spanish" monarch from becoming the "Spanish" Empire' (Armitage 1998, xviii–xix). Under his person, ideas for establishing a universal monarchy were current as, for example, that proposed by his own chancellor Mercurino Gattinara that Charles could materialize Dante Allighieri's vision stated in his book *Monarchia*, a pan-European empire based in Italy (Allighieri 1995; Davis 1957; as cited by Armitage 1998, xix). 'Sire,' wrote Gattinara to the Emperor shortly after his election, 'now that God in His prodigious grace has elevated Your Majesty above all Kings and Princes of Christendom, to a pinnacle of power occupied before by none except your mighty predecessor Charlemagne, you are on the road towards Universal Monarchy and on the point of united Christendom under a single shepherd' (Braudel 1995, 476–7). Such visions, however, did not include the Castilian territorial claims in the New World, since the chief political concern in the Catholic European imaginary of the time concerned its external threats: the growing power of the Ottoman Empire and the Protestant enemies of Catholicism (Headley 1998; as cited by Armitage 1998, xix).

The real opportunity for a creative understanding of empire involving the New World, as noted by Armitage and shown by Frankl, arose through the 'eccentric as it was original' invocation by the conqueror of Mexico, Hernán Cortés, in 1519. In his first letter to the King (*Carta Relación*), he appealed to a legal doctrine contained in the thirteenth-century *Siete Partidas* of Castillian King Alfonso X (The Wise), and suggested that two of the Alfonsian legal principles could be applied in order for the King to adopt a doctrine of multiple empires to incorporate the possessions of Moctezuma, the now subjugated Aztec Emperor, into his realm: (i) the unconditional superiority of the common good of all men over the good of some and (ii) the legitimate derogation of current laws in case they went against God's Law, seignorial right or the communal good of all earth, or against known goodness (Frankl 1963, 111, my translation). In his second letter to the King, he promised that 'he might call [him]self emperor of this kingdom with no less glory than that of Germany, which, by the Grace of God, Your Majesty already possesses' (Pagden 1986, 48; as quoted by Armitage 1998, xix). This 'implied the existence of multiple empires for Charles's glory, one acquired by election from the German princes, the other by donation by his new vassal, Moctezuma, or by his faithful servant Cortés's conquest'. Conquest implied the defeat of a worthy enemy; donation implied a secular juridical basis for Charles's dominion in New Spain, distinct from the Papal grant of new territories in the Antilles and Tierra Firme (continental land) to the Castilian Crown in 1493 (Armitage 1998, xxi). Frankl then goes on to examine the evolution and morphing of this idea in Cortés's letters to his King.

Cortés's suggestion is very illustrative of a combination of knowledges that interact in making a novel imperial space. His training and experience as notary in Valladolid and in Hispaniola allowed him to combine legal doctrine and jurisprudence with grounded military experience of conquest (Wilkes 1971). Taking as his spatial imaginary that which resulted from living and working in the New World, his view of a universal empire was not limited to Europe. In fact, he likened the Aztec Empire to a European Empire based on the sheer size and wealth he found there. As an indication, the estimated population of the Aztec capital, Tenochtitlán, was 200,000 inhabitants (Denevan 1992), a large city with regard to Seville (126,000) and Lisbon (100,000), and comparable to London (187,000), Paris (245,000) and Naples (224,000). The largest European city of the time was Constantinople (700,000; Chandler 1987). Nonetheless, Charles and his court did not follow Cortés's suggestions, and by the time of his abdication, his son Philip inherited Spain and his Italian possessions, and his brother Ferdinand the Holy Roman Empire, putting an end to the particular and limited empire with universal aspirations.

Regardless of how scholars have approached Charles I's theory and model of empire, the conundrum that resulted from combining the old world, with its foes and allies, and the New World with the opportunities and challenges it brought, can be explored, in my opinion, in a more fruitful way, by approaching mapping examples from his time as sites of experimentation. The example explored here, that of the 'Spanish' *Padrón Real*, relates to a rather atypical mapping phenomenon, not circumscribed to cartography alone. It relates mostly to the realm of Charles I from 1516 onwards, although the mapping process began already in 1508. It is a different kind of map from that of Juan de la Cosa's in the sense that it was not a single piece of cartography but a process of mapping the world which included charts, knowledges, administrative forms and practices, sailing itineraries, navigational routes, amongst other elements, as recently explored in great detail in books by José María García Redondo (2018a) and Antonio Sánchez Martínez (2013). We do not have, as in de la Cosa's case, a definitive cartographic item representative of this process, partly due to the fact that the Padrón Real was more of an aspiration to concentrate all cosmographical and geographical knowledge of the world into a single (imperial) map, that new maps would render previous ones obsolete and would be subject to destruction, and partly due to its character of secret of state which impeded publication and distribution (Portuondo 2009).

The *Padrón Real* (Royal Register) was conceived as a master map under continuous actualization. It provided a unique cartographic model for the Crown to know its territorial domains and to strategize around them in an expansionist, evangelizing and globalizing context (see Sánchez Martínez 2013). As noted by García Redondo, the word *padrón* had 'a clear sense of territorial inventory, but also, of textual nature' (2018a, 69). It also served political purposes in the European context. Depictions of the *Padrón* would have been used to impress diplomats, courts and powerful merchants around Europe. In that respect, 'The notion of *padrón* performed a role of overseas sovereignty' (García Redondo 2018a, 72). Consequently, the 'Spanish' *Padrón* must be approached as a complex instrument of knowledge(s), practices and devices that contributed to defining what the nascent 'Spanish' Empire was about, and most importantly for the case of this analysis, as a vehicle for the invention of the New World. Not solely territorial, but also economic, cultural, religious and overall, spatial in character, the knowledge produced through and in the *Padrón* would be a central element in the constitution of the object of governance of the 'Spanish' monarchies in the XVIC.

In order to understand the character of the *Padrón*, and its relationship to the composite form of empire it was meant to sustain, it is important to understand the institutions and the practices out of which it arose. In epistemological terms, it is possible to assert that the *Padrón Real* operated both as a condition of possibility and also of operability of the very idea of the Indies, its governance, the operation of transport routes and the very existence and operation of a 'Spanish' empire during the Hispanic Monarchies. Once claims are made on a new world as a new empirical space (see Brendecke 2012), which only really happens, as seen in Vespucci's letter opening this chapter, toward the end of the 1490s and early 1500s, what follows is a rapid process of stabilizing the claim, a process of invention of the New World. This is done by creating means that monopolize the interpretation of realities in the newly created space. Technically put, this is the result of stabilizing the empirical domain whilst setting up the epistemological frame that determines what is to be known, how and by whom. This is all accompanied by legal (and cultural) processes which seek to create, borrowing Niklas Luhmann's phrase, a security of expectation (Luhmann 2013, 78), that allow, in turn, for the recognition of an established order. In this process of stabilization, practices begin to be standardized (such as those involved in oceanic sailing by the training of pilots and the production of sailing itineraries and rutters), narratives begin to be legitimized by resort to (newly) accepted knowledge (e.g. chronicles and descriptions of the nature of the Indies), institutions of control are established (e.g. the Council of Indies and the *Casa de Contratación de Sevilla*), legal codes and jurisprudence are created (e.g. *Leyes de Indias*), professions are adapted to support the endeavour (e.g. cosmographers, cosmologists and geographers), standards of measurement and for the depiction of phenomena are introduced or adapted and enforced (e.g. marine astrolabe, nautical knots, nautical miles) and systems of circulation with their means for communication and command and control are introduced (e.g. *Carrera de Indias, Galeón de Manila*).

The empirical evidence of this process is ample. By 1516, the time of the coronation of Charles I, a complex system of governance had already been put into place to organize and control all issues related to the Indies. Key to this organization was the establishment of the Council of the Indies, originally created as part of the Council of Castile in 1503, and since 1524, as a separate council in its own right. The Council of the Indies was a special case in the councils of the Realm which were normally of territorial or of thematic character (cf. Gil Pujol 2004). In this case, the Council was both territorial and thematic and was in charge of providing counsel to the Crown on judicial, legislative and executive matters on all Indian issues (see Diego 1985). It had jurisdiction over all aspects related to the New World, was in charge of supervising the *Casa de Contratación* – as will be expanded on later – nominated candidates for viceroys, appointed generals and captains of fleets and armadas as well as bishops and bishoprics in the Indies. It also operated as a court of appeal and regulated ecclesiastical issues in line with royal patronage. It was presided by a bishop or a noble, and amongst its permanent staff were included, amongst others, an astronomer, a cosmographer and a chronicler, roles that already denote the importance of geographic, cosmographic and historical knowledge in the conception and governance of the New World. The business and tasks it concerned itself with grew exponentially as years progressed. As noted by Maria Portuondo, the Council of the Indies and the *Casa de Contratación* created a world which never stopped growing (Portuondo 2009).

The second institution, which depended on the Council of the Indies, was the *Casa de Contratación de Sevilla* (House of Trade of the Indies), established in 1503. The *Casa*[4] was created following the example of the Portuguese *Casa da Guiné e Mina*, later called *Casa da India*, with the purpose of organizing and governing all merchant relations with the Indian Ocean basin (see Acosta Rodríguez 2003). Based in Seville, the only legal port of departure to and arrival from the New World, the *Casa de Contratación* had powers over financial and legal matters regarding American trade. It was responsible for authorizing emigration, the training and licensing of pilots, the making of maps and navigational instruments, as well as the managing of estates of Spaniards deceased in the Indies. According to Turnbull, the *Casa de Contratación*, together with the *Casa da India*, was the first scientific institution of Europe (Turnbull 1996, 7). The science it sponsored and cultivated was of applied and practical nature, as will be noted later.

One of the most important figures within the *Casa*, which contributed greatly to the creation of the world Portuondo referred to, and to the invention of the Indies as such, was that of the *Piloto Mayor* (Pilot Major). This role emerged out of the *Junta de Navegantes* (Board of Navigators), a scientific meeting celebrated in Burgos in 1508 which included the four top navigators of the Realm (Juan Díaz de Solís, Juan de la Cosa, Vicente Yáñez Pinzón and Americo Vespucci), and was tasked with exploring ways of reaching the Molucca islands (the Spice Islands, or *especiería*) by sailing west as not to violate the Tordesillas Treaty that had allocated the Indian Ocean to the Portuguese. As a result, the *Junta* agreed to the creation of a new role, that of *Piloto Mayor* which should reside in Seville and coordinate cosmographical knowledge with regard to the Indies and further explorations. The role was given to Americo Vespucci. By 1510, King Ferdinand transferred the office of the *Piloto Mayor* to the *Casa* and tasked it with planning further explorations, examining pilots, drawing and updating charts, building and calibrating nautical instruments and creating and updating the *Padrón Real*. The *Casa*, under its Pilot, would ensure the monopoly of nautical knowledge and cartographic information, would supply such information on the basis of need under strict protocols of secrecy and would ensure that relevant knowledge would feed an updated version of the *Padrón* (see Sánchez 2013, 128–36).

In practical terms, the *Padrón* would operate as a sum of edited cosmographical and nautical knowledge coordinated through the figure of the *Piloto Mayor*. Through his tasks of training and examining (licencing) pilots for the Atlantic crossings, he would frame the operation of an epistemic community with shared knowledge, practices and traditions which would in principle materialize in the continuous creation of the *Padrón*. Licenced pilots departing to the Indies would be provided with a copy of the segment of the map relevant to their voyage which they should correct and augment through their experience and report their findings to the *Piloto Mayor* at their return. The continuous updating of the cartographic registry would lead to the destruction of erroneous and outdated maps. There were clear procedures for doing so, as described by García Redondo (García Redondo 2018b, 49, chap. 1). In practice, as Arndt Brendecke argued (Brendecke 2012, 190–226), the system did not always work since pilots found ways to operate beyond and around the established system using alternative maps produced on the black market and trading information otherwise rendered as secret. As noted by García Redondo, it would not be surprising that the most beautiful and desired copies of the *Padrón* would find themselves into a black market of spies, courtiers and collectionists (García Redondo 2018b, 49, chap. 1).

The appointment of the *Piloto Mayor* and its commission alert us to an important element in the political economy of knowledge which characterizes the idea of 'Spanish' Empire at the time. As such, the office had no precedent in Europe where, as noted by García Redondo, cartography had been an eminently private enterprise (García Redondo 2018a, 48). When the Castilian crown undertakes the monopoly of cartography appointing cosmographers to its service, it is claiming property and sovereignty over cartographic knowledge. The move is of great importance because it signals a shift in cartographic knowledge, from private wealth to common wealth in the figure of the monarch, expressing an idea of empire that combines both dominion – property rights – with imperium – sovereign rights (cf. Pagden 2005). The role of the *Piloto Mayor* operates as a centralizing figure in such a conception of empire, that in its empirical character claims property and sovereignty over knowledge, and governs through it.

One of the key tasks of the *Piloto Mayor*, part of the monopolization of cartographic knowledge and practice, was to build and calibrate nautical instruments for oceanic navigation. These instruments, rudimentary as they might seem today, constituted the European state of the art for calculating location at sea. Different to Mediterranean sailing, where navigation through dead reckoning based on direction and distance was usually enough to know a ship's location, oceanic voyages required methods and instruments for celestial navigation. Whereas only rough estimates of time could be had with regard to longitude (see Leitão 2018), a problem which would only be solidly solved in the XVIIIC, latitude could be calculated using various methods and instruments, central to which were the marine astrolabe, the quadrant and the cross-staff. Readings taken with these instruments required tables and almanacs that would allow pilots to plot them into their maps and have an idea of their relative location. Their use, therefore, demanded knowledge of some practical cosmography as well as training on their handling and operation. Between 1510 and 1552, this role lay on the *Piloto Mayor*, but due to the wealth of information gathered in Seville and the complexities of the tasks involved in the role, it was decided that a chair of cosmography would be established, commission by which a professor would continuously develop and adapt cosmographical science for the use of celestial navigation in the 'Spanish' routes in the training and licensing of pilots (Sánchez Martínez 2010, 624).

Cosmographical knowledge is a prolific site from which to observe tensions between the experiential knowledge derived from oceanic navigation and exploration, and theoretical cosmography based on treatises and the teaching of the ancients. By the 1550s there were at least two chairs of cosmography in Castile. One, based at the University of Salamanca, was concerned with theoretical cosmographic knowledge and worked with ancient and medieval treatises such as those of Ptolemy and Sacrobosco. The second, based at the Casa de Contratación, was tasked with devising practical applications of cosmographical knowledge and rendering it useful in the crafting of cartography and instructions for navigation. Whereas the figure of the *Piloto Mayor* had initially brought together empirical and scientific knowledge, an important characteristic given that most pilots at the time were mostly illiterate (Pérez Mallaína 2005, 229–31), specialization and bureaucratization of tasks led to a distancing of them. This differentiation matters with regard to the crafting of maps. Oceanic navigation demanded the adaptation of Portolan maps, which were mostly focused on practical navigation by dead reckoning, and transformed them into more technical devices which were difficult to use and interpret. The use of navigational instruments made the task even more complex, making some pilots seek alternative charts, of more practical use. This led to the emergence of a black market of information which rivalled and challenged the Crown's monopoly intended through the *Padrón Real* (Brendecke 2012, 191–202).

A visual representation of the complex ensemble of cosmographic knowledge represented through the *Padrón Real* can be observed in Diego Ribeiro's World Map of 1529 (figure 2.2). The map, claimed by some to be part of the *Padrón Real*, was a diplomatic depiction of the world demarcating 'Spanish' claims invoking the latest cosmographic knowledge and practices of the time. It is used here, not as an archetypical case of the *Padrón* but as a site of experimentation from which to explore the idea of empire represented through it. Ribeiro, Portuguese by origin, and then royal cosmographer at the service of the *Casa de Contratación*, was a seriously experienced navigator who had travelled to India with Vasco da Gama in 1497 and with Alfonso de Alburquerque in 1503, had prepared the maps used by the Magellan-Elcano

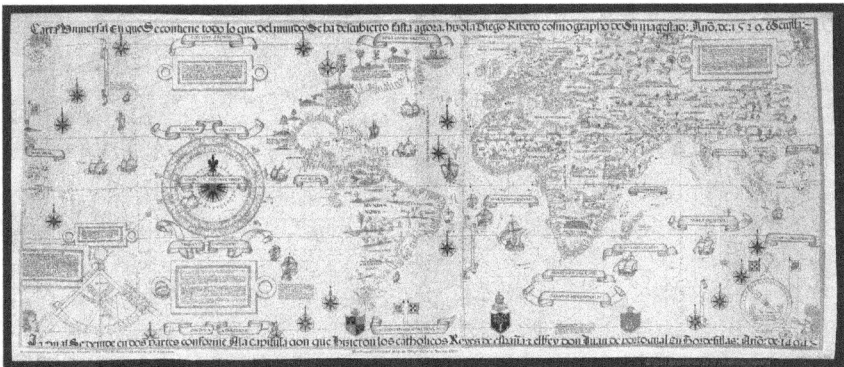

Figure 2.2. World Map by Diego Ribeiro, 1529 (The Second Borgian Map). From a facsimile by W. Griggs, 1886. Original in the Museum of Propaganda in Rome.

circumnavigation of 1519, and had participated in the *Junta de Badajoz-Elvas* of 1524 where 'Spanish' and Portuguese cosmographers had gathered to determine the location of the Tordesillas Anti-Meridian so as to settle a dispute over territorial claims on the Philippines and the Molucca Islands. He was also a member of the 1526 *Junta de Pilotos* gathered by Ferdinand Columbus (son of Christopher) to update information for a revision of the *Padrón Real*. As such, his authority in producing a world map was unchallenged. However, and in the spirit of this chapter, the map must not be taken to be a faithful representation of a geographical status quo, but be approached as a site of experimentation. What is experimented with here is the invention of a new world and its derivatives in the Pacific Ocean.

Two issues stand out in the 'Spanish' Imperial claim depicted in the map. The first is the political claim to world-space, represented by two features. First, a large legend framing the bottom of the map which reads 'General chart containing the whole of the world that has hitherto been discovered; compiled by Diego Ribeiro, cosmographer to His Majesty, which is divided into two parts according to the agreement made by the Catholic Majesties of Spain and King John of Portugal at Tordesillas, A.D. 1494'. Here, the imaginary of discovery mentioned in the introduction with regard to Vespucci's letter, is explicitly present. Rendering the map as 'General chart containing the whole of the world that has hitherto been discovered', presents the world as discoverable, parts of which have already been so, and are claimed as political spaces demarcated in the map; other parts remain to be discovered and the division of the world, 'according to the agreement made by the Catholic Majesties of Spain and King John of Portugal', sets what is to belong, in principle, to which power. In this respect, the map portrays a bipolar imaginary of discovery and conquest legitimated by law according to an international treaty, that of Tordesillas. On this matter, the demarcation of the Tordesillas line is very important. The Atlantic portion of the meridian line crossing Brazil is indicated at the bottom of the map with the flags of Castile to the west and that of Portugal to the east. The Pacific part of the line, the Anti-Meridian is, however, not clearly demarcated. Only the two flags appear at the south-east bottom part of the map without a line which corresponds to the lack of agreement at the *Junta de Badajoz-Elvas* of 1524. The issue would be settled only through the Treaty of Zaragoza of 1529 by which Spain ceased claims over the Moluccas and kept what was later to be known as the Philippine islands.

The second remarkable issue relates to claims to epistemological novelty. Here, a bold statement is made with regard to the scientific character of the map. The map does not contain any religious references, saints or Madonnas, which were a distinguishing feature of older Portolan maps such as de la Cosa's. In their absence, and most likely in their stead, the map is decorated in its lower corners with two very detailed and large navigational instruments: a quadrant (left) and an astrolabe (right) with some instructions on their use. The two instruments can be interpreted as making a claim to the scientific character of the map representing the celestial navigation techniques employed in sailing the world and plotting it (cf. Davies 2003). The main wind rose, of remarkable size and located in the middle of the Pacific, contains in this case a detailed depiction of the zodiac, and the time cycle it represents. This is a typical feature of cosmographic and geographic treatises of the time, and its inclusion in the map adds a dynamic temporal dimension to the geographical space depicted there (the world that does not cease to grow). The epistemological novelty claimed by invoking the authority derived from the use of navigational instruments and the zodiac is, therefore, a partitioning of the world according to scientific techniques which render a world-space, under growth, as governable.

## THE INDIVIDUAL EMPIRE OF PHILIP II AND THE DIEGO GUTIERREZ MAP OF AMERICA

The third conception of empire, according to Frankl in relation to the Catholic monarchies, was that of individual empire. It came in the figure of Philip II, son of Charles, who came to be recognized as the king of all Spains, an idea that did not acknowledge colonies but kingdoms under a single monarch. Under his realm, Spain was recognized as the largest and most powerful European kingdom, including Spain, Portugal, the Low Countries, Sicily and Naples, Franche-Comté in France, the Rhineland in Germany, most of the American continent, the Philippines with the 'Spanish' East Indies, trading ports in India and South Asia and parts of Guinea and North Africa (Parker 2001). The conception of empire underlying this model, as shown in great detail in the work of Arndt Brendecke, relied intensely on the capacity of the King to know and administrate through dedicated institutions, similar to contemporary ministries, which in turn relied on strategies for knowing, involving innovations such as printed forms for administration and the systematic collection of data (Brendecke 2012; also in English 2016). This individual idea of empire was premised on the capacity to transform empirical knowledge into power resources and action, but also, of laying explicit claim on its territories and spaces of political action.

The geopolitical circumstances regarding the access of Philip to the 'Spanish' throne are of particular interest here. After the abdication of Charles I in 1556, and his subsequent death two years later, a long period of war with France, partly related to the French wars of royal succession, was brought to an end with the Treaty of Cateau-Cambresis signed in 1559. As part of the treaty an agreement was reached between Spain and France whereby Elizabeth of Valois, daughter of Henry II of France, would marry Philip II in the summer of 1559. The agreement, which stabilized monarchic territorial claims in Europe until around the Thirty Years War, detailed the realms of influence of Spain and France in Europe, including agreements with England. It did not, however, settle disagreements between Spain and Portugal and the rest of European powers with regard to trade in most of their extra-European spheres of influence, particularly in the New World. As a consequence, the Treaty settled in principle a form of European peace whilst creating a de facto space for imperial European confrontation. To deal with this issue, as has been allegedly historically supported by some circumstantial evidence, a verbal agreement was reached between Spain and France in the course of negotiations of the Treaty so that its agreements would not apply in the zone west of the Prime Meridian and south of the Tropic of Cancer (Mattingly 1963, 148–58). Although this agreement does not appear in the Treaty's text, according to Mattingly, evidence to it can be found on diplomatic correspondence between the French, 'Spanish', and English in the mid to late XVIC, and, as will be noted in the following, in cartographic depictions on imperial zones of influence (Mattingly 1963, 148–58). The problem concerning the location of the Prime Meridian remained a highly political issue.

The implications of the establishment of such lines of demarcation and the zone of perpetual imperial confrontation it tolerated cannot be overstated. They created a de facto division of the (European dominated) world, which together with the still claimed order resulting from the Treaty of Tordesillas, partitioned the Atlantic in three parts, as will be detailed in the following. It would take forty years for Hugo Grotius's thesis of Mare Liberum to openly challenge the Portuguese policy of *Mare Clausus* in the Indian Ocean basin and the 'Spanish' legal claims based on the Tordesillas Line, and many more years for it to be adopted and recognized, if at all (cf. Benton 2010, 104–61).

Under such a context, mapping was used as a diplomatic and cultural instrument with which and through which to claim and reclaim possession of spaces, disseminate and reinforce a historiography of how such spaces were found and conquered, and establish spheres of imperial domination. Such form of mapping can be explored, experimentally, in Diego Gutierrez's map of America of 1562 (figure 2.3). Here, the imperial possessions of the recently crowned Philip II get represented by claims over the New World as well as the Atlantic and Pacific waters that surround it (see Sánchez Martínez 2013, 280–82). The claims rely, once again, on issues of epistemological novelty and an imaginary of discovery.

The map resulted from a collaboration between Diego Gutierrez, a royal cosmographer working for the *Piloto Mayor* at the *Casa de Contratación*, and Hieronymus Cock, an Antwerp engraver who had one of the most advanced

Figure 2.3. America's Map by Diego Gutiérrez, Antwerp, 1562 (Americae Sive Qvatae Orbis Partis Nova et Exatissima Descritptio). Courtesy of Library of Congress, Geography and Map Division.

printing workshops of the time. The map was entitled *Americae Sive Qvatae Orbis Partis Nova et Exatissima Descritptio* (Part of the new and the most exact description of America or of the fourth of the world). The reference to the fourth part of the world corresponds to an expression used in the context of Martin Waldseemüller's 1507 printed wall map of the world, the first to use the name 'America' for the continent. In its accompanying *Cosmographiae Introductio*, it was stated that America, as an island surrounded by the seas, constituted the fourth part, the first three being Europe, Asia and Africa (Waldseemüller *et al.* 1907, chap. 9). Gutierrez's explicit use of the expression to qualify the term 'America' can be interpreted as reinstating the 'Spanish' claim to having discovered the *continent* (a claim to epistemological novelty), and of projecting and promoting their imaginary of the New World as a discovery subject to conquest. This is evidenced on an inscription at the very top of the map, in Latin, which translated into English reads: 'This fourth part of the world remained unknown to all geographers until the year 1497, at which time it was discovered by Americus Vespucius serving the King of Castile, whereupon it also obtained a name from the discoverer'.

The map can be interpreted as presenting the known parts of the New World as shared with the Portuguese, in the area of Brazil, and with the French, in North America. The main spatial contentions come in the ways in which Atlantic ocean-space is depicted. In general terms, the Atlantic can be observed as divided into two parts. The first was constituted by an area west of the Prime Meridian – located on this map explicitly crossing Ferro on the Canary Islands – and north of the Tropic of Cancer, where European agreements would stand. As such, it was an area of peace. Here, Philip II is represented close to the coasts of Florida riding a carriage behind Poseidon, god of the sea, as if making a claim to modernity (epistemological novelty) by which Spain discovers a world unknown to the ancients and challenges the myths governing their Thalassic order. Such an imaginary is reinforced on a panel of script in the lower left part of the map, where the conquests of Alexander the Great are mentioned by way of comparing the magnificence of the 'Spanish' Empire with those of ancient rulers. At the same time, the 'Spanish' Habsburg coat of arms is shown next to that of the French crown, perhaps in recognition of the marriage between Philip II and Elizabeth of Valois, in what is now the United States, depicting the amity between the two powers, north of the Tropic of Cancer, that resulted from the Treaty of Cateau-Cambresis (see Hébert 1999). On the same year the map was printed, however, France started its colonial presence in parts of today's South Carolina and Florida forcing Spain to defend its space.

The second partition corresponds to the area west of the Prime Meridian and south of the Tropic of Cancer. Here, the order of the Cateau-Cambresis Treaty does not apply, although the order of the Tordesillas Treaty is observed by Iberian powers. This is symbolized by a depiction of a man riding a sea monster and holding the Portuguese coat of arms, located at the bottom of the Atlantic, representing the Tordesillas Line. A fleet north of the Equator in the proximity of the African coast and south of the Cape Verde Islands is used to represent Portuguese claims on those waters and is accompanied by the legend 'the Portuguese Fleet going to Calicut'. However, in the mid-South-Atlantic just under the Tropic of Capricorn, a naval battle involving a caravel and two naos, apparently from Spain and Portugal, and a Mediterranean-style galley with a different flag, represents the geopolitical instability and contestation in this part of the world. Such depiction, however, could also represent conflicts arising from the difficulties of ascertaining one's position, particularly in relation to longitude, through celestial navigation. Spain's claims on the Pacific coast of the Americas and its surrounding ocean are represented as uncontested and challenged only by nature as depicted by shipwrecks, sirens and seamonsters.

The 1562 Diego Gutierrez map represents Philip II's American empire as contested by European rivals and anticipates the geostrategic contestation of Atlantic ocean-space in the centuries to come. The way in which it represents partitioned spatial orders at sea illustrates the individual conception of empire where unity without uniformity seemed to have been the strategic motto. By 1580, however, such strategy was to be tested to the limit. A great war between European powers had commenced. As noted by Braudel, it 'was fundamentally a struggle for control of the Atlantic Ocean, the new centre of gravity of the world. Its outcome would decide whether the Atlantic was in future to be ruled by Catholics or Protestants, northerners or Iberians, for the Atlantic was now the prize coveted by all' (Braudel 1995, 482–83).

## CONCLUSION: THE 'SPANISH' EMPIRE AS EPISTEMOLOGICAL FORMATION

Perhaps, in a way, Pagden was right. There was never such a thing as a 'Spanish' Empire. In fact, it could be argued, there were never European empires. There were, instead, empires in the making, imperial projects and aspirations in a continuous process of becoming and actualization. However, central to understanding the making of European empires is the problem of knowledge and not simply of political authority. In the XVIC 'Spanish' case explored in this chapter, such process involved two core issues: claims to epistemological novelty, on the one hand, and an imaginary of discovery on the other. Whereas the former prepared the ground for the invention of new spaces, new orders and new forms of governance, the latter revealed the epistemological conditions that legitimated the first.

This can be seen in the three mapping examples explored earlier. In times of the Catholic Kings, the epistemological novelty claimed for the New World relied on the idea that there was a world out there that could be discovered, a frontier that could be colonized. Such a world was conceived already as part of a Christian order whose limits were being pushed beyond the Pillars of Hercules. It implied already a Christian faith to be promoted; a political economy to be implemented, exploited and developed; and a political order to be imposed. In the case of Charles I, epistemological claims relied on the empirical and technical capacity to depict and master global spaces so as to produce a master map of the world. Such claims relied on the sophistication and organization of cosmographic knowledge, bureaucratic creativity and oceanic navigational skill. It implied a conception of world-space, terrestrial and landed, that could be conquered, defended and governed (e.g. the circumnavigation of the globe, the establishment of global trading circuits through the *Carrera de Indias* in the Atlantic and the Galeón the Manila in the Pacific). In the case of Philip II, epistemological claims came around the idea of America as the fourth part of the world, as a continental space mostly under 'Spanish' rule, and of an Atlantic ocean-space partitioned in such a way that continental European agreements applied in principle to the north-west, and the rest was subjected to the erosion of the Tordesillas order giving rise to an ocean-space of imperial contestation. The imaginary of discovery now relied on the capacity of intra-European imperial rivalry to project naval and diplomatic power across contested and legally unregulated ocean-spaces. It implied, de facto, the invention of the Atlantic as a space of imperial confrontation that was to last well into the twentieth century.

This is to say that the idea of empire in the 'Spanish' monarchies of the XVIC, in relation to America, is not a stable one and defies typological classifications. Whereas the chapter has used conceptions of Catholic, composite and individual empire, the analysis of the maps reveals that such neat categories do not necessarily match the power struggles at play. Aimed at differentiating political authority between the three monarchs, this classification simplifies the complexity of forms of authority, the legitimacy of power and the effectiveness of rule in each of the cases, and does not contribute much to understanding the rationalities upon which novel spaces of governance were created. Approaching maps as sites of epistemological experimentation allows us to challenge such neatness and observe and learn from power struggles at play by de-naturalizing detail, interrogating form, de-constructing style and technique, enquiring about the complexity of authorship and exploring the authority that legitimated the production of the map. Such analysis assumes maps, not as sources of knowledge and fact, but as empirical sites from which original questions can be posed.

The three mapping cases analysed here become fertile grounds from which to foster the interrogation of political imaginaries of empire in specific historical settings. As such, they become empirical sites from which to begin to develop a form of political theory that transcends the written text and affords an engagement with experiments of power.

## NOTES

1. The term *'Spanish' Empire* is used in this chapter in a very general and anachronistic manner. There was no such thing as Spain until the reforms of the House of Bourbon in the early eighteenth century. The unity of the Catholic Queen Isabel and King Fernando in 1469 was dynastic, not territorial. The Indies, as America was

called at the time, was part of the Kingdom of Castile, not 'Spanish', and as such, was not part of the Habsburg composite empire as was, for example, Naples. What is referred to in this chapter as the early 'Spanish' Empire is really a XVIC Castilian empire with very strong inputs of other parts of the Hispanic monarchy, mostly peninsular, as well as from what today constitutes Italy.

2. I am grateful to Ricardo Padrón, Antonio Sánchez Martínez and the co-editors of this volume who made very useful comments on an earlier version of this chapter.

3. Vespucci, regardless of his doubtful reputation as mariner and cosmographer (see Fernández-Armesto 2007), was by then an experienced European explorer who had participated of Atlantic crossings twice under 'Spanish' sponsorship, and his latest trip was under commission of Manuel I of Portugal. His authorship of this letter known as *Mundus Novus*, translated from Latin and published in pamphlet form, is disputed (cf. Omodeo 2014). However, and regardless of the authenticity of Vespucci's authorship, its text influenced European intellectual and political circles and reveals an important epistemological tension prevalent in the (Western) European imaginary well into the XXC.

4. There were other houses of trade in Spain at the time, e.g. the *Lonja de Barcelona*, *Casa de Contratación de Perpignan*, *de Zaragoza*, *de Bilbao*, *de Burgos*. In this chapter the use of *Casa* refers to the *Casa de Contratación de Sevilla*.

## REFERENCES

Acosta Rodríguez, Antonio. 2003. *La Casa de la Contratación y la Navegación entre España y las Indias*. Sevilla: Universidad de Sevilla.

Akerman, James R. 2009. *The Imperial Map: Cartography and the Mastery of Empire*. Chicago: University of Chicago Press.

Allighieri, Dante. 1995. *Monarchia (ca. 1320)*, edited and translated by Prue Shaw. Cambridge: Camrbidge University Press.

Alvarez, Aldo. 2003. 'Geomagnetism and the Cartography of Juan de La Cosa: A New Perspective on the Greater Antilles in the Age of Discovery'. *Terrae Incognitae* 35 (1): 1–15.

Armitage, David, ed. 1998. *Theories of Empire, 1450–1800*. London: Routledge.

Bacchi, Carol. 2012. 'Why Study Problematizations? Making Politics Visible'. *Open Journal of Political Science* 2 (1): 1–8.

Barrera-Osorio, Antonio. 2006. *Experiencing Nature: The 'Spanish' American Empire and the Early Scientific Revolution*. Austin: University of Texas Press.

Benton, Lauren. 2010. *A Search for Sovereignty: Law and Geography in European Empires, 1400–1900*. Cambridge: Cambridge University Press.

Braudel, Fernand. 1995. *The Mediterranean and the Mediterranean World in the Age of Philip II*. 2 vols., translated by Siân Reynolds. Berkley: University of California Press.

Brendecke, Arndt. 2012. *Imperio e información: Funciones del saber en el dominio colonial español*. Madrid: Iberoamericana Editorial Vervuert.

———. 2016. *The Empirical Empire: 'Spanish' Colonial Rule and the Politics of Knowledge*. Berlin: Walter de Gruyter.

Cañizares-Esguerra, Jorge. 2002. *How to Write the History of the New World: Histories, Epistemologies, and Identities in the Eighteenth-Century Atlantic World.* Stanford: Stanford University Press.

———. 2006. *Nature, Empire, and Nation: Explorations of the History of Science in the Iberian World.* Stanford: Stanford University Press.

Casey, Edward, S. 1998. *The Fate of Place: A Philosophical History.* Berkley: University of California Press.

Chandler, Tertius. 1987. *Four Thousand Years of Urban Growth: An Historical Census.* Lewiston, NY: The Edwin Mellen Press.

Craib, Raymond B. 2000. 'Cartography and Power in the Conquest and Creation of New Spain'. *Latin American Research Review* 35 (1): 7–36.

Davies, Surekha. 2003. 'The Navigational Iconography of Diogo Ribeiro's 1529 Vatican Planisphere'. *Imago Mundi* 55 (1), 103–112.

Davis, Charles Till. 1957. *Dante and the Idea of Rome.* Oxford: Clarendon Press.

Del Val-Valdivieso, M. I. 2004. 'La Reina Isabel en las Crónicas de Diego de Valera y Alonso de Palencia'. In *Vision del Reinado de Isabel la Catolica*, edited by Julio Valdeón Baruque, 63–91. Valladolid: Ambito.

Deleuze, Gilles, and Felix Guattari. 1994. *What Is Philosophy?*, translated by Graham Burchell and Hugh Tomlinson. London: Verso.

Denevan, William. 1992. *The Native Population of the Americas in 1492.* Madison: University of Wisconsin Press.

Derrida, Jacques. 2007. *Psyche: Inventions of the Other, Volume I*, edited by Peggy Kamuf and Elizabeth Rottenberg. Stanford: Stanford University Press.

Desai, Gaurav. 1993. 'The Invention of Invention'. *Cultural Critique* 24: 119–42.

Diego, Alfonso García Gallo de. 1985. 'El consejo y los secretarios en el Gobierno de Indias en los siglos XVI y XVII'. *Revista Chilena de Historia del Derecho* 11: 329–53.

Dodge, Martin, Rob Kitchin, and Chris Perkins, eds. 2009. *Rethinking Maps: New Frontiers in Cartographic Theory.* London: Routledge.

Fernández-Armesto, Felipe. 2007. *Amerigo: The Man Who Gave His Name to America.* New York: Random House.

Foucault, Michel. 1972. *The Archaeology of Knowledge.* New York: Pantheon Books.

———. 1989. *The Order of Things.* London: Routledge.

———. 1994. 'Polemics, Politics, and Problematisations: An Interview with Michel Foucault'. In *Michel Foucault: Essential Works of Foucault 1954–1984, Vol. 1 Ethics*, edited by Paul Rabinow, 111–19. London: Penguin.

Frankl, Víctor. 1963. 'Imperio Particular e Imperio Universal en las Cartas de Relación de Hernán Cortés'. *Cuadernos Hispanoamericanos* CLXV(1): 443–82.

García Redondo, José María. 2018a. *Cartografía e Imperio: El Padrón Real y la Representación del Nuevo Mundo.* Madrid: Ediciones Doce Calles.

———. 2018b. *Cartografía e Imperio: El Padrón Real y la Representación del Nuevo Mundo.* Madrid: Ediciones Doce Calles.

Gil Pujol, Xavier. 2004. 'Un Rey, Una Fe, muchas Naciones. Patria y Nación en la España de Los Siglos XVI–XVII'. In *La Monarquía de Las Naciones: Patria, Nación y Naturaleza en la Monarquía de España*, edited by Antonio Antonio Álvarez-Ossorio Alvariño and Bernardo J. García García, 39–76. Madrid: Fundación Carlos de Amberes.

Goodman, David C. 2002. *Power and Penury: Government, Technology and Science in Philip II's Spain*. Cambridge: Cambridge University Press.
Hardt, Michael, and Antonio Negri. 2001. *Empire*. Cambridge, MA: Harvard University Press.
Harley, John Brian. 1989. 'Deconstructing the Map'. *Cartographica* 26 (2): 1–20.
Headley, John M. 1998. 'The Habsburg World Empire and the Revival of Ghibellinism'. In *Theories of Empire, 1450–1800*, edited by David Armitage, 45–80. London: Routledge.
Hébert, John R. 1999. *The 1562 Map of America by Diego Gutiérrez*. Washington, D.C.: Library of Congress.
Hispalensis, Isidorus. 2014. *Historia de Regibus Gothorum, Vandalorum et Suevorum*. CreateSpace Independent Publishing Platform.
Kamen, Henry. 2014. *The 'Spanish' Inquisition: A Historical Revision*. New Haven: Yale University Press.
Ladero-Quesada, M. A. 2004. 'La Reina en las Crónicas de Fernando Del Pulgar y Andrés Bernáldez'. In *Vision y Reinado de Isabel La Catolica*, edited by Julio Valdeón Baruque, 13–61. Valladolid: Ambito.
Lefebvre, Henri. 1991. *The Production of Space*, translated by Donald Nicholson-Smith. Oxford: Wiley-Blackwell.
Leitão, Henrique. 2018. 'Instruments and Artisanal Practices in Long Distance Oceanic Voyages'. *Centaurus* 60 (3): 189–202.
Lobo-Guerrero, Luis. 2019a. 'Novelty and the Creation of the New World in XVI C Spain'. In *Imaginaries of Connectivity: The Creation of Novel Spaces of Governance*, edited by Luis Lobo-Guerrero, Suvi Alt, and Maarten Meijer, 13–37. London: Rowman & Littlefield.
———. 2019b. 'On the Epistemology of Maps and Mapping: De La Cosa, Mercator, and the Making of Spatial Imaginaries'. In *Mapping and Politics in a Digital Age*, edited by Pol Bargués-Pedreny, David Chandler, and Elena Simon, 20–38. London: Routledge.
Luhmann, Niklas. 2013. *A Sociological Theory of Law*. London: Routledge.
Maravall, José Antonio. 1966. *Antiguos y Modernos: La Idea de Progreso en el Desarrollo Inicial de una Sociedad*. Madrid: Sociedad de Estudios y Publicaciones.
———. 1972. *Estado Moderno y Mentalidad Social Siglo XV a XVII. Book 1*. Madrid: Libropolis.
Martínez, Ricardo Cerezo. 1993. 'La Carta de Juan de la Cosa (II)'. *Revista de historia naval* 11 (42): 21–44.
Martín-Merás, María Luisa. 1993. *Cartografía marítima hispana: la imagen de América*. Barcelona: IGME.
———. 2000. 'La Carta de Juan de La Cosa: Interpretación e Historia'. *Monte Buciero* 4 (1): 71–85.
Mattingly, Garrett. 1963. 'No Peace beyond What Line?' *Transactions of the Royal Historical Society* 13: 145–62.
Miravalle, Mark I. 2006. *Introduction to Mary: The Heart of Marian Doctrine and Devotion*. Goleta: Queenship Publishing.
Mudimbe, Valentin-Yves. 1988. *The Invention of Africa: Gnosis, Philosophy, and the Order of Knowledge*. Bloomington: Indiana University Press.

Muldoon, James. 1999. *Empire and Order: The Concept of Empire, 800–1800*. Basingstoke: Palgrave Macmillan.

———. 2015. *The Americas in the 'Spanish' World Order: The Justification for Conquest in the Seventeenth Century*. Philadelphia: University of Pennsylvania Press.

Naipaul, V. S. 1988. *The Enigma of Arrival*. New York: Vintage.

North, Michael. 2013. *Novelty: A History of the New*. New edition. Chicago: University of Chicago Press.

O'Gorman, Edmundo. 1961. *The Invention of America: An Inquiry into the Historical Nature of the New World and the Meaning of Its History*. Bloomington: Indiana University Press.

Omodeo, Pietro T. 2014. 'The Authenticity of Amerigo Vespucci's Mundus Novus and Information Untold about His Third Journey'. *Nuncius* 29 (2): 359–88.

Oro, José Garcia. 1971. *Cisneros y la Reforma del Clero Espanol en el Tiempo de los Reyes Catolicos*. Madrid: CSIC.

Padrón, Ricardo. 2004. *The Spacious Word: Cartography, Literature, and Empire in Early Modern Spain*. Chicago: University of Chicago Press.

Pagden, Anthony, ed. 1986. *Hernán Cortés: Letters from Mexico*. New Haven: Yale University Press.

———. 1998a. *'Spanish' Imperialism and the Political Imagination: Studies in European and 'Spanish'-American Social and Political Theory 1513–1830*. New Haven: Yale University Press.

———. 1998b. *'Spanish' Imperialism and the Political Imagination: Studies in European and 'Spanish'-American Social and Political Theory 1513–1830*. New Haven: Yale University Press.

———. 2005. 'Fellow Citizens and Imperial Subjects: Conquest and Sovereignty in Europe's Overseas Empires'. *History and Theory* 44 (4): 28–46.

Parker, Geoffrey. 2001. *The World Is Not Enough: The Imperial Vision of Philip II of Spain*. Waco: Baylor University Press.

Pérez, Joseph. 2005. *The 'Spanish' Inquisition: A History*. New Haven: Yale University Press.

Pérez Mallaína, Pablo E. 2005. *Spain's Men of the Sea*. Baltimore: Johns Hopkins University Press.

Portuondo, María M. 2009. *Secret Science: 'Spanish' Cosmography and the New World*. Chicago: University of Chicago Press.

Rey, Eusebio. 1952. 'La Bula de Alejandro VI Otorgando el Título de "católicos" a Fernando e Isabel'. *Razón y Fe* 146: 59–75, 324–47.

Robles Macias, Luis A. 2010. 'Juan de La Cosa's Projection: A Fresh Analysis of the Earliest Preserved Map of the Americas' Available electronically from https://hdl.handle.net/1969.1/129190

Sáenz-López, Sandra. 2006. 'La Carta de Juan de La Cosa (1500), Colofón de La Cartografía Medieval'. *Piezas Del Mes – Museo Naval de Madrid 2003–2005*, no. 1: 10–31.

Sánchez Martínez, Antonio. 2010. 'Los artífices del Plus Ultra: pilotos, cartógrafos y cosmógrafos en la Casa de la Contratación de Sevilla durante el siglo XVI'. *Hispania* 70 (236): 607–32.

———. 2013. *La Espada, La Cruz y El Padrón: Soberanía, Fe y Representación Cartográfica en el Mundo Ibérico bajo la Monarquía Hispánica, 1503–1598*. Madrid: CSIC.
Solórzano Pereira, Juan de. 1629. *De Indiarum Jure Sive Dejusta Indiarum Occidentalium Inquisitione, Acquisitione, & Retentione. 2 Vols.* Madrid: Ex typographia Francisci Martinez.
Steinberg, Philip E. 2001. *The Social Construction of the Ocean*. Cambridge: Cambridge University Press.
Todorov, Tzvetan. 1984. *The Conquest of America: The Question of the Other*. New York: Harper & Row.
Turnbull, David. 1996. 'Cartography and Science in Early Modern Europe: Mapping the Construction of Knowledge Spaces'. *Imago Mundi* 48 (1): 5–24.
Vespucci, Americo. 1503. 'Mundus Novus in Translation'. In *Vespucci Reprints, Text, and Studies*, translated by Tyler Northup. Princeton: Princeton University Press.
Waldseemüller, Martin, Charles George Herbermann, Joseph Fischer, Franz Wieser, and Edward Burke. 1907. *The Cosmographiæ Introductio of Martin Waldseemüller in Facsimile, Followed by the Four Voyages of Amerigo Vespucci, with Their Translation into English*. New York: The United States Catholic Historical Society.
Wilkes, John. 1971. *Hernán Cortes, Conquistador in Mexico*. Cambridge: Cambridge University Press.
Yun-Casalilla, Bartolomé. 2019. *Iberian World Empires and the Glonalization of Europe 1415–1668*. Houndmills: Palgrave Macmillan.

*Chapter 3*

# Freezing Cartographic Imaginaries

## *Mapping the Rediscovery of Greenland and the Restoring of the Danish Monarchy*

Jeppe Strandsbjerg

In August 1582, the Danish King Frederik II, residing in his fashionable castle *Kronborg*, wrote a letter to Queen Elizabeth of England to ask her permission to employ the English 'military man' Captain Martinus Frobisher for one or two years. The letter emphasizes Frobisher's intelligence and knowledge of seafaring (Letter from Frederik II in Bobé 1936b, 11). Frobisher had led the expedition licensed by the Muscovy Company, in search of the North-West Passage, that first 're-encountered' Greenland in 1576 after contact had been lost between Denmark-Norway and Greenland since the 1420s. Whereas Frobisher's expedition, along with those of most contemporary European sailors, was concerned with discovering new routes and lands, the Danish king was concerned with how to re-connect to old Crown Lands. And Frobisher could well hold the key after years of fruitless efforts by the Danish court. Rather than keep relying on old sources and written directions from the Norse settlers and optimistic sailors who might have sighted Greenland, here was somebody who had actually stepped foot on Greenland and knew how to get there.

Seen from a perspective that equals territorial possession with occupation and control, the situation at the court was a bit bizarre. During the Viking Age, at least two settlements had been established in Greenland. Now, in his capacity, among many other titles, as king of Norway, the Danish king considered Greenland as part of the realm (*domæne*) because the Norse settlers had submitted to the Norwegian king in 1261. However, the court had lost the know-how to reach the island and re-establish contact with the old Norse settlements. That is, sovereignty was claimed over unreachable land. Other countries also recognized Danish sovereignty over Greenland. It was thus part of the realm but inaccessible and largely unknown. This poses some interesting questions to our usual narratives and perceptions of imperial mappings. Whereas most of the mapping – which attracts scholarly attention – taking place during the fifteenth, sixteenth and seventeenth centuries is driven by a desire to discover, govern and rationalize new sites and lands, the Danish-Norwegian mappings of Greenland, and the route to the island, were driven by a desire to re-establish contact, ensure sovereignties and thus secure dominion over these faraway and mythical lands. In that respect, the mappings of Greenland and of the travel routes to get there were more concerned with restoring the kingdom than establishing a new empire.

The re-connection of Greenland to Denmark-Norway is, however, an important case to discuss in the context of European mapping and empire-building because it both nuances and illustrates how cartography played a central role in claiming control over overseas areas – whether these were imperial or state-making exercises. After several attempts and planned but not executed voyages, Greenland was eventually reached by three expeditions leaving from Copenhagen in 1605, 1606 and 1607. According to the established historiography, the English chief pilot James Hall, who oversaw the navigation on all three expeditions, was instrumental to the success in reaching Greenland. His reports to the Danish kings after the first two journeys have been preserved, and in this chapter I want to focus mostly on four sketch maps of the Greenlandic coast that Hall included in the first report, especially the first and the latter map because they include most signs and iconography (see figures 3.1 and 3.2). Usually the historiography of the mapping of Greenland focuses on the drawing and placing of the island by European map-makers.[1] But in this chapter, I will focus on the two large-scale maps of the coastline in order to draw out some arguments about European imperial space-making. The maps are drawn following contemporary standards of geometric cartography[2] and tie the crown to the land in a fashion that follows a pattern similar to that of contemporary European imperial practices.

I see these maps as small examples of what Patricia Seed (1995) calls 'ceremonies of possession'. As such, the maps connect royal insignia to the specific landscape with its inhabitants. The maps visualize a royal presence and generate imaginaries of the land as known and ordered. What is found on the map all appears to belong to the king. First, these maps highlight an epistemological shift connecting, disconnecting and reconnecting Denmark-Norway and Greenland. The renewed attempts in the sixteenth century coincide with a new standard of mapping and recording positions and travel routes. These allowed smaller 'discoveries' to be connected to wider continental map-making activities that aimed to produce ever more accurate maps of the north. I will focus on what these maps tell us in connection with the report written for the king, and his instructions to the expedition prior to their departure. Second, they contribute to a changing conception of Greenland. During the century after it is reconnected to the kingdom in 1605, the perception of the land starts to change from being a dependency (*biland*) to being a territory

**Figure 3.1.** 'The Kinge Christianus His Forde: Names of Rodestes, Havens, and Soundes within This Ford'. With permission by Hakluyt Society.

with a colonial potential for Denmark-Norway (Mølholm Olesen 2019). Most importantly, however, is how the reconnection of Greenland is tied up in an epistemological transformation where cartography starts to play a different role in the shaping of global space as well as political ordering. This eventually leads to a territorialized imaginary of Greenland corresponding to an emerging territorial colonial order, as I will explain in the last section of this chapter.

However, the overall concern for the kings seems to have been a desire to reconnect and re-establish old obligations and tax duties. This took place under the increasing fear of losing sovereignty because of Russian, Iberian, British and Dutch activities in the north. The general cartography started to show Greenland as landlocked with North America and sometimes Norway or Russia. This could have implications for Danish claims. At the same time, the expeditions seem also to have been guided by imaginations of a cold and mythical kind – why not a Northern Eldorado? In his instructions for the 1607 expedition, the king notes how the old texts mention silver mountains (Instruction from Christian IV in Bobé 1936b, 15–17). Captains brought back various rock samples to show the richness of the new shores. But, whereas the

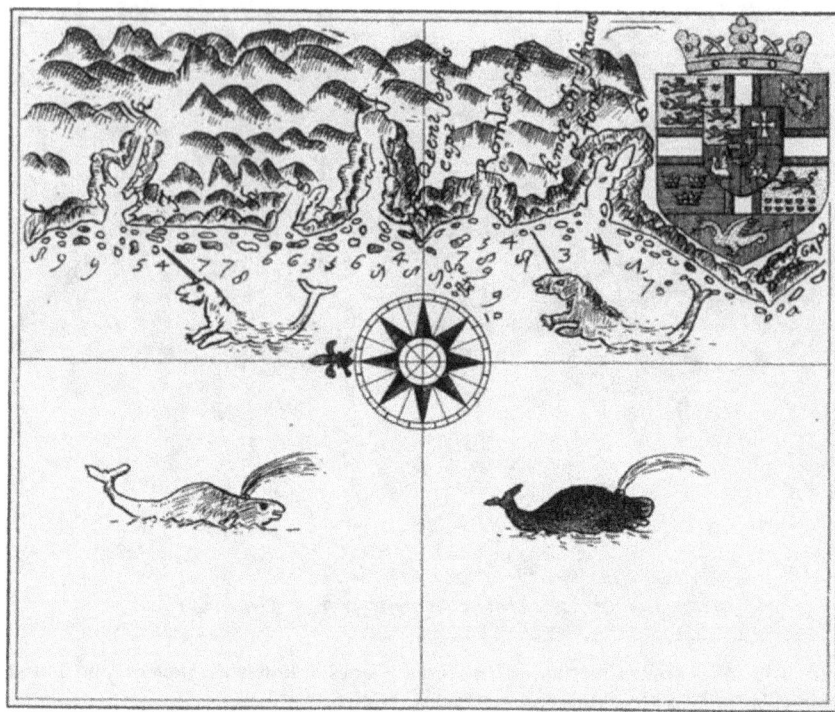

**Figure 3.2.** 'The Coast of Groineland: With the Lattitudes of the Havens and Harbors as I Fovnde Them'. With permission by Hakluyt Society.

voyages set out to reconnect lost populations and travel routes, they started to assemble Greenland as a cartographic space. In that way, attempts to map can be seen as attempts to bring back and make real, and remember spaces of obligation and duties and contact. In making these arguments, I draw on my own previous work on cartography, space and sovereignty (Strandsbjerg 2010, 2012, 2017) which again draws heavily on the works of Bruno Latour and historical cartographers such as Brian Harley, David Woodward and Matthew Edney as I will elaborate subsequently.

To begin the chapter, I first discuss the origin of the Danish-Norwegian claim to Greenland. It is relevant both for understanding the epistemological transformation from what can be called a *map-less empire*, or maybe more precisely, a *networked polity* based on ocean navigation and settling land, to a territorialized colonial relationship in the making. It provides an interesting invitation to reflect on the connection between cartography and empire. Second, I discuss how I see different cartographies as different modes of making space real and present. Maps mediate the relationship between people and their environment. And different ways of making space real through mappings condition different imaginaries of political organization and connectivity. This is illustrated through the Danish Court's attempts, during the sixteenth century, to find the Norse settlements with aid from the old written travel descriptions. It was not possible to translate these descriptions into renaissance navigation practice and the attempts to complete the realm remained unsuccessful until British mariners with personal experience were hired. This leads us to the last section of the chapter, where I discuss the purpose and effects of the expedition in 1605, where finally I interpret Hall's map as a ceremonial attempt to restore the crown's claim which, in effect, thereby contributed to a new territorialized understanding of Greenland which gave way to new imaginaries of the old dependency as a potential colony.

## CONNECTING THE NORTH

This chapter is about making space by connecting sites, places, things and people as well as the role maps play. It is also about different ways of connecting. I will gradually elaborate my theoretical take on mapping throughout the different sections. But for a start, the story could begin in 986 when Erik Thorvaldsson (known as Eric the Red) set off from Iceland with a fleet of more than thirty vessels loaded with entire households and husbandry in order to settle in Greenland. This was a continuation of established practices of travelling to settle in new lands. During the tenth century, Vikings or Norse traders, raiders, settlers and farmers were connecting large parts of Northern Europe and also, less successfully, tried settling in North America (Seaver 1996). They did so without maps of the kinds that we tend to think of as maps today. Indeed, the old Norse language did not have a word for maps (Seaver 1996, 24). And by today's standards they established an empire, sometimes referred to as the North Sea Empire including England, Norway, parts of Sweden, Iceland and eventually the Greenlandic settlements, as I will discuss in the following text. Whether this was indeed an empire or something else is less important than the notion of controlling other lands and kingdoms at a distance, and the ability to travel regularly across large distances and maintain contact.

According to the sagas, Eric was born in Norway. His father was made an outlaw for crimes and sought refuge in Iceland. Eric took up the same habit. After being engaged in a feud with neighbours, he killed two men, was expelled and re-settled in the north-west of Iceland. This did not, however, end the brawls, and he was made an outlaw around 982 because of homicide. Almost a hundred years prior to these events, a sailor called *Gunbjørn* was set off course by a storm and encountered a great new landmass (Rasmussen 1932, 21). Hence, Erik possibly knew about new lands, when he – after becoming an outlaw – explored the coast of Greenland. And when he gathered a large fleet in 986 and returned to the southern fjords of the big island, they found more fertile and better grassland than in northern Iceland. Hence the name Greenland. Here, two settlements were established: *Østerbygd* (the larger) and *Vesterbygd* (close to the location of the current capital Nuuk) on the south-western coast of Greenland. The two settlements maintained an Icelandic system of government; they became Christian under the auspices of the archbishop of Hamburg-Bremen and later, Trondheim, Norway, and maintained contact with the other North Atlantic polities.

This happened during a time of Viking expansion, when the Norse among other places raided and eventually conquered England, raided and settled in Normandy and during the late 800s settled in the North Atlantic Islands: The Hebrides, the Orkney, Shetland and Faro Islands and Iceland during a process called *landnam*, which literally means 'land-taking', that is, to take and settle uninhabited lands. In that light, Eric's Greenland fleet was a continuation of established practices. From the outset, the settlements in Greenland were a sort of free-state, or self-governing societies, up until the mid-thirteenth century. They kept close ties to Iceland and Norway and attempted settling and resource gathering in North America. However, in 1261 the Norse Greenlanders submitted to the Norwegian king (Ørebech 2016, 24). The wording of the agreement is not known but in a similar agreement with Iceland the following year, the king was obliged to supply Iceland with essentials in return for the acceptance of chieftainship and tax privileges (Mølholm Olesen 2019, 77). The Greenlanders' submission became the basis of subsequent Danish claim to sovereignty and also the eagerness to reconnect to Greenland because this claim relied on the crown's ability to supply it.

Accepting Norwegian kingship altered the character of connectivity from one based on mutual benefit and exchange to a more hierarchical relation based on a mutual obligation. With the agreement, the settlements became part of a North Atlantic Norse polity. The Norse *landnam* in the ninth and tenth centuries can probably not be described as an empire from the outset but rather a vast North Atlantic network of settlements, farms, towns, markets, courts and so forth. But over time it became more institutionalized with the international recognition of the Norwegian claim to these settlements and possessions. The key to this network was, of course, the ability to connect the dots. The ability to navigate, trade and maintain continued contact. This ability was maintained for 400 years. But from the early 1400s there are no records of contact between Scandinavia and Greenland until the expedition in 1605, which I will discuss later in this chapter. The destiny of *Østerbygd* and *Vesterbygd* remains unresolved but generally, it is considered that the settlements declined – this is also supposedly a reason why they accepted the authority of the Norwegian crown – and after the government of Greenland moved to the Danish court[3] attention towards Greenland was even less prominent (Bjørnbo 1910, 8).

The purpose of discovery, as Bruno Latour notes, is not only to find new places but to bring them 'back home' in a form that allows a return voyage (Latour 1987, 223–24). But how did the Vikings navigate? How did they come back? It is believed that they passed on itineraries by word of mouth. In the 1300s some of these were recorded in Norwegian and Icelandic sagas. It is believed that they relied on knowledge of currents, debt soundings, the sun and the Polar Star, on sensorial skills (smells, taste of salt content in the water, etc.) as well as personal experience. This is sometimes called empirical navigation. There is also archaeological evidence that they utilized a kind of sun compass – or bearing dial – that might have been useful for setting a course to a known destination but was particularly useful for finding a way back from unknown locations (Seaver 1996, 17).[4] Regardless of whether, and to what extent, they used instruments, it is to stress important that they did not record the routes to connect in any way that would resemble our current understanding of maps or written itineraries. Only from the thirteenth century onwards do we find records of these. *Hauksbogen*, written in the fourteenth century, contains a description of the route from Norway to Iceland and Greenland:[5]

> Starting from Hernum in Norway one must sail straight West to reach Hvarf on Greenland. When you have done this, you have sailed north of Hetland [Shetland Islands] but close enough to see them in clear weather. You have sailed south of the Faro Islands at a distance where half the mountains can be dimly seen, and far enough south of Iceland to still observe whales and birds from there.

I have previously associated such ways of navigating space as a functional understanding of space as opposed to a rational one to capture the way in which space and spatial relationships and connection would be understood and conceptualized by means of a social functionality (Strandsbjerg 2010). That is, distance measured in travel times, agrarian land measured by the time it took to work it (carucate) or the amount of seed needed to sow (barrel of land). Functional perceptions represent a different epistemology of space with less uniform measures, standards or templates.

The literature on cartography and empire tends to present cartography as either a very powerful instrument or set of practices that became instrumental for European empire-making; or as inherently imperial and ingrained in the very fabric of empire (see, e.g. Akerman 2009). Facing this literature, the history of Norse North Atlantic domains connecting remote places with no trace of the use of, or even a concept of, maps provides an interesting reminder of how space can be organized socially and politically without maps. In effect the Vikings established a vast networked polity with no graphic records. And it was not because land was unimportant – as mentioned, the period of North Atlantic settlement was labelled *landnam*, a practice that was probably at the centre of all imperial projects where new lands and nodes of control and exploitation are sought. But it was the inhabited settlements that were connected and made up the framework of the 'empire'. Indeed, the Norse had a word for that which was outside the settlement. It was called uninhabited land, *óbigðir* (Bjørnbo 1910, 4). It was the sea around the settlements that were valuable hunting and fishing grounds. And later, the expeditions to Greenland were trying to locate these settlements.

The claim that the Norse-networked polity was a map-less empire of course depends on how we understand maps. I will discuss this in the following section where the emphasis will be on what I call the space-making function of maps. To an extent, it is not so important whether we can call the Norse mode of recording space and connecting maps or not. What is interesting is how they did it and how it changed and made it difficult for later renaissance sailors to follow in their wake.

## APPROACHING COLD MAPS

In an otherwise poor fantasy novel, *A Secret Atlas*, we find an interesting personage. The chief cartographer Qiro has the ability to draw maps that create new worlds and continents. From his workshop, Qiro thus plays a key role for the imperial ambitions of the ruling dynasty by creating new lands (Stackpole 2005). The ability of maps to conjure up new lands and shape the world is an old and popular one. In 1464, German-born Nicolaus Cusanus described the cosmographer as a creator in the shape of 'a man positioned in a city with five gates, representing five senses. Messengers bring him information in order to give a complete record of the external world' (Woodward 2007, 17). He compiles the received information into a map, and just like God preceded the world, the cosmographer exists prior to the mapped land (Woodward 2007, 18). In computer games, like World of Warcraft, the programmer, by shaping the world, constructs a playing field that conditions a possible range of actions by players (Strandsbjerg 2011). What these analogies allude to is how cartography plays a role in shaping geography and mediating the relationship between people and their environment. Likewise, as discussed in the opening chapters of this volume, it is common to associate or even inscribe imperial ambitions and powers into the map itself.

This depends on how we conceptualize mapping and cartography. Maps can, of course, be many things; as metaphors of knowledge, as practices of creating spaces or as simple maps on paper or other materials they appear for very different purposes and audiences. Generally, though, I believe it is possible to make some general statements about maps. They mediate the relationship between people and their surroundings. The majority known cultures have created visual representations of their relationship with their environment to varying degrees reflecting symbolic significance and practical utility. While Harley and Woodward define maps as 'graphic representations that facilitate a spatial understanding of things, concepts, conditions, processes, or events in the human world' (1987, xvi), I like to focus on what maps do. Maps reify spaces, maps prioritize spaces, maps subdue spaces, maps assemble spaces of control, maps make spaces familiar and the list goes on. However, what unites many of these processes is the mediation of the spatial relations of people. This is another way of saying that maps create space. Maps are about space-making. But maps are not one thing.

We can understand the different media and systems that people use to navigate, orientate, locate and understand their environment for mappings. In that respect, mapping is a way of establishing a spatial relation. This is relevant for understanding how the Vikings navigated the North Atlantic. They had a detailed understanding of how to get from one point to another without using drawn maps and with any resemblance to fourteenth-century portolan charts or geometric or measured maps that we see in Europe from the fifteenth century onwards. We can of course understand the oral- and experience-based knowledge system of navigation as mapping because it was about navigation and connecting remote places into a coherent polity. To support this suggestion, a feudal lord form Iceland, Christopher Huitfeldt, brought old travel route descriptions back to Norway and described these itineraries as a 'sea chart to navigate Greenland' (Bobé 1936a, 6). Rather than assessing whether such narratives can be considered maps or not, the key point to discuss is how different ways of making maps, different modes of mapping, should be considered as different ways of making space real, or present (Strandsbjerg 2010).

Cartography represents spaces, but more importantly, cartography conditions different ways, or modes, of connecting things, places, people, and also authority, power and place. That is also to say that different mappings condition different modes of organizing and controlling space. Following this understanding, maps are not imperial or the opposite by themselves. But they always shape a geographic, or spatial, reality that connects to different ways of organizing space. Whereas the map-less connectivities of the Vikings went together with the seaborne polity or Northern Empire that tied different nodes of authority into a web of mutual obligations, geometric cartography developed in tandem with a territorialization of political authority both in Europe and overseas. And it is in this context that cartography is often seen as being imperial alongside the great surveying enterprises to make land governable, for example, in India (Edney 1997), North America (Goettlich in this volume) and South America (Lobo-Guerrero in this volume), and the link between the discipline of geography and empire has been well documented (Driver 2001). Yet, in the case that follows, cartography was not employed as an imperial practice but rather to restore a kingdom.

## RECONNECTING THE NORTH

If we return for a moment to King Frederik II and his attempt to secure the service of Frobisher, we find him at the newly rebuilt *Kronborg* castle, which at the time was one of the largest renaissance palaces in Northern Europe. A building of splendour and fortification beautifully combined in what is now a UNESCO heritage site. At the castle, one finds a series of delicate wall tapestries that construct a genealogy of Danish kings back to a somewhat mythical origin of the Danish state and provide a (fictional) unbroken line of kings. This illustrates a court culture of both time and space wherein the temporal lineage of the current kings was written back in time at the same time as the court sponsored both surveying of the territory as well as Tycho Brahe's scientific advances within astronomy. It also illustrates a more general Renaissance impetus at the Danish court both attaching themselves to new trends in European learning culture as well as a pre-occupation not only with the Greek and Latin classics but also with the Norse past through, especially, the Icelandic written sagas. This is to say that the Danish court was in tune with the general European Renaissance culture of knowledge and dynastic politics while at the same time being pre-occupied with the specific Norse past and the sources documenting the Greenlandic settlements.

In the early sixteenth century, the archbishop of Trondheim Erik Walkendorf – under whose auspices the bishop in Garðar operated – compiled the existing descriptions of travel routes from Iceland and Norway to Greenland. The descriptions were used as the basis for reaching the country and also for studying the possible locations of the two settlements (Bobé 1936a, 5). This reflects a dual pre-occupation both with rediscovering the route to Greenland and to know more about the Norse settlers and their location; an ambition that harmonized well with the Renaissance impulse to rediscover the knowledge and geography of aged classics.[6] During the sixteenth century there were several attempts to retrace the route but they all fell short for various reasons. Sometimes war, and other times more curious causes. For example, in 1514, newly appointed King Christian II asks the Pope for absolution in advance for the mariners supposed to participate in an expedition to the north (Pingel 1845, 631). But in February 1520 Søren Nordby, admiral of the navy, writes that he would be very happy to prepare his ships but unfortunately, they are in need of repair and he is struggling to get a mast big enough for his ship.

But he should be ready after Easter, he writes (in Bobé 1936b, 4). The expedition never leaves. Over the years, several expeditions are planned, royal travel passes are issued to secure the passage and provisions of the expeditions under way but they either never leave, or fail to reach Greenland or, in the cases where they sight Greenland, cannot get to land because of the ice. As such, the compiled descriptions of the Norse travel routes were insufficient for the new Renaissance court to fulfil their Nordic ambitions.

But why was it so important for the king to reach Greenland? Of course, the obvious reason was that the court wanted control of its dependencies but there was more to the story. During the sixteenth century, sailors from the other European powers, especially Britain, the Netherlands but also Spain and Russia, sailed further and further north in search of new routes, lands and whale-hunting grounds. In this context it became increasingly untenable for the Danish-Norwegian monarch not to be present and able to reach his lands. Obviously, there was a risk that other states would make landfall and colonize but, more importantly, the crown had obligations to the old Norse settlements and if the Danish king did not fulfil these obligations, the inhabitants of Greenland were free to enter an agreement with other kings (Mølholm Olesen 2019). The relationship between the king and his dependency was based on mutual obligations and an ability to uphold connection. In 1579, Frederik II issues an instruction and travel pass to the Brit Jacob Allday. The instruction states that Greenland by right and equity 'is subject to our realm [*rige*] Norway' but has not been visited by kings from Denmark or Norway for many years. It is important now that 'this country' again becomes subject to the right authority, that the subjects in the country are supplied and supported for their most basic needs and brought to the right Christian faith (Letter 1579 in Bobé 1936b, 8). This clearly asserts that Greenland belongs to the Danish crown via Norway and also, in a way that might sound comical to the modern ear, that it just happened not to have been supplied by ships for some years (more than 150 years).

The effort to reach the lost settlements was thus made more and more urgent by increasing maritime traffic and competition from the others. England had reached Russia to the north. The Muscovy Company, established in 1555, opened trade between England and Russia bypassing the Danish sound toll applying to all Baltic trade. It was therefore not only the status of Greenland that caused anxiety at the Danish court but also generally their dominance at sea and substantial income from the international Baltic trade. The control of the North Atlantic became a declared goal of the Danish monarch. From the second half of the sixteenth century the seas between East Greenland, Jutland and the west coast of Norway were defined as royal currents and sovereignty was claimed over these waters expressed in the concept of *Dominium maris septentrionalis* (dominion over the Northern Seas). Not only did this cast the waters to the north as 'our streams and currents', it also played into an uncertainty of what Greenland was. No one at the time, of course, knew that Greenland was an island, and along with the general developments in European cartography, more and more maps showed Greenland in various shapes and forms. I will return to the discussion of what was actually connected by the claim to Greenland. For now, it is important to remember that the implications of claiming Greenland were uncertain.

In the Latin scholarly circles, knowledge of Greenland was limited, and schematic knowledge departing from the image of a spherical earth (*orbis terrarum*) centred on Jerusalem surrounded by circles of remote lands and seas. Greenland was at the edge of the inhabitable and known world (Bjørnbo 1911, 71–74). Because continental cartography came to define the theatre of Renaissance European politics, we should note how Greenland moved into the standard Latin world map as it developed during the age of *reconnaissance*, 1450–1650 (a term borrowed from Parry 2000). The first known written record of Greenland is *Adam of Bremen*'s description of the north from ca. 1075. He locates Greenland far away, as part of a dark borderland sea (Bjørnbo 1911, 70–71), and located, wrongly, to the north-east. When Ptolemy's *Geography* was first translated and reappeared in Latin scholarly circles, knowledge of Scandinavia was thus fairly anecdotal and theoretical. The geographical knowledge of the Scandinavian sailors was not integrated into European cartography until *Claudius Claussøn Swart*'s first additions to the Ptolemaic atlas. He travelled the Nordic countries, spent time in Italy and was connected to the Danish and Portuguese courts. In the 1420s, he had added Norway and Greenland to the Ptolemaic map in a way that combined Norwegian and Icelandic knowledge with the graticule (Bjørnbo 1911, 98). Swart very explicitly justifies his additions by (claiming to be) an eyewitness. In one of the key texts, he states that 'I, the Dane Claudius Claussøn Swart, ... have by meticulous drawing as well as written records aimed to give to the world a true picture of said countries known to me by personal experience, yet unknown to Ptolemy, Hipparch and Marinus'.[7] The most detailed study of Swart suggests that he drew on a combination of the old itineraries and his own travels. It is disputed whether he went to Greenland himself.[8] In that way, Swart translated the old sources into the new epistemology – or knowledge template – of European cosmographers and cartographers. Two maps are known from Swart (see figure 3.3 for the first one), and they are important because they integrate the practical knowledge of Icelandic and Norwegian sailors with Ptolemaic geography. Swart's cartography and descriptions undermine the schematic knowledge of an inhabitable earth surrounded by uninhabitable Polar region and sea. Greenland stretches far to the north and is inhabited (Bjørnbo 1911, 119).

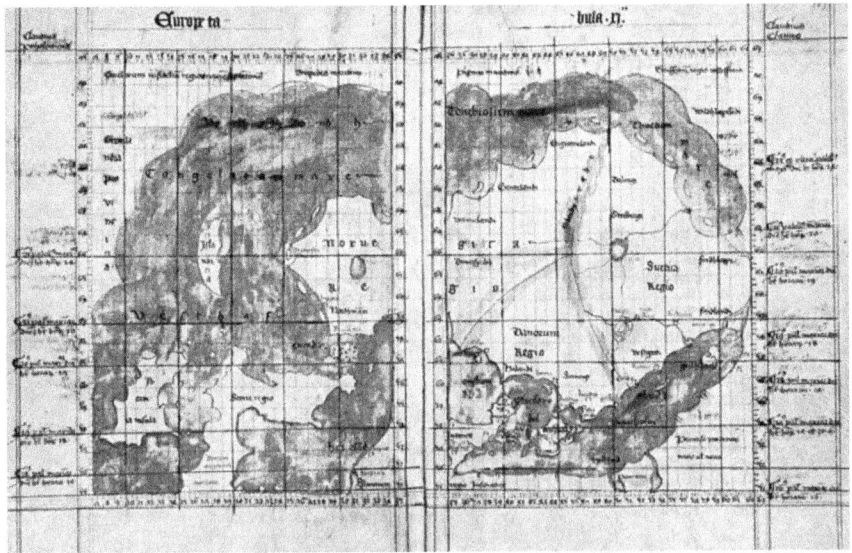

**Figure 3.3.** Swart's first map – the older one – adding Northern Scandinavia and Greenland to the Ptolemaic Map. The original from ca. 1424 is unknown but a copy from 1427 exists in a later edition. Bibliotheque municipale Nancy Manuscrit 441. By courtesy of the Danish Royal Library.

How Greenland and the North Atlantic more generally were mapped during the age of discovery is worth a chapter (or books) on its own with its combination of mythical islands, old tales, knowledge and fantastic narratives dressed up in the geometric reason of Renaissance cartography. We should note, however, how Greenland is integrated into European politics both through navigation and cartography. Even more important is the uncertainty over what Greenland is; sometimes it is represented cartographically as an island, and sometimes landlocked with North America, sometimes with Russia. Sometimes Greenland refers only to the East coast, because this was where the Norse descendants were mistakenly supposed to live, whereas the west coast was, for example, called *Terra Laboratoris* on Waldseemüller's *Carta Marina* from 1516 (Bjørnbo 1911, 199). In addition, the question of how to connect newly discovered coasts and islands – such as Svalbard in 1596 – remained unsolved in cartographic visions of the Arctic at the time. A famous and prevailing example is that of Gerardus Mercator's Arctic map (see figure 3.4) depicting a mountain on the North Pole surrounded by four lands. In addition, he split Greenland into two islands with a northern neighbour island called Groclant. This influenced geographic imaginaries at the courts, as it appears from a statement made by King Frederik's successor Christian IV, who already, prior to his ascension to the throne, drafts an

Figure 3.4. Section of Mercator's 1606 Map of the Arctic. Image in Public Domain.

agreement with a noble to 'win the already discovered but not for travel open countries Greenland and groclant for Denmark'.⁹ In line with Christian IV's Arctic ambitions, and the uncertainty of the Northern geography, he later – in 1624 – claims that he understands Greenland as including everything to the north of Iceland and the North Cape, and also claims that Svalbard is a Greenlandic island (Bobé 1936a, 14). In sum, during the sixteenth century, the understanding that Greenland is inhabited and is subject to Denmark-Norway is widespread in Europe. However, there is no agreement on what it is, and at the court in Copenhagen they have no ability to reach their lands nor their subjects.

## RECONNECTING GREENLAND

It was by accident that Greenland was reached again. In 1576 Martin Frobisher, as already mentioned, searching for a North-West passage, sighted Greenland's Coast. The English expeditions searching for a North-West passage generated a growing squad of British Mariners with experience of sailing the north, and several of them had encountered Greenland. They were thus attractive to the Danish court. As a curious illustration, a royal order exists dated May 1606 where the king demands from the custom house officers in Elsinore that they stop the first English mate suitable for royal service and send him to Copenhagen (Gosch 1897, xxxi). There were close ties between the two courts, and the Danish king Christian IV was brother-in-law to James I of England. The Scotsman John Cunningham was captain in the Danish Navy and became commander of one of the ships that left for Greenland in 1605. His first mate – the pilot of the expedition – was John Hall. It is not known on what credentials Hall was hired for the expedition, but it appears from his report that he knew the route to Greenland that would take them beyond the big ice sheets and reach the coast. Gosch (1897, xxxiv–xxxv) suggests that he most likely had travelled with Davis in his attempt to find a North-West Passage in 1586 in 1587 and thus was familiar with the waters around Greenland.

The expedition left Copenhagen in early May 1605 and consisted of three ships and, after a relatively uneventful journey, reached the coast of Greenland. Here they split up with the Danish supreme commander Godske Lindenov only staying briefly in Greenland after which he returned to Copenhagen, whereas Cunningham and Hall returned only in August having spent more time surveying the coast. In a royal letter of credence dated 18 April 1605 Godske Lindenov and his officers are instructed to find the sea route to Greenland and its harbours and report back to the king (Letter of credence 1605 in Bobé 1936b, 13–14). I read Hall's report as a response to this request. There is no explicit demand to include or make charts or observations in these instructions but, of course, reporting on the route and harbours warrants a kind of mapping. In a similar letter of credence for the following year – preparing the expedition in 1606 – there is a request to thoroughly explore 'this, our domain's present condition' (Letter of credence 1606 in Bobé 1936b, 15). The expeditions are thus aimed at reconnecting and exploring this somewhat mythical dependency. The interesting thing is what kind and in what form this exploration or mapping takes.[10]

Instead of relying on the old Norse travel descriptions, the expedition followed sailing directions that had been followed by the English explorers (Gosch 1897, xxxix). This appears to have taken the ships around the big ice sheets that had previously stopped expeditions from reaching the coast. In the report, Hall promises that he would bring the ships from the expedition 'saffe and sound to good harbors, without any pester of yce' (Hall in Gosch 1897, 6). I have not been able to find information on the mapping that Hall used to pilot the expedition but we know from his account that he did use maps. After a storm the three ships get divorced and upon meeting each other again, the Danish officers ask for a map in case they get lost again. A request which Hall very reluctantly accepts (Hall in Gosch 1897, 6). It might have been portolan-style charts with latitude added as developed by Iberian mariners during the sixteenth century (see, e.g. Waters 1970, 9–12). In any case, the success of Hall's piloting appears to derive from his experience with the waters and maybe also his access to and ability to chart the route. In his report to the king, Hall includes several sketches of contour forms of important coast formations both underway, for example, of Shetland, and the newly drawn coast of Greenland. These contour drawings are similar to the ones we know from late sixteenth-century rutters (the English adoption of the French *routier*; Ash 2007, 511).

The report written to the Danish king upon return was called *A Report to King Christian IV of Denmark on the Danish Expedition to Greenland, under the Command of Captain John Cunningham, in 1605 by James Hall, Chief Pilot*. It is fairly short – twenty-one leaves in original; sixteen pages in book reproduction – and describes the events, the route and, as mentioned, includes contour drawings of important coastal features. Apart from the route, Hall describes how they take possession of the land on behalf of the king, and how they deal with the people they meet there. Hall's report is most famous for the mapping expedition he undertakes on his own along the coast. He does not mention this trip in the report but documents it only through the four maps. According to Gosch (1897, vi), these maps represent the first attempt at an accurate mapping of Greenland. In the following I will focus on the acts of possession and thereunder how Greenland was reconnected; what was being connected and thereunder the dealings with the Greenlanders. After this I will spend the rest of the chapter reflecting on the four maps and what they tell us about European Imperial space-making.

At the time the Danes tried to reconnect with Greenland, most other European navigation, exploration and conquest were, of course, propelled by an expectation of finding new routes to Asian markets. Possession could be claimed of unknown and empty places, in the juridical sense of *terra nullius* which was land ungoverned (by 'civilized people' as it was deemed). For example, John Cabot, the first explorer in the service of an English monarch, was instructed in 1496 to discover and find only those regions uninhabited by Christian people and not already claimed by another Christian Prince (Keller, Lissitzyn, and Mann 1967, 50):

> Be it known and made manifest that we have given and granted . . . to our well-beloved John Cabot, citizen of Venice, and to Lewis, Sebastian and Sancio, sons of the said John, and to the heirs and deputies of them, and of any one of them, full and free authority, faculty and power to sail to all parts, regions and coasts of the eastern, western and northern sea, under our banners, flags and ensigns, with five ships or vessels of whatsoever burden and quality they may be . . . to find, discover and investigate whatsoever islands, countries, regions or provinces of heathens and infidels, in whatsoever part of the world placed, which before this time were unknown to all Christians. . . . And that the before-mentioned John and his sons or their heirs and deputies may conquer, occupy

and possess whatsoever such towns, castles, cities and islands by them thus discovered that they may be able to conquer, occupy and possess, as our vassals and governors lieutenants and deputies therein, acquiring for us the dominion, title and jurisdiction of the same towns, castles, cities, islands and mainlands discovered.[11]

In contrast, the primary concern of the Danish monarch was, as discussed, to recover the best route to the Greenlandic coast in order to re-establish contact with the settlements and locate Christian subjects to the crown and their lands. Greenland was thus not *terra nullius*; sovereignty, the destiny of the population and tax and other sources of revenue were a concern.

Again, in a wider European context, the mere sighting of land was not regarded as sufficient basis on which to make a claim to sovereignty, neither did penetration and exploration do it alone (Keller *et al.* 1967, 148). Instead, various symbolic acts of taking possession were regarded as sufficient and did not need to be accompanied by 'effective occupation'. Despite variation, these ceremonies had a similar legal effect (see also Seed 1995). In this light, it is interesting to note how James Hall, when they get clear of the ice and approach the coast, starts to name coastal features. A central mountain is named *Mounte Cunningham* after the captain, and on both sides the capes are named after the king's wife and mother. The central fjord, where they anchor the first time, is named after the king: 'your Maiesties ford' (Hall in Gosch 1897, 10). When they make landfall, they take the land into possession: 'when the Captaine and my selfe went a land, we ffalleinge downe on oure knees and thanked God for his goodness; the which donne, the Captaine tooke possession of the same in youre maiesties behalf, takeinge with him both earth and stones' (Ibid, original spelling preserved). Elsewhere, Keller *et al.* (1967, 57) mention how Cunningham also performed a turf and twig ceremony in Greenland thus mirroring common European ceremonies of sovereign acts.

As mentioned, the main concern of the expedition was to re-establish the travel route to the Norse settlements that were the foundation of the claim to sovereignty – and the right to call it 'our crown's land' (Mølholm Olesen 2019). The crown was, as we have discussed, obliged to supply these settlements, and it was the social bond, the contract, that sanctioned the claim to sovereignty. It was thus more about the people than the land which was only known from the old texts. In the instruction to the 1607 expedition, the crown cites the 'old documents' mentioning all the churches and locations, and all the precious goods that could be traded (in Bobé 1936b, 16). The king is particularly concerned with a fjord called 'Erichsfiord' (named after Eric the Red) where one would find the best land and the best people (Ibid, 16–17). However, the expeditions never meet descendants of the Norse settlers but they encounter the Inuit Greenlanders early on. And curiously, they are not treated as colonial others. In order to maintain the claim to sovereignty it is important to maintain the imagination of a Christian population subject of the Crown (Mølholm Olesen 2019, 83). The Europeans and the Inuit both trade and fight each other during these encounters occurring on the first expeditions (Gosch 1897, xliv). A couple of Inuit are kidnapped – or taken back – to Copenhagen and presented to the king as his subjects. As such, the Inuit population is formally considered subject to the crown although they are also sometimes in practice dealt with as inferior others. One was, for example, shot dead by Captain Cunningham because he was too violent after his abduction (Gosch 1897, lxxxiv).

Connection was never made with the Norse settlements, although the ambition lasted well into the eighteenth century. And, as I will argue subsequently drawing on the work of Simon Mølholm Olesen, the expeditions left in search of a lost dependency and a population, but the lasting legacy was an emerging understanding of Greenland as a space – or land – that could be mapped, understood and explored independently of the population. Of course, there was probably the hope and desire that the crown could find its own North Atlantic Eldorado; and indeed, large quantities of supposedly silver ore were brought back from the first expedition, and silver ore was also a main objective of the second expedition. However, none of this materialized in anything of value, and the efforts were subsequently down-scaled. Instead, the maps that we will focus on tie the crown to the land in a very particular way that is also symptomatic of wider imperial space-making practices.

## MAPPING GREENLAND

Renaissance, or geometric, cartography is characterized by its universal abstract mathematical principles. It is abstract in the sense that it represents the landscape without reference to a symbolic order, compared, for example, to medieval European world maps that would always centre the map on Jerusalem. It bears a universal[12] logic because the principles of making observation, calculation and measurements of location and distances are applicable everywhere and combinable with other observations and maps made according to the same principles. This means that maps made in this way in principle can transfer knowledge about space between people in a way that the old Norse narratives could not. Even more important, however, is the way in which Renaissance cartography represents space as a thing in itself. The territory achieves a life of its own through the map. The cartographic image is one that can be claimed. Generally, with the cartographic production of space, it became possible to tie sovereignty to territory without reference to the people or its specific locations (for a more elaborate discussion of this, see Strandsbjerg 2010, 2017). Now, where Hall as an able explorer probably just thought to give an account of the land, his maps also played an important role in territorializing the imaginary of Greenland.

The first of his maps (figure 3.1) shows the fjord named after the king, the first place of anchoring and the first haven or harbour that was named after the ship *Trost*. The map is accurate by the standards and the fjord has subsequently been identified as Itivdleq Fjord to the south of present-day Sisimiut. The king's monogram takes up a vast space in the top left corner emphasizing that the fjord is named after him and asserts his possession of the land. As opposed to the other maps, this one is populated. In his report, Hall only described the people he meets as 'them'. There might have been another word used omitted from the report. But I find it interesting that the derogatory term *skrælling* is absent even though this was the term used in the known contemporary descriptions. This supports the idea that the Greenlanders were formally treated more like royal subjects than colonial others. The map also features a hut that Hall describes as 'a kinde of tentes covered with seale skinnes' (Hall in Gosch 1897, 11) as well as seals swimming in water. It is thus a populated land that is presented as the king's domain.

The next two maps in the report show two other fjords. As the first map, they are centred on a compass rose, but there are neither royal iconography nor people. Only names and sea creatures. The names are interesting though and worth mentioning. There is a large literature on cartography and the power of naming (notably Mignolo 1995), and it is not surprising that the two fjords are named after Cunningham and a prominent member of the Danish Council, Breide Rantzau (Gosch 1897, lxviii). More interesting is an inlet named Catt Sound, probably after a small strait in Copenhagen *Kattesundet*, mirroring the capital on the newly mapped coasts, and thus symbolically strengthening the connection between the crown and Greenland.

The last map (figure 3.2) provides an overview of the section of the coast surveyed by Hall showing the different fjords and capes. The top right corner features the king's coat of arms again writing royal possession onto the surveyed areas. As a curious note, one might think of the unicorned hybrid between horse and whale drawn in the sea as one of the fantastic creatures that typically feature maritime zones of Renaissance maps, but they probably have a more specific value. Narwhals were also called sea unicorns at the time. Frobisher, for example, found a dead whale on one of his expeditions and reported how its 'horn is wreathed and straight, like in fashion to a taper made of wax, and may truly thought to be the sea-unicorn' (Zimmer 2014). To get access to rare commodities like the spiral narwhal tusks was also a motivation to recover the connection to Greenland (Mølholm Olesen 2019, 19).[13] And like many other explorer's cartographies at the time, this map issued promises of riches to be found. Not only did Hall and Cunningham bring back large quantities of supposed silver ore, they also indicated the presence of valuable whale resources under the royal seal.

When the navigator and explorer Jens Munk passed Southern Greenland in his search for a North-West Passage in 1619, he went ashore and erected two cairns displaying Christian IV's monogram. The use of the monogram was an established practice when demarcating the realm, that is, not taking new lands into possession. In contrast, when new colonial spaces were taken into possession in the West Indies in 1672 and 1718, this was symbolically marked with the planting of the Danish flag (Mølholm Olesen 2019, 71).[14] Cunningham's expedition had thus succeeded in restoring the kingdom and overcoming the epistemological challenges of mapping and navigation. On returning to the capital, a large map of Greenland was displayed at the prow of the ship *Trost* (Gosch 1897, lxxxv) according to two contemporary chroniclers, Jens Bielke and Claus Lyschander. They both popularized the events of the expedition (Gosch 1897, xviii–xix), as such translating it to a wider public audience both in Denmark and in Europe. And this is important because, whereas the old Norse *routiers* were incompatible with emerging Renaissance cartographic and navigational conventions, Hall's maps had rendered the west coast of Greenland both moveable and combinable in the language of Bruno Latour discussed previously, with its contemporary continental cartographic practice, and helped translate the old writings.

Soon after the return, Hall's place names start to appear on other maps of the North Atlantic, for example, the map by Gudbrand Thorlacius from 1606 that shows Britain, Scandinavia, Iceland, North America and Greenland combining old text and the new discoveries (Steenstrup 1885–1886). This shows how Hall's small detail maps became part of a wider assemblage of a new cartographic reality of space that developed alongside territorial sovereignty and overseas empires (Strandsbjerg 2010). Geometric cartography helped turn lands and places into cartographic spaces that could be both conceptualized and claimed at European courts. And while Cunningham's expedition in 1605 went out with the mission to re-trace forgotten routes and re-establish contact with the Norse settlers, the result was a new cartographic imaginary of Greenland. Rather than establishing contact with the old settlements, Hall's maps helped turn Greenland into a cartographic space subject to royal authority. Remember that it was the settlements that had submitted to the Norwegian king in the thirteenth century with no (at least not known) spatial demarcation of definition.

In 1660, in the wake of a decisive defeat to Sweden, Denmark underwent a constitutional change with the introduction of absolutism. This of course dissolved the role of the council in electing the king. It also undermined the old idea that the king had to meet obligations in order to claim kingship.

In parallel, the perception of Greenland changed from being a dependency tied to the crown by mutual agreement to a territory naturally subject to the king. This is clearly illustrated by Law Professor Peder Hansen Resen's treaty *Groenlandia* from 1687, in which he notes how this territory ought to be taken into possession in order to get access to the riches (still supposedly) found there and expand the realm by taking control from the 'natives' who unjustifiably live on 'Danish territory'. This also emphasizes the transformation of the perception of the Greenlanders from being subjects to the king – and at times seen as (maybe) descendants of the Norse settlers – to being seen as strangers living on Danish lands, that is, colonial others (Mølholm Olesen 2019, 91–92). The territorialization of Greenland can hardly be illustrated more clearly. And it provides the end of this narrative of cartography's role in transforming Greenland from a neglected dependency to a cartographic space which eventually was turned into a territorialized imaginary.

## CONCLUSION

This chapter revolved around a lost ability to connect and how this ability was recovered, and what the implications were for the relationship of power and authority in the North Atlantic. While there is large literature on the close relationship between empire and mapping, the Norse networked polity before 1400 was map-less in the way that we commonly understand maps today. Through the oral recording of travel routes and navigation by experience, populated centres were connected across vast distances. These connected centres, or nodes of population, can be said to constitute a map-less empire stretching into the Arctic, a seemingly well-functioning polity thriving over several hundred years. Eventually, however, after contact had been lost between the northern settlements, the old *routiers* and practices of connectivity were of little use for the Renaissance kings in Denmark who strived to re-connect to the old lands. Knowledge of mapping and navigation had taken on new forms.

When Greenland was eventually reconnected, it was recorded and taken back home in a new fashion that was compatible with renaissance spatial learning. The mapping of Greenland not only connected Greenland to the court but also connected it to a wider European cartographic theatre occupied with imperial rivalry alongside a territorialization of sovereignty. The process also shows how the knowledge of Greenland, and of how to get there, was connected with a European scholarly network of cartographers and chroniclers. This process further highlights how changes in cartographic practices are linked to modes of connectivity because in the – maybe somewhat mundane – endeavour to reconnect Greenland to Denmark, Greenland was also connected to Europe and, not least, to a continental cartographic practice.

In that context, Hall's cartography served to translate the old written sources in a manner that made them combinable with a new European tradition of geographical knowledge. This did not invent and create imperial control but it conditioned a new way of organizing political space at a distance. Greenland was formally colonized in 1721 by the Norwegian missionary Hans Egede. Prior to that, the perception of Greenland had undergone a transformation in Denmark from being an old dependency – or tax-land – which the crown had obligations to support and respect its autonomy to a Danish territory open for various commercial and religious enterprises. The conquest of land was at the centre of the Viking expansion 700 years prior to Greenland's colonization, but political order was about connecting inhabited centres across ocean space. The marriage between geometric cartography and the ambition to re-establish sovereignty over lost land reconditioned this relationship. In a subtle way it paved the way for a spatial – or territorial – understanding of what eventually became colonial rule.

## NOTES

1. It is not uncommon, though, to read analyses that interpret the desire by the court to reconnect Greenland as general European imperial ambitions (see, e.g. Etting 2009). This, however, oversees the whole point of restoring the kingdom.

2. I use the term *geometric cartography* for what is typically – in the traditional history of cartography – called *modern cartography*. I do that to emphasize that this way of mapping is based on geometry, and at the same time, I try to avoid ascribing normative connotations to any mapping discourse or regime.

3. In 1396 Norway, Denmark and Sweden were united in the Kalmar Union under Queen Margrethe I. Under various configurations Norway remained attached to the Danish Crown until 1814, when Norway came under the Swedish rule, though, without its North Atlantic dependencies (Iceland – until independence 1944, the Farao Islands and Greenland) which remained under Danish rule in what is now known as *Rigsfællesskabet* (Community of the Realm).

4. See, for example, Bernáth *et al*. (2013) for different interpretations.

5. My translation from 'Af Hernum i Norge skal man seile lige mod Vest til Hvarf paa Grönland; og da seiler man norden for Hetland, dog saaledes at man netop kan det, fordi at man har klar Udsigt over Havet, men sönden om Færöerne, saa at man over Söen kun ser Fjeldenes halve Höide, men saaledes sönden for Island, at dets Söfugle and Hvalfiske lade sig see' (Pingel 1845, 213).

6. For a related argument, see Dalche who argues that the initial renaissance preoccupation with Ptolemy was not so much the math and instructions for map-making as a concern with the lived geography of the classical thinkers.

7. My translation from 'Jeg Danskeren Claudius Claussøn Swart . . . har ved omhyggelig Tegning saa vel som ved skriftlig optegnelse søgt at give Efterverdenen et tro billede af de mig ved Selvsyn nøje bekendte nedennævnte Lande, som var

Ptolemæus, Hipparch og Marinus ukendte' (quoted by Nørlund 1943, 13). For more on Swart's different sources, see Bjørnbo and Petersen (1904, 146–96). This translation is copied from Strandsbjerg (2010, 139).

8. Bjørnbo and Petersen (1904, 184–96) suggest that he did, while Bjørnbo (1912, 108–114) in his later study is less certain.

9. My translation from 'at vinde de allerede opdagede, men for samfærslen åbnede lande Grønland og groclandt for Danmark' (Bobé 1936a, 10).

10. I am incredibly grateful to Anders Kirk Borggaard for translating these letters from Latin to Danish.

11. From H. P. Biggar, *The Precursors of Jacques Cartier, 1497–1534* (Ottawa: Government Printing Bureau, 1911), 8–10. Available online at http://www.bris.ac.uk/Depts/History/Maritime/Sources/1496cabotpatent.htm.

12. It is important to remember that even though the principles or the logic informing the map are universal, this does not mean that the maps are universal in the sense that all people, cultures or societies can or should agree that this is the right way to make maps. Of course, the principles and the map always develop in a particular historical context. But one of the subtle powers of the geometric map is indeed that its principles are universal (see Strandsbjerg 2010, 108–11, for a more elaborate discussion).

13. There is an alternative interpretation of the meaning of the unicorn in the context of the Danish Greenland voyages. Danish historian Lars Bisgaard has identified and interpreted an early sixteenth-century emergence of unicorns in church painting as relating to the ambition to reconnect Greenland. At the same time, the unicorn, according to some tales, being native to India, would tie Greenland to India and again the wider travels of exploration (Bisgaard 2008).

14. Mølholm Olesen is drawing on Gøbel and Sebro (2017, 52) who note how Denmark-Norway's colonization in the West Indies in 1672 was marked by the planting of the Danish flag as the first ritual of possession when the expedition went ashore on St. Thomas on 26 May that year.

# REFERENCES

Akerman, James. 2009. *The Imperial Map: Cartography and the Mastery of Empire*. Chicago: University of Chicago Press.

Ash, Eric H. 2007. 'Navigation Techniques and Practices in the Renaissance'. In *Cartography in the European Renaissance*, edited by David Woodward, 509–27. Chicago: University of Chicago Press.

Astrid E. J. Ogilvie. 2014. 'Norse Greenland: Selected Papers from the Hvalsey Conference 2008'. *Arctic, Antarctic, and Alpine Research* 46, no. 4: 1013–18.

Bernáth, Balázs, Miklós Blahó, Ádám Egri, Barta András, and Gábor Horváth. 2013. 'An Alternative Interpretation of the Viking Sundial Artefact: An Instrument to Determine Latitude and Local Noon'. *Proceedings of the Royal Society A: Mathematical, Physical and Engineering Sciences*. 469, no. 2154.

Biggar Henry Percival. 1911. *The Precursors of Jacques Cartier, 1497–1534*. Ottawa: Government Printing Bureau.

Bisgaard, Lars. 2008. 'Kampen om enhjørningen. Christian IIs planlagte Grønlandstogt 1514–22 i danske kalkmalerier'. In *Renæssancen i svøb: Dansk renæssance I europæisk belysning 1450–1550*, edited by Lars Bisgaard, Jacob Isager, and Janus Møller Jensen. Odense: Syddansk Universitetsforlag: 245–77.

Bjørnbo, Axel Anthon. 1910. 'Historisk overblik over landets opdagelse'. In *Meddelelser om Grønland* vol. XLVIII (1912). København: C. A. Reitzel.

———. 1911. 'Grønlands Kartografi i perioden 1000–1576'. In *Meddelelser om Grønland* vol. XLVIII (1912). København: C. A. Reitzel.

Bjørnbo, A. A., and C. S. Petersen. 1904. *Fyenboen Claudius Claussøn Swart 'Claudius Clavus', Nordens ældste Kartograf*, København, Det Kongelige Danske Videnskabernes Selskab, Høst & Søn.

Bobé, Louis. 1936a.: *Opdagelsesrejser til Grønland 1473–1806*, København: C. A. Reitzel.

———. 1936b. *Diplomatarium Groenlandicum*, København: C. A. Reitzel.

Driver, Felix. 2001. *Geography Militant: Cultures of Exploration and Empire*. Basingstoke: Blackwell.

Edney, Matthew H. 1997. *Mapping an Empire: The Geographical Construction of British India, 1765–1843*. Chicago: University of Chicago Press.

Etting, Vivian. 2009. 'The Rediscovery of Greenland during the Reign Christian IV'. *Journal of the North Atlantic*. Special Volume 2: 151–60.

Gøbel, Erik, and Louise Sebro. 2017. 'Danmark. Norge I Vestindien 1672–1720'. In *Vestindien – St. Croix, St. Thomas og St. Jan*, edited by Poul Erik Olsen, 50–95. København: GAD.

Gosch, C. C. A. 1897. *Danish Arctic Expeditions 1605–1620*. London: Hakluyt Society (reprinted by Cambridge University Press 2010).

Hall, James. 1897. 'A Report to King Christian IV of Denmark in the Danish Expedition to Greenland, under the Command of Captain John Cunningham, in 1605'. In *Danish Arctic Exditions 1605–1620*, C. C. A. Gosch, 1–20. London: Hakluyt Society.

Harley, John Brian, and David Woodward. 1987. 'Preface'. In *Cartography in Prehistoric, Ancient, and Medieval Europe and the Mediterranean*, edited by John Brian Harley and David Woodward, 3–24. Chicago: University of Chicago Press.

Kejlbo, Ib Rønne. 1980. *Map Material from King Christian the Fourth's Expeditions to Greenland*. Land- und Seekarten im Mittelalter und in der frühen Neuzeit. C. Koeman. München: Kraus International Publications. 7: 193–212.

Keller, Arthur Schopenhauer, Oliver James Lissitzyn, and Frederick Justin Mann. 1967. *Creation of Rights of Sovereignty through Symbolic Acts, 1400–1800*. New York: AMS Press, Inc.

Latour, Bruno. 1987. *Science in Action: How to Follow Scientists and Engineers through Society*. Milton Keynes: Open University Press.

Mignolo, Walter. 1995. *The Darker Side of the Renaissance: Literacy, Territoriality, and Colonization*. Ann Arbor: University of Michigan Press.

Mølholm Olesen, Simon. 2019. '"Vor och Cronens Land" Dansk-norske forestillinger om retten til Grønland, ca. 1550–1700'. *TEMP tidsskrift for historie* 10, no. 19: 71–101.

Ørebech, Peter Thomas. 2016. 'Terra nullius, Inuit Habitation and Norse Occupation: With Special Emphasis on the 1933 East Greenland Case'. *Arctic Review on Law and Politics* 7, no. 1: 20–41.

Parry, John Horace. 2000. *The Age of Reconnaissance 1450–1650*. London: Weidenfeld & Nicolson.

Pingel, Christian. 1845. "Om de vigtigste Reiser, som i nyere Tider ere foretagne fra Danmark og Norge for igjen at opsøge det tabte Grönland og at undersöge det gjenfundne" in *Grønlands Historiske Mindesmærker*, edited by Finn Magnussen, vol. 3, 625–794. København: Det kongelige Nordiske Oldskrift-Selskab.

Rasmussen, Knud. 1932. *Polarforskningens saga*. København: Chr. Erichsens Forlag.

Seaver, Kirsten A. 1996. *The Frozen Echo: Greenland and the Exploration of North America ca. A.D. 1000–1500*. Stanford: Stanford University Press.

Seed, Patricia. 1995. *Ceremonies of Possession in Europe's Conquest of the New World 1492–1640*. Cambridge: Cambridge University Press.

Stackpole, Michael A. 2005. *A Secret Atlas*. New York: Bantam Dell.

Steenstrup, Knud Johannes Vogelius. 1885–1886. 'Om Østerbygden', *Geografisk Tidsskrift* 8: 123–34.

Strandsbjerg, Jeppe. 2010. *Territory, Globalization and International Relations*. Basingstoke: Palgrave.

———. 2011. 'World of Warcraft™ and the State of Territory in International Relations'. Paper presented at the *52nd ISA Annual Convention: International Studies Association Conference 2011*. Montreal: Canada.

———. 2012. 'Cartopolitics, Geopolitics and Boundaries in the Arctic'. *Geopolitics* 17, no. 4: 818–42.

———. 2017. "The Space of State Formation". In *Does War Make States*, edited by Lars Bo Kaspersen and Jeppe Strandsbjerg. Cambridge: Cambridge University Press.

Waters, David. 1970. *The Iberian Bases of the English Art of Navigation in the Sixteenth Century*. Lisboa: Junta de Investigacoes do Ultramar.

Woodward, David. 2007. 'Cartography and the Renaissance: Continuity and Change'. In *Cartography in the European Renaissance*. Edited by David Woodward, 3–24. Chicago: University of Chicago Press.

Zimmer, Carl. 2014. 'The Mystery of the Sea Unicorn". *National Geographic*. 17 March. https://www.nationalgeographic.com/science/phenomena/2014/03/18/the-mystery-of-the-sea-unicorn/.

*Chapter 4*

# Surveying in British North America
## *A Homology of Property and Territory*
### Kerry Goettlich

Without explaining why, Lewis Evans's 1749 'Map of Pensilvania, New-Jersey, New-York, and the Three Delaware Counties' shows the colony of Pennsylvania as having two different northern boundaries. One of them is the boundary of the colony's patent, given by an imperial declaration. The other is the limit of Native American land purchases. The former boundary is labelled 'the Bounds of Pensilvania by Patent', while the latter has no label, but the name 'Pensilvania' in large letters is clearly confined deliberately within it. Which one was the real boundary of Pennsylvania?

Pennsylvania's two northern boundary lines in this map illustrate the ambiguous relationship between spaces of landownership and those of colonial authority. But beyond simply representing this ambiguous relationship, the map also contributed to it. On seeing the new map displayed in a New York print shop shortly after its publication in 1749, an anonymous landowner of New York Province wrote to the *Pennsylvania Gazette* complaining that New Jersey's northern border was shown too far north and that the cartographer must have been employed by the East Jersey proprietors to try to steal more land (Klinefelter 1971, 22). The East Jersey proprietors were only owners of the land, and had no powers of government, yet it was the East Jersey proprietors and not the provincial government that the anonymous writer was concerned with. As with many of the boundaries on the Evans map, the New Jersey-New York boundary was both a property boundary and an intercolonial one, and as this episode suggests, property boundaries could be more important than intercolonial boundaries. This chapter explores that ability of maps to make connections between different kinds of socio-political activities.

One of the most distinctive aspects of the English settler colonies in America, some historians have argued, was its emphasis on control of land.

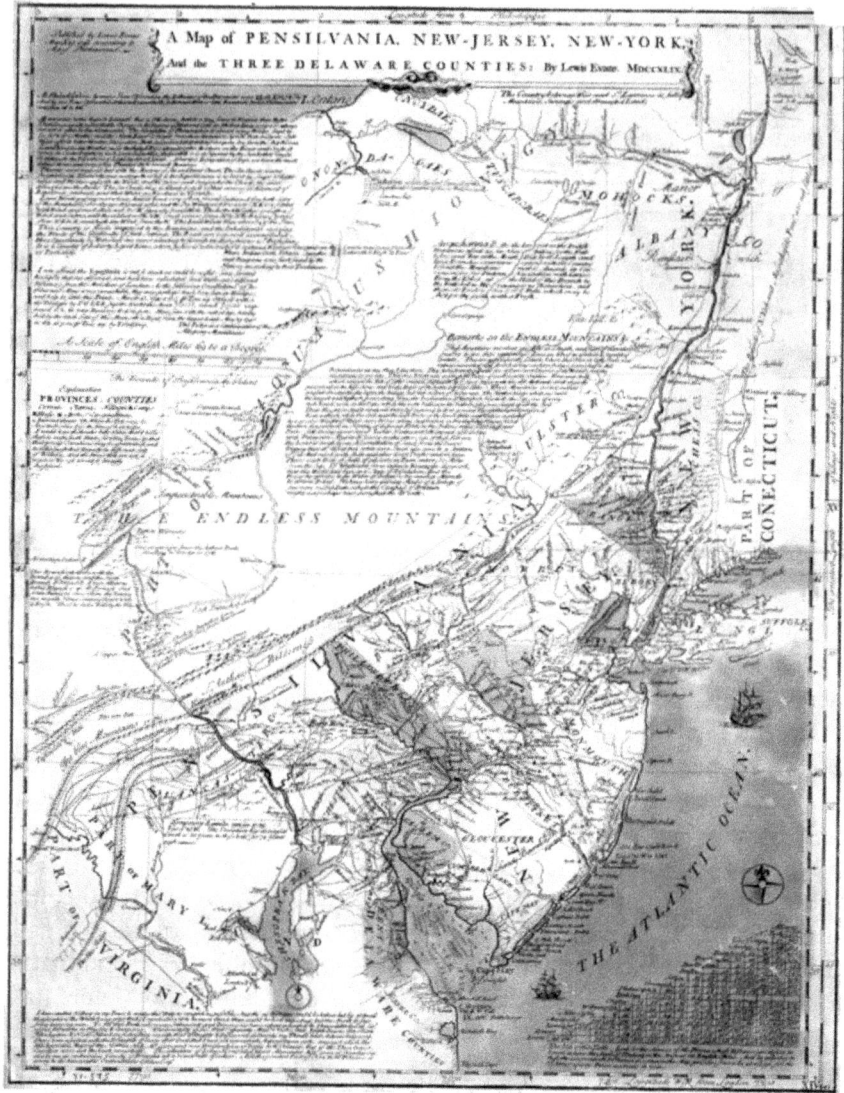

**Figure 4.1.** A Map of Pensilvania, New-Jersey, New-York, and the Three Delaware Counties (Evans and Hebert, 1749).

While other European empires in America laid claim indiscriminately to mountains, rivers and souls, English settlers explicitly coveted the land of Native Americans and worked to justify methods of separating them from their land (Greer 2017, 191). At the same time, the English colonies, particularly in the seventeenth century, lacked a great deal of military might, and were populated to a large extent by newly created landowner settlers (Keene

2002, 62). In this context, cartography, and even more so, the surveying work which went into it, became a crucial element in the making of empire (Brückner, 2006). With many settlers emigrating to these colonies in pursuit of land, governments found regulating the process of tracing, memorializing and increasingly marking and mapping property boundaries to be crucial to avoiding civil disputes that could cripple the nascent colonies.

While there is much scholarship on the role of private property within colonialism (Blomley 2003; Bhandar 2018), the relationship between individual property claims and other concurrent forms of colonial spatial claims, such as the colonial charters of the English North American colonies, has not always been fully addressed. In particular, the technologies and practices of surveying provided a crucial connection between property boundaries and intercolonial boundaries, which resulted in a mutual reinforcement. This kind of connectivity I call a 'homology', a 'correspondence in type and function' which goes beyond analogy to denote a historical linkage between practices, ideas or structures (Owens 2015, 6). Far from being a coincidence that both property boundaries and intercolonial boundaries were surveyed, often by the same people, the growing hegemony of surveyed mapping meant that practically any kind of boundary, large or small, in any part of the world, was in principle amenable to the same kinds of techniques.

From this historical basis, in this chapter I argue that mapping and surveying can be important for the making of empire in two distinct ways which are yet related. On the one hand, surveying was an instrument of settlers aiming to become landowners, as well as an instrument of colonial governments attempting to expand their settler populations without collapsing in a mess of property disputes. Surveying was used for a variety of purposes, some legal and institutional, and some more rhetorical and symbolic. On the other hand, however, committing a colony to an institution of surveyed private property had larger consequences that could scarcely have been intended. In the process of committing the colonies to the spatial grammar of surveying, the territories of entire colonies became tied to the same process of boundary surveying. Not only did property in land have to be surveyed, but the competition for land between neighbouring colonies came to be plagued by much the same kinds of disputes. In understanding the relationship between mapping and empire in the English North American colonies, then, we must attend to both the rhetoric and the unintended consequences of surveying.

I proceed in four main sections. First, I engage with two different understandings of the relationship between mapping and empire, which I refer to as 'rhetoric' and 'unintended consequences'. Second, I elaborate on how the idea of homology can illuminate the connection between those two understandings of mapping and empire. In the third and fourth sections, I investigate in more historical detail how each of these logics worked in the English North American colonies.

## IMPERIAL CARTOGRAPHY: TWO PERSPECTIVES

How can we conceptualize the significance of maps and surveying in the making of empire? One well-known paradigm through which scholars of cartography have theorized the significance of maps is what I will call 'rhetoric'. This was one of the main contributions of J. B. Harley, who in many ways instigated systematic inquiry into the role of mapping and surveying in politics and society (Harley 1989). Harley criticized the discipline of cartography for its dogmatic scientism and its denial that social theory had anything to say about maps. The main characteristic of this scientific view of cartography was an epistemology which defined truth in terms of mathematical accuracy and correspondence with systematic observation.

While Harley opened up many avenues for those interested in maps and social theory, his focus was on the rhetorical power of maps. As he puts it,

> My position is to accept that rhetoric is part of the way all texts work and that all maps are rhetorical texts. Again we ought to dismantle the arbitrary dualism between 'propaganda' and 'true,' and between modes of 'artistic' and 'scientific' representation as they are found in maps. All maps strive to frame their message in the context of an audience. All maps state an argument about the world and they are propositional in nature.
>
> (Harley 1989, 11)

His argument used the language of textual criticism, but it extended beyond visual representations themselves to the surveying techniques that lay behind many of them, which he argued conveyed a 'rhetoric of neutrality'. Indeed, his intervention was intended not only for an academic field of study but also those within the community of practitioners whose aim it was, through technological means, to eliminate rhetoric from maps.

The meaning of any particular text or map, with Derrida, might be 'undecidable', or in other words, 'enigmas, problems to be explained, prisonhouses which lock the understanding away from the world' (Harley 1989, 8). But at the same time, Harley's main concern was, with Foucault, to show how maps are enmeshed in historically particular power struggles, and are never neutral reflections of an external world. This was not necessarily limited to instrumental uses of maps, in which the cartographer is fully aware of and in control of the intervention that the map makes, and makes the map expressly for the purpose of bringing about some particular outcome. Yet the suggestion remained at least of a general alignment between the positionality of the cartographer and the political significance or effect of the map. For example, 'maps of local estates in the European *ancien regime*, though derived from instrumental survey, were a metaphor for a social structure based on landed property' (Harley 1989, 10). In other words, while the immediate concerns of the map-maker in these cases may have been limited to representing individual measurements, their broader significance in underpinning an agrarian system supported those who paid for the maps. Likewise, a map purporting to show particular borders as a neutral reflection of the world might in fact represent an aspiration rather than a reality. In this case, the map would have to be understood as a means toward the making of a 'spatial reality' (Strandsbjerg 2010) by using the grammar and techniques of science to convince an audience of its truth.

This model of mapping and surveying as rhetorical has, from its beginning, been a key contribution to the study of how empires are made. As Harley noted, maps have long been 'weapons of imperialism', particularly in that lands were 'claimed on paper before they were effectively occupied' (Harley 2001, 57). Taking the example of colonial North America, he argued that it was cartography that allowed Europeans 'to say, "This is mine, these are the boundaries"'. In other words, cartography compensated with rhetorical power where empires were lacking in other forms of power. Even surveying that was less specifically tied to visual representation in maps, such as the ancient Roman centuriations that laid out land in geometrical grids, was 'an expression of power'.

Sometimes, however, maps have significance exceeding the cartographer's purposes. Consider the map commissioned by Louis XIV in the 1680s which, because of its superior accuracy, decreased the apparent size of France (Konvitz 1987, 7–8). More generally, the rapid increase in map-making activity in Europe beginning in the late fifteenth century, including many state maps, initially had very little state sponsorship. It was only by the end of the sixteenth century that rulers regularly took an active interest in having maps made (Biggs 1999). One reason for this is the extreme expenses required for large-scale projects to measure the size and dimensions of an entire state. If geometrically representative maps had rhetorical value which could be deployed politically, a potential patron would have to be convinced that this was worth its production costs. While no doubt maps were implicated in political struggles, it cannot be assumed that any particular powerful interest was behind their creation, or that a map had any particular effect that it appears to intend.

Against this backdrop, Jordan Branch has argued that important effects of mapping that occurred in international relations were indeed political but do not seem to have been intended by anyone (Branch 2014, 88). In particular, in the sixteenth and seventeenth centuries, European maps began to show authority as bounded by carefully drawn borderlines, and only afterwards in the eighteenth century, these precisely delimited borderlines began to appear in treaties as well. Branch shows that new mapping practices led to a change in authorities' background knowledge about how authority was held, which then in turn led to a change in territorial practices that resembled mapping practices. These changes were certainly political, because if maps were taken for granted as true depictions of the world, polities that could not be mapped in the new way would simply disappear. This would happen not only to the temporal authority of the Roman Catholic Church but also to countless minor princes and lords whose authority depended more on feudal relations with a superior than on precise territorial boundaries. Nor were the advantages of having accurate maps unnoticed by those polities that were becoming increasingly territorial, such as France. Despite their territory being apparently shrunk by more accurate cartography in the 1680s, French authorities found that maps were extremely useful for projects such as tax reform and simplifying administrative divisions.

Again, this way of understanding the significance of maps had important consequences for the study of empire, but at the same time brought to light consequences which went beyond rhetoric. Two particular contributions can be noted here. First, as Branch noted, European empires were making imperial claims in the Americas using cartographic lines several centuries before they were expressing state boundaries within Europe using the same techniques. What this suggested for the making of empire was that this was not a process of simply applying age-old European techniques of rule, but that imperial construction was in some sense a laboratory of new technologies of domination. Second, it also suggested that in some cases cartography could actually be quite counterproductive for certain kinds of empires. In particular, with the popularization of a map-based worldview, types of authority which were less amenable to depiction through these new technologies became delegitimized, such as the Holy Roman Empire's claim of rulership over all Christendom, or the city-league of the Hansa (Branch 2014, 27).

On one hand, Branch's account shows how the importance of maps for the making of empire may be more than rhetorical, having wider implications beyond the intentions of the map-maker. Despite the shift in the nature of authority toward linearly defined territory being in the interests of states such as France, these states do not seem to have promoted this particular effect of cartography beyond their own frontiers. On the other hand, the advantage of the rhetorical model, in relation to the notion of unintended consequences, is its focus on power and its scepticism of any claims of innocence on the part of maps.

These two ways of understanding maps are not mutually exclusive, as the remainder of this chapter will try to show. In the next section, I interrogate the intersection between them conceptually, before examining the colonial maps of British North America in order to illustrate how these two models might be connected.

## CARTOGRAPHIC REPRESENTATION AS ENABLER OF HOMOLOGIES

While all cartography in principle can be used in multiple kinds of social contexts simultaneously, this chapter focuses on particular features of Ptolemaic mapping. *Ptolemaic* here means following broadly many of the techniques of cartography set out by the ancient Greek writer Claudius Ptolemy in his *Geography*, including longitude and latitude, projection and proportional representation. These techniques in various ways, at various times, became more common in European mapping during the fifteenth and sixteenth centuries (Branch 2014, 51–55). Homogenization is a crucial implication of many of these techniques. Unlike in many early medieval European maps of the world which were explicitly centred on Jerusalem, every point on the map is, in theory, of equal significance, and it is centred nowhere (Goettlich 2019, 212–218). With proportional representation, things are represented according to quantitative measures, rather than qualitative characteristics or relations, and so one set of measuring principles in theory suffices for everything.

To take this a step further, where Ptolemaic mapping flattens out and obscures qualitative differences between represented objects, it creates a certain kind of connectivity among those objects that appear the same. So not only does the space within a territory appear homogenous, suggesting that power is evenly spread within that space, but it may also do this for all territories within the scope of the map in the same way (Strandsbjerg 2010, 83). The linearization of borders which took place after linear borders began appearing on maps was not an isolated process in each individual state, but instead the homogeneity of Ptolemaic mapping suggested that if territory could be linearly defined in one territorial unit of authority, then this could be done in all of them. The same technological instruments and techniques of measurement could be used in any part of the world, and in many cases this created connections across distance.

To take the case of colonial North America, the borders established by English charters in the seventeenth and eighteenth centuries created a relatively regular pattern of parallel east-west lines across the eastern part of the continent, along with the occasional diagonal line (Sack 1986, 10). While these colonial lines were being drawn, and as they took on more importance, a practice of boundary surveying emerged which was increasingly professionalized and homogenized. By the late eighteenth century, for example, it was possible for one surveyor, David Rittenhouse, to have personally surveyed boundaries for more than half of the Thirteen Colonies (Cazier 1976, 13). In defining the particularly difficult Maryland-Pennsylvania border, the empire had to draw on the best of its network of scientific expertise. Introduced to them by the Astronomer Royal in London, the colonial proprietors selected astronomer Charles Mason and surveyor Jeremiah Dixon, who had just returned from observing the transit of Venus in Cape Town for the Royal Society (Danson 2017, 74). The spatial homogenization of Ptolemaic mapping thus in principle puts all borders in connection with a range of scientific practices which seem to be global in remit, unlimited by local particularities.

This particular kind of connectivity that Ptolemaic mapping makes possible through homogenization can be called a *homology*. A homology is similar to an analogy, as Patricia Owens explains, which is 'a likeness in form or function', but makes a stronger claim than analogy (Owens 2015, 6–7). Claiming that a homology exists goes beyond analogy in that it involves an actual, not just comparative, relation between two things. When biologists say there is a homology between organs in two animals, for example, it means not just that there is a similarity but that this is due to the two animals having a common ancestor. Similarly, to say that modern territorial borders are homologous is not just to say they have common characteristics but that they are historically related to one another, in this case through the technologies of surveying and mapping that make them possible.

Importantly for our purposes here, Ptolemaic mapping is not just used for mapping states and the boundaries of their sovereign territory. Instead, the proportional representation of three-dimensional space as two-dimensional and seen from above is the default mode of representation in many very different contexts, from road maps used for navigation to university campus maps. Floorplan diagrams of houses or other buildings which state explicitly that they are 'not to scale' indicate an anticipation that the viewer would normally expect to see such diagrams drawn to scale. Many of these proportional maps show linear boundaries not related to sovereign territoriality, whether to do with administrative units, districts or other divisions. Many early modern maps using Ptolemaic methods also showed regions as being linearly bounded such as Germany or Italy which at the time did not correspond to any existing political institutions (Biggs 1999). If there is a basic homology among modern territorial borders which has to do with how they are mapped, does this also extend to all linear borders cartographically shaped by Ptolemaic mapping, no matter the size or nature of what they bound?

Such a far-reaching question is beyond the scope of this chapter, but in the following sections I examine the colonial maps of British North America to show how the two models of rhetoric and unintended consequences might be connected together homologically. Whereas the initial territorial claims made by the English and British Empires were bounded on only some sides, and overlapped each other, the colonies that emerged over time tended toward more precise and narrow boundaries (Hubbard Jr. 2009). The United States, at independence, had territorial boundaries specified in painstaking detail, although it was later discovered that even the degree of specificity in the 1783 Paris Treaty was far from sufficient, and it took many decades to survey them. To a large extent this was linked to the growing importance of geometrical private property surveying.

These two logics link directly to the question of how the practices of surveying were connected to the making of empire. On one hand, the rhetorical impact of surveyed mapping on empire was felt in the legitimacy it afforded to what were, in practice to a large extent, property titles newly created out of dispossessed Native American land. Surveying, promoted by the colonial state, attempted to be as precise and geometrical as possible in order to reinforce private property. Governing at a distance without great means of direct coercion, a surveyed property regime attempted to bring stability to the masses of often overlapping individual claims. Moreover, it helped protect the private property of many of the officials in colonial governments, leaving poorer settlers to usurp more Native American land rather than pay increasing prices for already colonized land (Zinn 2003, 54).

But on the other hand, the concern for precision in surveying and mapping spilled over into intercolonial struggles, having implications on the kinds of surveys required for these boundaries as well, and in turn on the politics of competition for land among colonies. In the last section, then, I explore some of the consequences of surveying which were not necessarily productive of empire. While relying on surveys facilitated colonial control in many areas, it also helped determine the limits of the geographical reach of colonial governments and pitted them against each other.

## THE RHETORIC OF GEOMETRIC PROPERTY MAPPING

The rhetorical effect of geometrical maps, in terms of reinforcing the status and property of landowners in North America, can be traced back to profound changes occurring in the English surveying practice beginning in the sixteenth century. Surveying in England before that time was a multifaceted practice which included investigating boundaries by interviewing tenants and reviewing whatever written records might exist but also providing advice on farming, manuring, draining and irrigating (Darby 1933; Taylor 1947). Surveyors were well versed in law and agricultural techniques, and measured the extent of the land often by estimation, sometimes without visiting all the premises. Quantitative measures were required by statute only for 'improved' areas, and even then were often done by counting strips of land. By the early sixteenth century, many of the astronomical and mathematical techniques needed for accurate surveying existed, but this knowledge had so far remained academic and in Latin (Lindgren, 2007). Numerical measurements and calculations made up a relatively small part of the surveyor's job, and the ability to do advanced kinds of computations was generally unnecessary.

This changed during the enclosure movement, the process beginning in the sixteenth century of fencing and walling in previously open lands, in which landowners absorbed much land that had been held in common (Darby 1933; Taylor 1947). In this context, surveys provided landowners with an opportunity to increase their holdings under the pretext of seeking greater accuracy and knowledge of their property. Many feared that peasants had been 'concealing' part of the land by living on it. The rhetoric of property mapping, in this context, was a way of justifying dispossession, as well as providing a narrative for a rising agrarian bourgeoisie.

When English settlers came to North America, they had partially different reasons for implementing surveys (Greer 2017). Unlike the surveys of the English enclosure movement, which were often done in order to strengthen and expand property titles, in colonial North America surveys were done in order to alienate land which was in theory owned only by the Crown, creating new titles. Whereas landownership in England was derived from the conveyance of rights from person to person from time immemorial, settlers were self-consciously moving in and replacing the existing inhabitants of the land. Whether surveys were done prior to or after settlement, there were no apparently ancient rights to simply measure out more accurately.

Surveys were nevertheless equally important in underpinning the rapid redistribution of land that occurred in the colonies, although here it was mainly Native Americans who were dispossessed. One reason for this was that the precision of surveys implied fairness and justice, something which many of the English settlers identified with themselves. According to historian Allan Greer, the Protestant empires with colonies in North America more generally, including also the Netherlands and Sweden, believed that a market system of property gave them a moral high ground over their Catholic rivals (Greer 2014). If Native Americans had freely sold the land and had been given adequate compensation, they could not be accused of theft. The French, Portuguese and Spanish, by contrast, declared sovereignty over indigenous peoples without sharply distinguishing them from their land. As one English observer put it, the French in Canada and Louisiana 'have scarce any other title to the country than what they obtained by usurpation, very seldom asking leave of the natives' (Greer 2014, 76–77). Despite vast differences in circumstances, the free market in property played a similar role of justifying dispossession in North America as it did in England.

The practice of surveying also came with a kind of social capital among the landowning class. By the time of U.S. independence, knowledge of the surveying practice, or at least a passing familiarity with it, to a certain extent pervaded the colonial elite. Both George Washington and Thomas Jefferson, the first and third presidents, had direct experience with surveying (Cazier 1976). Surveying manuals such as John Wing's *The Art of Surveying* and John Love's *Geodaesia* were widely popular among gentlemen planters. Surveying was comparable in social status with other professions which required technical knowledge and could come with formal certification, such as the medical and legal professions. 'Their satin waistcoats, brocaded vests, patent slippers, and powdered wigs were of the latest English fashions' (Hughes 1979, 156).

It was more difficult to find skilled and well-equipped surveyors in the colonies than in England, and the new and somewhat rapidly created colonial property boundaries were constantly in dispute (Greer 2017, 346–54). Yet this only made it more necessary for landowners to learn the practice themselves and further cemented a connection between landowning and surveying. With landowning, a general aspiration for white male settlers, surveying became widely dispersed enough that it could be called 'a new form of popular literacy' (Brückner 2006). Less geometric techniques for fixing boundaries persisted, for example, in New England, townspeople would perform perambulations, collectively walking the town boundaries together. But these were stripped of their older religious meaning by Puritans, and made to resemble as much as possible the surveyor's blank page with connected lines.

One of the most important surveying manuals published in England in the seventeenth century, John Love's *Geodaesia*, was specifically aimed at settlers in North America (Richeson 1966, 126–27). As the author wrote, he had seen surveyors in the colonies struggle to apply English surveying principles to their fields. So, for example, in the 'thick woods of Jamaica, Carolina, &c', where there are no iron ore deposits, he suggests using a magnetic needle to measure angles (Love 1768, 59). One way to read *Geodaesia* is as a way of bringing the pure, almost metaphysical conceptions of geometry to apply to a particular practical pursuit done by people with no particular level of education beyond basic literacy. In this respect it can be seen within a Protestant religious context in which worldly labour, as opposed to ascetic contemplation, was given an increasing spiritual significance, and in which one's practical vocation was the highest aspiration available (Weber 2001). Love refers to geodesy as 'a study so pleasant, and affords such wholesome and innocent exercise, that we seldom find a man that has once entered himself into the study of Geometry or Geodaesia, can ever after wholly lay it aside' (Love

1768, preface). Yet he takes it upon himself to answer questions that mathematicians, in their academic isolation, would find trifling, but which have left 'young men in America so often at a loss ... (particularly in Carolina)', such as how to lay out a field five or six times wider than its length (Love 1768, preface). It is perhaps owing to its exceptional clarity and practical utility that the book was published in thirteen editions over more than 100 years after its first publication in 1688 (Richeson 1966, 126).

While settlers on their own looked for ways to solidify their newly invented property claims, some being more concerned with quantitative measures than others, it fell mostly to the colonial governments to try to ensure that these claims did not overlap with each other, and surveying was seen as an important part of achieving this goal. While maintaining a scientifically surveyed property order would privilege wealthier landowners connected to the government and able to obtain skilled surveying, it was mainly thought to reduce the amount of necessary litigation, and potential frontier conflict. This

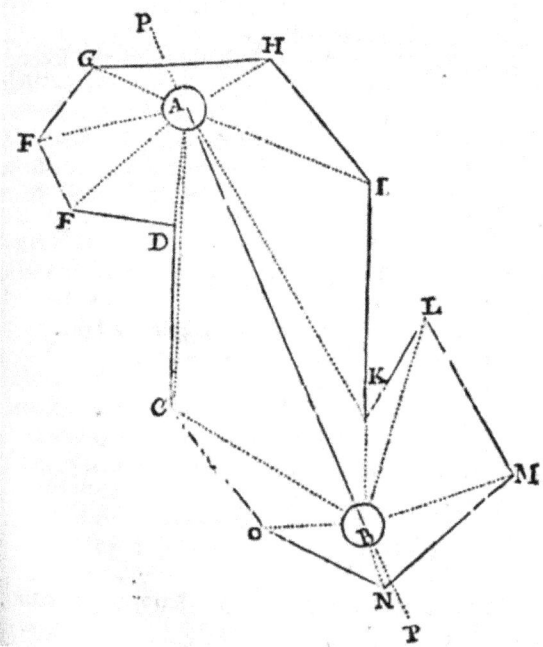

Figure 4.2. Illustration in John Love (1768, 83), *Geodaesia: Or, the Art of Surveying and Measuring Land Made Easy*. Image in Public Domain.

meant that surveying became an important problem for colonial governments. We can see a good example of this at work in seventeenth-century Virginia, where a surveyor general was appointed in 1621 to control the appointment of county surveyors, who would in turn control how crown lands were parcelled out to private owners (Hughes 1979, 8–19). Because the allocation of land was so contentious, surveyors general had support from a sizeable faction in the Virginia Assembly and by the end of the century, this position grew to be one of the most powerful offices in the colony. Suspicions grew that the surveying profession was being used for personal gain rather than purely scientific purposes, and this contributed to popular discontent with the government which threatened to escalate into a full-scale rebellion. In response, then, laws were enacted, in Virginia and in other colonies, which mandated that surveyors perform their work up to certain scientific standards and using specific kinds of equipment (Kain and Baigent 1992, 269). The rhetorical force of these laws, and the kind of surveys that they mandated, was to create a distribution of property which was fixed and fair, or at least had this appearance.

These rhetorical effects continued as settlers transitioned from small, weak coastal footholds toward a continental hegemony, and these issues continued to be debated. After independence, Congress saw surveys as part of what would entrench its power over far-away settlers and the Native Americans with whom they often came into violent contact. Much of the land ceded to the United States by Britain, in the western parts of the area between the Mississippi River and the Atlantic Ocean, was at first claimed by but not fully under the control of various individual states. For example, Connecticut and Massachusetts both continued their northern and southern borders westward, in accordance with their original grants, which were specified by lines of latitude going all the way to the Pacific Ocean (Gates 1968). Virginia claimed all of the U.S. territory north of the Ohio river, including the land claimed by Connecticut and Massachusetts. In consolidating the confederation of states, these western lands were ceded to Congress, which would then create new states out of them.

To this end Congress agreed on the Land Ordinance of 1785, which detailed the methods to be used in dividing up this vast area into ranges of townships running north to south (Onuf 1987; Hubbard, 2009). By this time the perceived importance of the technical practices of surveying had become so great that roughly the first third of this semi-constitutional piece of legislation consisted of detailed instructions on surveying methods:

> The lines shall be measured with a chain; shall be plainly marked by chaps on the trees and exactly described on a plat; whereon shall be noted by the surveyor, at their proper distances. . . .

> The plats of the townships respectively, shall be marked by subdivisions into lots of one mile square, or 640 acres, in the same direction as the external lines, and numbered from 1 to 36; always beginning the succeeding range of the lots with the number next to that with which the preceding one concluded. . . .
> The geographer and surveyors shall pay the utmost attention to the variation of the magnetic needle; and shall run and note all lines by the true meridian, certifying, with every plat, what was the variation at the times of running the lines thereon noted.
>
> (White 1983, 11–12)

These surveys had at least three results from the rhetorical point of view (see figure 4.3). First, this process of surveyed settlement was designed to contain disputes and conflicts which could proliferate violence and legal complications (Onuf 1987, 88). Colonial elites imagined the frontier as a violent space and viewed both Native Americans and many settlers as uncivilized, and they hoped that fixing clear property boundaries would reduce the potential for conflict between them. It was assumed that there would be a mad rush for this land once it was opened to settlers, as myths spread about its ideal qualities and, very much mistakenly, how this land was spared the harsh winters of the north-east. While the British Empire had tried to simply prevent settlers from going beyond the Appalachian Mountains, Congress decided to have the western lands surveyed in advance. Boundary disputes also arose between new states, as they had existed between colonies before independence, and some of these threatened to turn violent. With Congress's power and constitution on unstable ground, surveys could provide a kind of scientific certainty.

Second, Congress badly needed money in the wake of its War of Independence, and selling off the western lands was a major opportunity to fulfil this need. Other ideas existed of how to use the land, such as using it to pay soldiers' bounty claims or to maintain a kind of middle ground between wilderness and civilization which was thought to help preserve the liberty of the republic. These ideas lost out to a general acceptance that the land would pay for the war. Moreover, selling the land to individual citizens was promoted ideologically as a means to stimulate the emergence of a free market in land, if done in a controlled way (Onuf 1987, 35; Festa 2013). Congressional leaders saw the sale of land to individuals, and thus the cultivation of docile yet industrious developer-settlers, as productive for the common good. Many of them, such as George Washington, themselves having a history of involvement in land speculation, knew that an unrestrained scramble for wealth could destroy wealth and take control away from Congress. Speculators threatened to take up all the best land, and as a product of fierce competition drive the price of land down to a point where it would not pay for Congress's war debts. Meanwhile the land would sit in the hands of speculators rather than being developed, and would remain defenceless against Native Americans or other

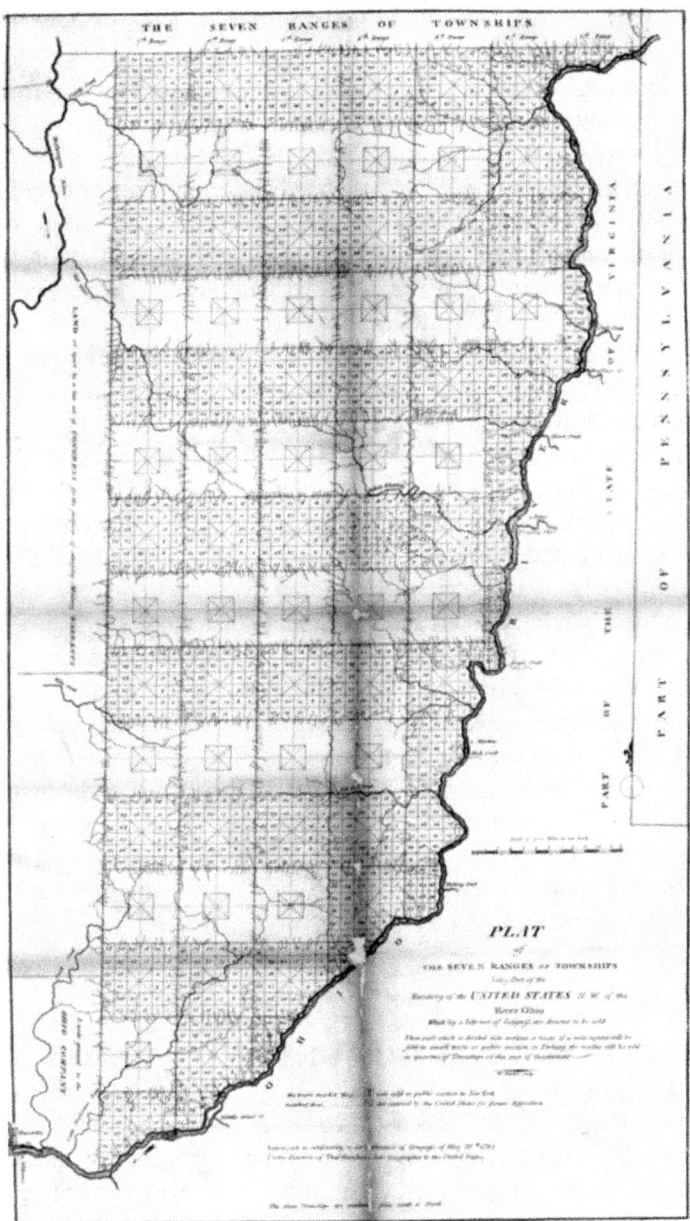

Figure 4.3. Plat of the Seven Ranges of Townships (Hutchins, Barker, and Carey 1796).

European empires. As always, alienating the land into a free market in property required commodifying it by geometrically surveying it, and only surveys could serve to divide up vast areas of land into small pieces in a way that could be controlled by the central authority of Congress.

Third, Congress needed to prevent groups of separatist settlers from breaking out of its control. Groups of settlers were organizing their own governments, with Vermont being the only successful instance. As another example, a group of colonists in Western Virginia had been trying in the decades preceding the War of Independence to create a new colony there within the British Empire, to be named Vandalia in honour of the queen consort of Great Britain, Charlotte of Mecklenburg-Streilitz, who was supposedly descended from the Vandals (Anderson 1979). While the initiative mostly faded away during the War of Independence, the threat of separatist movements was apparent enough for Rhode Island's Congressional delegates to predict that 'in the course of a few years the [Ohio] country will be peopled like Vermont. It will be independent, and the whole property of the soil will be lost forever to the United States' (Onuf 1987, 29). In addition to Native Americans, other European empires, and speculators, even the settlers themselves were potential threats to Congressional authority. Many, especially those who travelled the furthest from settler-populated areas, were considered by elites to be 'corrupted', 'disorderly' or 'nearly related to an Indian' in manners (Onuf 1987, 31).

Yet the emergence of a widespread concern with accurate surveying, and the normalization of referring to fixed and mapped linear boundaries in property disputes also had consequences that are not so easily seen as instrumental or purposeful. In particular, the transformation of landscapes into geometrical spaces eventually necessitated a transformation in the kinds of territorial agreements and disputes that could take place. In the next section I examine how the connection between property boundaries and intercolonial boundaries, through mapping, had important consequences for the international politics of British North America.

## UNINTENDED CONSEQUENCES: THE LINEARIZATION OF TERRITORIALITY

Modern territoriality, as defined by linear boundaries, was not brought over from Europe by settlers. In Europe at the time, such precise linear borders were not commonly agreed between polities, with major peace agreements concerning territory being phrased almost exclusively in lists of objects and places (Branch 2014, 125). In contrast to this, linear definitions of authority predominated in the English North American colonies in the seventeenth century, as an outcome of property surveys. In this way the rhetorical logic of property surveying was transferred in its application to colonial jurisdiction. Disputes between colonies tended to result from disputes over the ownership of specific lands, and so addressing these disputes involved similar surveying practices, writ large.

We can see an early example of this in a property disagreement between colonists of Plymouth and Massachusetts Bay colonies, two of the first English colonies to survive permanently, in the 1630s shortly after they had been established. In the predominantly Congregationalist New England colonies, lands were granted to individuals by townships, which retained much autonomy. A dispute arose between the inhabitants of Scituate, a Plymouth town, and Hingam, a Massachusetts town, over some meadow grounds. Some Hingam people 'presumed to alotte parte of them to their people, and measure & stack them out', but then some Scituate people took the stakes out and threw them away (Bradford 1856, 368). Because the two towns were in different colonies, a new practice had to be improvised. In this context the colonial governments decided to appoint commissioners to determine a line, and a 'mathematician' was sent to survey this line (Dean 1897, 170). This would serve for the 'avoiding and preventing of all differences and controversies that might arise about or concerning the extents and limits of the patents of New Plymouth and Massachusetts Bay' (Shurtleff 1855, 127).

In 1641 the same surveyor was sent to survey the Massachusetts border with Connecticut, addressing a dispute that was also instigated by private property claims (Shurtleff 1853, 323). The town of Springfield, on the Connecticut River and governed by Connecticut, had already been experiencing strained relations with the government in Hartford, which disapproved of Springfield's dealings with the nearby Pocumtuc Native Americans (Green 1888, 58–61). Springfield was charged with buying maize from the Pocumtucs for Connecticut, but the Pocumtucs did not want to sell maize at the price being offered, and in response Connecticut sent up an armed contingent to force the sale. Upset by this interference, Springfield requested that Massachusetts include it within its boundaries, in order to cut ties with Connecticut. Massachusetts' subsequent letter to Connecticut reveals the assumptions underlying the politics of space between colonies, focusing on recent land grants made by Connecticut that it believed 'to bee within our patent' and 'to belong to us', and informing Connecticut that 'wee intend (by Gods help) to know the certeinty of o$^r$ limitts, to the end that wee may neither intrench upon the right of any of o$^r$ neighbo$^{rs}$, no$^r$ suffer o$^r$selues & o$^r$ posterity to bee deprived of what rightly belongeth unto us' (Shurtleff 1853, 324).

In accordance with its colonial charter, then, Massachusetts sent surveyors to find the point three miles south of the southernmost point on the Charles River, and then run a line due west from there. When the survey found Springfield to fall on the Massachusetts side of that line, Connecticut's response was not to rely on Springfield's having been founded under Connecticut jurisdiction or its lack of authority to unilaterally secede. Instead, Connecticut disputed the credentials of the surveyors, calling them 'obscure sailors' who had apparently not even run the line at all but instead sailed around Cape Cod and up the Connecticut River to a point they thought was at the same latitude as their starting point but was actually some seven or eight miles to the south (Bowen 1882, 19).

This linear geometric logic also affected some inter-imperial boundaries, but this applied unevenly, depending on where settlements, and thus property surveys, were. We can see this by contrasting two agreements made by New Englanders, one with the French and one with the Dutch. The Dutch in New Netherlands pursued a kind of settlement similar to that emerging in New England, leading the settlers of the two empires to attempt to negotiate a linear boundary. In contrast, the French presence in Maine did not involve a significant settler population, and by extension, it did not involve property surveys, making a linear boundary unnecessary.

In the Treaty of St. Germain in 1632, England returned Canada and Acadia to France after having briefly seized them, but did not define their boundaries (Davenport 1917, 347). In 1635 the French co-lieutenant-general Charles d'Aulnay captured and fortified an English trading post at Penobscot, or Pentagoet, marking the westernmost extent of French control on the North-eastern coast (Faulkner 1981). Strife had broken out between the two co-lieutenant-generals of Acadia, and the other, Charles de la Tour, attacked Pentagoet in 1643 with the help of some Massachusetts colonists. The embarrassed Massachusetts government sued for peace, while still complaining about the French seizure of Penobscot. This resulted in a 1644 agreement between the New England Confederation and New France which established peace and free trade, and that 'if any occasion of offence shall happen, neither of them shall attempt anything against the other in a hostile way.' No boundary or frontier was mentioned in the treaty, and the only contact between the English and French implied by it was through trade. With the area surrounding Pentagoet controlled by Etchemin Native Americans, and with few French settlers coming into contact with the English by land, there was little French influence on property boundaries in the area (Price 1995, 77). As a result, it should be no surprise that there seems to have been no perceived need for a French-English boundary.

The Dutch Empire, however, did alienate land to private owners in the lower Hudson river valley, and in this context we do see a linear border emerging between the Dutch and the English. While the Dutch West India Company was initially motivated primarily by Native American trade, especially in fur, this failed to produce suitable profits, and so in order to facilitate trade, the company introduced settlers (Rink 1978). In theory, properties would come with obligations to feudal lords called *patroons*, but this proved difficult to implement in practice, because of the availability of land and the nearby presence of non-feudal colonies, and so the Dutch system, like New England, approached individual ownership of land (Keene 2002, 66–67). In 1650, then, representatives of the Dutch and English settlers agreed on a boundary:

> The bounds upon the mayne to begine at the west side of Greenwidge Bay, being about 4 miles from Stanford, and soe to runne a northerley lyne twenty miles up into the cuntry, and after as it shalbee agreed by the two goverments of the Duch and of Newhaven, provided the said lyne com not within 10 miles of Hudsons river.
>
> (Davenport 1929, 5)

The distance of twenty miles inland makes sense as an outcome of settlement, as this was roughly the extent of the patroonships concentrated into one area. Unlike the absence of French settlement in the area of Acadia nearest to New England, Dutch landowners did have an important influence on the layout of towns and properties that remains today (Price 1995, 220).

In creating a linear boundary, the settlers were imagining dividing up this land between their respective empires in the same way that they would between individual landholders, as if on a survey map. This is illustrated further by a dispute over this border that later emerged between the colonies of Connecticut and New York (Bowen 1882, 69–72). In 1664, during the Second Anglo-Dutch War, England conquered New Netherland from the Dutch, leading to a renegotiation of the boundary, which was now to run north-northwest. It became apparent, however, that the 1664 line was agreed on the false assumption that it would not give Connecticut any land within twenty miles of the Hudson River. In fact, that line would not only have crossed the Hudson but would have included most of the European-occupied area of the province of New York. At the same time, New York's claim included several Connecticut coastal towns, where it tried and failed to extend its jurisdiction by issuing arrest warrants. A compromise, then, was agreed on in 1683 which would rely on abstract geometry rather than conflicting claims and evidence. Connecticut was allowed to keep most of the coastal towns it claimed, but in exchange, if that land should

> Diminish or take away any Land within twenty miles of Hudsons River that then soe much as is in Land Diminished of twenty miles from Hudsons River thereby shall be added out of Connecticut bounds unto the Line aforemenconed & Parallel to Hudsons River and Twenty miles Distant from it the addition to be made the whole Length of the said Parallel line and in such breadth as will make up Quantity for Quantity what shall be diminished as aforesaid.
>
> (Van Zandt 1976, 73)

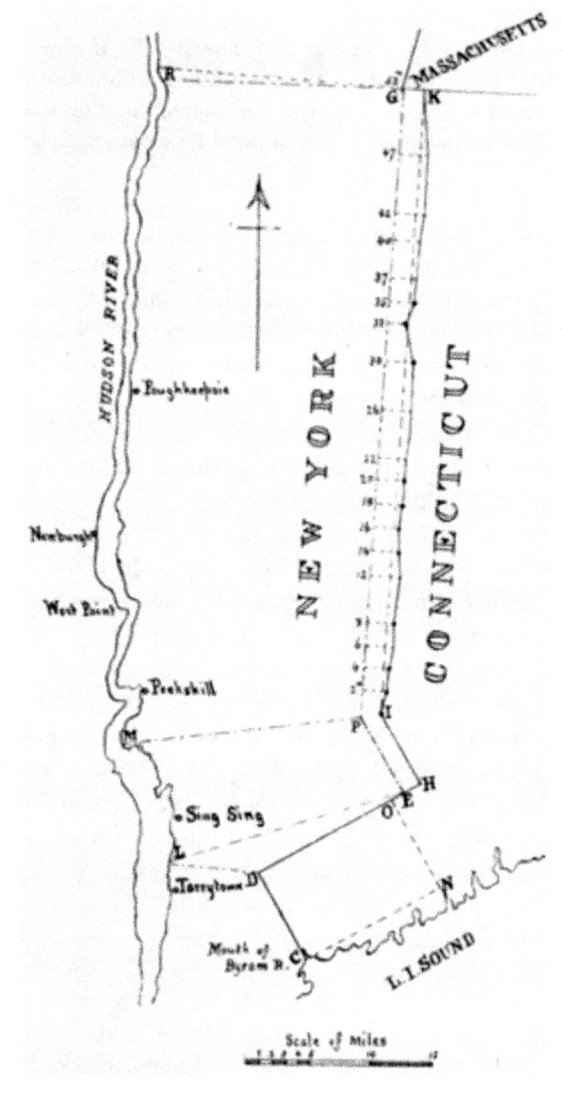

Figure 4.4. Illustration in Clarence Bowen (1882, 75), *The Boundary Disputes of Connecticut*. Image in Public Domain.

In other words, in exchange for the coastal area, Connecticut would have to give to New York a very thin strip of land all along the rest of the border, of which the quantitative area, calculated on paper, would be equivalent (see figure 4.4: Connecticut ceded area EHIKGP in exchange for area CDON). Agreements such as this tried, and at least in the case of the 1664 agreement, failed to reduce colonial authority to geometrical space as it existed on a property-surveying map. While officials debated over the intentions of the 1664 negotiators to include particular areas of settlement, they did not question the type of agreement itself, which did not mention any of these settlements in the actual text. Rather than taking up problems of representation as such, the structure of the 1683 compromise resembled more closely to the concerns of John Love in *Geodaesia*, such as how to impose pure and calculable mathematical forms onto a landscape that defied such purity.

Yet although the rhetoric of quantitative survey maps was one of stability, purity, abstraction and precision, and many looked to them as the natural solution to disorder of various kinds, surveys did not always work this way. In fact, the growing expectation that quantitative surveys were the only source of geographical knowledge often contributed to the conditions which were imagined as disorderly and called for surveys in the first place. One source that historians have often looked to for settlers' ideas of order on the frontier is the writings of William Byrd II, a Virginia squire who was part of a boundary survey between Virginia and North Carolina (Boyd 1929). In his *History of the Dividing Line*, he recounts how a territorial dispute between the two colonies arose. When the Province of Carolina was created in 1663, with a northern boundary of 36° N, the most recent southern boundary of Virginia had been set by its third colonial charter at 30° N, leaving a very large potential overlap of six degrees of latitude (Van Zandt 1976, 92).

This numerical overlap was a somewhat common occurrence among English colonial charters in the seventeenth century. Virginia's northern boundary, as set in its second charter of 1609, was a line running from a specified point on the Atlantic coast 'West and Northwest' all the way to the Pacific Ocean (Van Zandt 1976, 92). Such a boundary would, in theory, overlap with any of the more northerly colonies established in the following decades which were defined by latitudes stretching to the Pacific Ocean. The revealing aspect of these geometrical overlaps is that the reason for the confusion was not because of a lack of available geographical knowledge. If this had been the case, we could draw the conclusion that such problems are only a temporary limitation on the power of cartographic boundaries, which can be overcome by gathering some additional amount of knowledge. Instead, the abstract, numerical nature of the boundaries given in the overlapping colonial charters shows that empirical knowledge of particular locations was not lacking but was simply irrelevant to several of these disputes, and that these territories overlapped not only in practice but also in theory. These were contradictions that no amount of surveying could resolve.

In response, King Charles II issued a second charter in 1665 which specified that the boundary between Virginia and Carolina would be a latitude defined by 'Weyanoke Creek, lying within or about' the latitude 36° 30' N (Boyd 1929, 10). The identity of this creek, however, was contested in the following decades, with fifteen miles between two different possible creeks. Byrd claimed that settlers entering the area 'took out Patents by Guess', either from Virginia or Carolina, and that Carolina benefitted from this arrangement because the taxes and the terms of taking up land were easier under Carolina law (Boyd 1929, 11). Yet when Carolina sent the English authorities a request that a boundary survey be done, as early as 1681, there was no reply (Boyd 1929, xvii–xix). Only in 1705 did Virginia agree to a boundary commission, and an attempt in 1710 at a joint survey failed. This was for various reasons, for example, the Carolina representatives found the Virginia commissioners' instruments faulty. Only in 1728 was part of the line actually surveyed.

William Byrd II, who was eventually assigned to the commission which finally carried out the survey, left an account of the expedition which consistently portrays the boundary region as one of utter disorder and full of lazy inhabitants. He considered all the inhabitants of the area to be Carolinians, 'Apprehensive lest their Lands Should be taken into Virginia. In that case they must have submitted to some Sort of Order and Government' (Wohlpart 1992, 8). He imagined North Carolina as a state of nature, where people live off of nature's bounty and produce nothing of value. Because pork was 'the staple Commodity of North Carolina', for example, he wrote that this made the inhabitants 'extremely hoggish in their Temper, & many of them seem to Grunt rather than Speak in their ordinary conversation' (Boyd 1929, 55).

The growing expectation that borders were created by official surveys, which had to be both accurately mapped and clearly marked, could not always be fulfilled, sometimes creating confusion to the point of violence. The most prominent example of this is the 'Conojocular War', a conflict between Maryland and Pennsylvania settlers in the 1720s and 1730s. In terms of casualties it was miniscule compared to many of those fought between settlers and Native Americans, but it involved militias of hundreds of men and blocked further settlement except by those willing to risk their lives (Spero 2012; Dutrizac 1991). By 1682 it had been discovered that due to a cartographic error the Maryland-Pennsylvania border, written in the colonial charters at 40° North, excluded Pennsylvania's capital from its territory. In 1732, the proprietary governors came to an agreement addressing this problem, but were unable to implement it due to an ambiguity in that agreement over whether a 'twelve-mile circle' in the eastern part of the border referred to the radius or circumference of the circle (Wainwright 1963). As a result, over decades these technical problems prevented any possibility of a formal settlement. Representatives of both colonial governments repeatedly tried to arrest each other and use armed force to evict settlers holding land titles from the other government, leading to a constant threat of violence.

It is difficult to say whether or not some other kind of effective jurisdiction, if it had been imaginable at the time, could have been successfully imposed. By the time of the 1732 agreement, enough settlers from both sides were entrenched and determined to evict the others that some kind of unrest seems to have been likely. At the same time, if European settlement had from the beginning proceeded, for example, as it did in early New England, on the basis of relatively cohesive townships rather than individual plots of land, perhaps the two colonies could have governed their respective townships wherever they emerged. Allowances would have had to be made for enclaves and exclaves, but perhaps no more than those that persisted within the French-Spanish border, which was without a defined linear border until the late nineteenth century (Sahlins 1989). Territorial discontinuity did not prevent Connecticut from surveying and sending settlers to the land it claimed in what is now Pennsylvania in the 1770s, resulting in a similar kind of war (Ousterhout 1995). In any case, an expectation was created in the seventeenth century that only a surveyed boundary line could be the basis of any agreement between the colonies, and as long as this technical process was frustrated, any jurisdiction in the disputed area could only be provisional, providing for circumstances that permitted this particular type of conflict.

Surveyed boundaries did, in many cases, make resistance to settler colonialism difficult, as it did in England during the enclosure movement. But dependence on the very particular practices involved also afforded new opportunities for Native American resistance that would not otherwise have existed. One example of this can be seen in the ending of the Mason-Dixon Line, which settled the Maryland-Pennsylvania border in response to the Conojocular War (Strang 2012). Because the Mason-Dixon Line ran across the Appalachians and into the land set aside for Native Americans, Iroquois observers were sent to accompany the survey. Rumours had been spreading of the potentiality of a general war between Natives and settlers which would engulf all the sporadic violence that had long been taking place, and the settler authorities were cautious to avoid such a war. The Iroquois Confederacy, the main Native American power in negotiations with the British, had agreed to allow the extension of the Mason-Dixon Line into the lands of the Delaware people over whom they claimed authority. But as some of the surveyors' diaries show, the western expedition of the Mason-Dixon party was subject to ongoing negotiations between Iroquois in the surveying party and groups of Delaware people with whom they came into contact. At a certain point, after crossing a particular warpath, the Iroquois felt they could no longer defend the survey's further progress, and refused to continue along with it. Although it had been intended for the line to continue on another thirty miles, this forced Mason and Dixon to turn back (see figure 4.5: the line ends just west of a 'War Path').

## CONCLUSION

This chapter has examined the colonial maps of British North America, showing how they made possible a certain kind of connectivity between property and colonial territoriality. Through maps, as well as the many practices surrounding their making and use, spaces of property and of colonial authority became linked, with intercolonial boundaries having to be surveyed and mapped in a similar way. Where colonial authority and knowledge depended on property surveys, ideas and practices were transferred from the making of property boundaries to that of intercolonial boundaries. Based around this historical investigation into the English colonies of North America, the chapter has aimed to make a more general argument about the relationship of mapping and the making of empire. While maps do have rhetorical power and are embedded in particular contexts and struggles, the significance of maps may go beyond this, and they can have effects which appear unrelated to or even contrary to their aims. The notion of homology helps conceptualize how these things may not be mutually exclusive. Through the apparently universal ability of surveying practices to translate proprietary, colonial and imperial spaces into spaces on the surface of a map, these spaces become historically linked.

This chapter has also inquired into the relations between mapping and empire with attention to imaginaries of connectivity over time and space. In particular, it examined a system of surveying which emerged throughout the English colonies, despite many differences in government and particular institutions. It approached the mapping-empire relation through an investigation into a particular moment in history. The connections and practices it revealed, of course, may not have surfaced in other contexts where surveying emerged as a practice. To some extent a similar logic could possibly be applied to the neighbouring French and Dutch empires, where surveying was also an important part of landownership (Price 1995). New France was divided into administrative units based on *seigneuries*, which were surveyed according to government regulations, and as we have seen before, Dutch settlers in New Netherlands negotiated a linear boundary with New England, which might have been surveyed if it had been ratified by both imperial centres (Greer 2017, 335). Yet due to the much more centralized nature of both of these empires, we do not see the kind of territorial competitions among autonomous governments that we see in the English colonies.

Maps such as that of the Seven Ranges of Townships in figure 4.3 reveal a progressive, rational and orderly settlement of the Northwest which hides

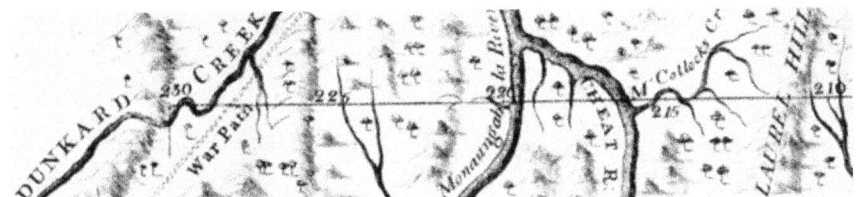

Figure 4.5. A Plan of the West Line or Parallel of Latitude, Which Is the Boundary between the Provinces of Maryland and Pensylvania (Mason, Dixon, Smither, and Kennedy 1768).

the violent and unstable realities of its history. While in some ways maps certainly aided the making of empire, the expectation that property boundaries and colonial boundaries would be as stable in reality as they appeared on maps may have made possible territorial conflicts that might not otherwise have occurred. Scholars should thus not only be aware of the extent to which maps are successful in achieving their aims but also ways in which they might unintentionally affect the politics of space, and in this way we can avoid being misled by maps that served imperial purposes.

## REFERENCES

Anderson, James Donald. 1979. 'Vandalia: The First West Virginia?' *West Virginia History* 40, no. 4: 375–92.

Bhandar, Brenna. 2018. *Colonial Lives of Property: Law, Land, and Racial Regimes of Ownership*. Durham, NC: Duke University Press.

Biggs, Michael. 1999. 'Putting the State on the Map: Cartography, Territory, and European State Formation'. *Comparative Studies in Society and History* 41, no. 2: 374–405.

Blomley, Nicholas. 2003. 'Law, Property, and the Geography of Violence: The Frontier, the Survey, and the Grid'. *Annals of the Association of American Geographers* 93, no. 1: 121–41.

Bowen, Clarence. 1882. *The Boundary Disputes of Connecticut*. Boston: James Osgood.

Boyd, Kenneth. 1929. *William Byrd's Histories of the Dividing Line Betwixt Virginia and North Carolina*. Raleigh: The North Carolina Historical Commission.

Bradford, William. 1856. *History of Plymouth Plantation*. Boston: Massachusetts Historical Society.

Branch, Jordan. 2014. *The Cartographic State: Maps, Territory, and the Origins of Sovereignty*. Cambridge: Cambridge University Press.

Brückner, Martin. 2006. *The Geographic Revolution in Early America: Maps, Literacy, and National Identity*. Chapel Hill: University of North Carolina Press.

Cazier, Lola. 1976. *Surveys and Surveyors of the Public Domain*. Washington, DC: US Department of the Interior, Bureau of Land Management.

Danson, Edwin. 2017. *Drawing the Line: How Mason and Dixon Surveyed the Most Famous Border in America*. Malden, MA: John Wiley & Sons.

Darby, H. C. 1933. 'The Agrarian Contribution to Surveying in England'. *The Geographical Journal* 82, no. 6: 529–35.

Davenport, Frances, ed. 1917. *European Treaties Bearing on the History of the United States and Its Dependencies to 1648*. Washington, DC: Carnegie Institution.

———, ed. 1929. *European Treaties Bearing on the History of the United States and Its Dependencies*, vol. II. Washington, DC: Carnegie Institution.

Dean, John Ward, ed. 1897. *The New England Historical and Genealogical Register, Volume LI*. Boston: N.E. Historic Genealogical Society.

Dutrizac, Charles. 1991. 'Local Identity and Authority in a Disputed Hinterland: The Pennsylvania-Maryland Border in the 1730s'. *The Pennsylvania Magazine of History and Biography* 115, no. 1: 35–61.

Evans, Lewis, and L. Hebert. 1749. *A Map of Pensilvania, New-Jersey, New-York, and the Three Delaware Counties*. Philadelphia: Library of Congress. Accessed 8 March 2020. https://www.loc.gov/item/gm71000595/.

Faulkner, Alaric. 1981. 'Pentagoet: A First Look at Seventeenth Century Acadian Maine'. *Northeast Historical Archaeology* 10, no. 10: 51–57.

Festa, Matthew. 2013. 'Property and Republicanism in the Northwest Ordinance'. *Arizona State Law Journal* 45, no. 2: 409–70.

Gates, Paul Wallace. 1968. *History of Public Land Law Development*. Washington, D.C.: Public Land Law Review Commission.

Goettlich, Kerry. 2019. 'The Rise of Linear Borders in World Politics'. *European Journal of International Relations* 25, no. 1: 203–28.

Green, Mason. 1888. *Springfield, 1636–1886: History of Town and City*. Springfield, MA: C. A. Nichols & Co.

Greer, Allan. 2014. 'Dispossession in a Commercial Idiom: From Indian Deeds to Land Cession Treaties'. In *Contested Spaces of Early America*, edited by Juliana Barr and Edward Countryman, 69–92. Philadelphia: University of Pennsylvania Press.

———. 2017. *Property and Dispossession: Natives, Empires and Land in Early Modern North America*. Cambridge: Cambridge University Press.

Harley, John Brian. 1989. 'Deconstructing the Map'. *Cartographica* 26, no. 2: 1–20.

———. 2001. 'Maps, Knowledge, and Power'. In *The New Nature of Maps: Essays in the History of Cartography*, edited by Paul Laxton. Baltimore, MD: Johns Hopkins University Press.

Hubbard Jr., Bill. 2009. *American Boundaries: The Nation, the States, the Rectangular Survey*. Chicago: University of Chicago Press.

Hughes, Sarah. 1979. *Surveyors and Statesmen: Land Measuring in Colonial Virginia*. Richmond: Virginia Surveyors Foundation.

Hutchins, Thomas, W. Barker, and Mathew Carey. 1796. *Plat of the Seven Ranges of Townships Being Part of the Territory of the United States, N.W. of the River Ohio*. Map. Philadelphia: M. Carey. Library of Congress. Accessed 7 March 2020. https://www.loc.gov/item/99441743/.

Kain, Roger, and Elizabeth Baigent. 1992. *The Cadastral Map in the Service of the State: A History of Property Mapping*. Chicago: University of Chicago Press.

Keene, Edward. 2002. *Beyond the Anarchical Society: Grotius, Colonialism and Order in World Politics*. Cambridge: Cambridge University Press.

Klinefelter, Walter. 1971. 'Lewis Evans and His Maps'. *Transactions of the American Philosophical Society* 61, no. 7: 3–65.

Konvitz, Josef. 1987. *Cartography in France, 1660–1848: Science, Engineering, and Statecraft*. Chicago: University of Chicago Press.

Lindgren, Uta. 2007. 'Land Surveys, Instruments, and Practitioners in the Renaissance'. In *The History of Cartography, Volume III: Cartography in the European Renaissance*, edited by David Woodward, 477–508. Chicago: University of Chicago Press.

Love, John. 1768. *Geodaesia: Or, the Art of Surveying and Measuring Land Made Easy*. London: J. Rivington.

Mason, Charles, Jeremiah Dixon, James Smither, and Robert Kennedy. 1768. *A Plan of the West Line or Parallel of Latitude, Which Is the Boundary between the Provinces of Maryland and Pensylvania: A Plan of the Boundary Lines between the Province of Maryland and the Three Lower Counties on Delaware with Part of the Parallel of Latitude Which Is the Boundary between the Provinces of Maryland and Pennsylvania*. Map. Philadelphia: Robert Kennedy. Library of Congress. Accessed 7 March 2020. https://www.loc.gov/item/84695758/.

Onuf, Peter. 1987. *Statehood and Union: A History of the Northwest Ordinance*. Bloomington: Indiana University Press.

Ousterhout, Anne. 1995. 'Frontier Vengeance: Connecticut Yankees vs. Pennamites in the Wyoming Valley'. *Pennsylvania History: A Journal of Mid-Atlantic Studies* 62, no. 3: 330–63.

Owens, Patricia. 2015. *Economy of Force: Counterinsurgency and the Historical Rise of the Social*. Cambridge, MA: Cambridge University Press.

Price, Edward T. 1995. *Dividing the Land: Early American Beginnings of Our Private Property Mosaic*. Chicago: University of Chicago Press.

Richeson, A. W. 1966. *English Land Measuring to 1800: Instruments and Practices*. Cambridge, MA: MIT Press.

Rink, Oliver. 1978. 'Company Management or Private Trade: The Two Patroonship Plans for New Netherland'. *New York History* 59: 5–26.

Sack, Robert. 1986. *Human Territoriality: Its Theory and History*. Cambridge: Cambridge University Press.

Sahlins, Peter. 1989. *Boundaries: The Making of France and Spain in the Pyrénées*. Berkeley: University of California Press.

Shurtleff, Nathaniel B., ed. 1853. *Records of the Governor and Company of the Massachusetts Bay in New England, Vol. I*. Boston: William White.

———, ed. 1855. *Records of the Colony of New Plymouth in New England, Vol. I*. Boston: William White.

Spero, Patrick. 2012. 'The Conojocular War: The Politics of Colonial Competition, 1732–1737'. *The Pennsylvania Magazine of History and Biography* 136, no. 4: 365–403.

Strandsbjerg, Jeppe. 2010. *Territory, Globalization and International Relations: The Cartographic Reality of Space*. New York: Palgrave Macmillan.

Strang, Cameron. 2012. 'The Mason-Dixon and Proclamation Lines: Land Surveying and Native Americans in Pennsylvania's Borderlands'. *The Pennsylvania Magazine of History and Biography* 136, no. 1: 5–23.

Taylor, E. G. R. 1947. 'The Surveyor'. *The Economic History Review* 17, no. 2: 121–33.

Van Zandt, Franklin. 1976. *Boundaries of the United States and the Several States*. Washington, DC: United States Government Printing Office.

Wainwright, Nicholas. 1963. 'Tale of a Runaway Cape: The Penn-Baltimore Agreement of 1732'. *The Pennsylvania Magazine of History and Biography* 87, no. 3: 251–93.

Weber, Max. 2001. *The Protestant Ethic and the Spirit of Capitalism*. London: Routledge.

White, C. Albert. 1983. *A History of the Rectangular Survey System*. Washington, DC: U.S. Dept. of the Interior, Bureau of Land Management.

Wohlpart, A. James. 1992. 'The Creation of the Ordered State: William Byrd's (Re)vision in the "History of the Dividing Line"'. *The Southern Literary Journal* 25, no. 1: 3–18.

Zinn, Howard. 2003. *A People's History of the United States*. New York: HarperCollins.

*Chapter 5*

# Empires of Science, Science of Empires

## *Mapping, Centres of Calculation and the Making of Imperial Spaces in Nineteenth-Century Germany*

Filipe dos Reis

### INTRODUCTION

In the years around 1850, an ongoing tragedy caught the attention of the British public. Two ships, the *Erebus* and the *Terror*, had left Britain in May 1845 for an Arctic exploration under the command of Captain Sir John Franklin to sail, chart and map the North-West Passage. A navigable North-West Passage, it was believed, would not only shorten the distance between Asia and Europe but also provide Britain with a monopoly on this sea route, and thereby facilitate trade within the British Empire. Consequently, the expedition's departure was accompanied by major ceremonies and became a mass spectacle. Although the journey was planned meticulously – with the crew well equipped and with Franklin being one of the most experienced Polar navigators of the Royal Navy, who had served on three previous Arctic expeditions – the two ships were seen by Europeans for the last time in July 1845. As no new information arrived, the British public became increasingly concerned with the fate of the two ships and, initiated by Franklin's wife Lady Jane, the 'search for Franklin' turned into an unprecedented media event, in the course of which the British Admiralty offered a reward of £20,000, and numerous government-sponsored search missions departed over the years. These missions collected significant information about the geographical condition of the Arctic. What they could not find, however, was any information about Franklin and his crew. The fate of the *Erebus* and the *Terror* remained untraceable. It was only in 1854, almost a decade after the ships had disappeared, that a search mission received information from local Inuits that the ships and their crews must have been lost near King William Island in the

Canadian Arctic. Finally, in 1857 first relics were found in this area. As we know today, the two ships must have frozen unprepared in the ice near King William Island during the first year of their expedition, where Franklin died in 1847 and all members of his crew, nearly 130 men, in the coming years, turning this episode in the end into a 'lost passage' (Hill 2008, 3).[1]

Yet, at the beginning of the 1850s, when the fate of Franklin and his crew was still unknown, many theories circulated in the British public speculating about the exact position of the two ships. The most 'spectacular and far-reaching' (Felsch 2010, 102) of these theories came from August Petermann (1822–1878), a young German cartographer who lived in London at the time and worked closely with the Royal Geographical Society, where he was awarded the honorary title of a 'Physical Geographer to the Queen' in 1852. August – or Augustus, as he called himself at the time in order to anglicize his name – Petermann was one of the leading representatives of the theory of an Open Polar Sea. In January 1852, Petermann presented this theory for the first time in a letter to the British Admiralty. He also passed it on to the newspaper *The Athenaeum* (Petermann 1852c). In the months that followed, more letters, speeches to the Royal Geographical Society and publications were circulated. Petermann used these publications to further substantiate his theory and, finally, develop a concrete plan to set up a mission to 'search for Franklin' (Petermann 1852a, 1852b, 1853).

In Petermann's view, it was 'a well-known fact that there exists to the north of the Siberian coast, and, at a comparatively short distance from it, a sea open at all seasons; it is beyond doubt that a similar open sea exists on the American side to the north of the Parry group; it is very probable that these two open seas form a navigable Arctic ocean' (Petermann 1852c, 82). The 'Polar is open and free from ice. It *never freezes*' (Petermann 1852b, 11; emphasis in the original). Petermann based his theory on two – already for his contemporaries counterintuitive – assumptions. Firstly, the temperatures near the North Pole are significantly warmer as commonly assumed. As Petermann wrote, it 'has been a too common error, in matters regarding the natural features of the Arctic Regions, to take into account the lines of latitude only, and to disregard the lines of temperature altogether; *the equator and the poles are too frequently considered the centres of the greatest heat and the greatest cold*. In no other regions are the inferences drawn from such views more mischievous than in the Arctic Regions, where the temperature corresponds less with latitude than in any other part of the globe, and where . . . the temperature chiefly depends on the currents and the drift ice, the influence of which is remarkable' (Petermann 1852b, 18–19; emphasis added). Thus, the temperature in the Arctic is warmer as believed and, as a result, for example, the number of animals, which could serve as food, increases toward the poles (Petermann 1852a). Secondly, it is possible to access the Open Polar Sea. The commonly held assumption of an 'impenetrable ice-barrier across the sea' needs to be considered as 'groundless, and as resting on prejudice' (Petermann 1853, 131); there exists only an 'imaginary barrier', which is 'even in these our enlightened days held up, by some' (Petermann 1853, 133). However, according to Petermann, the ice-barrier is open only during a few months. The access points are not navigable during the summer and autumn as they are blocked by 'floating ice which in the preceding months breaks loose from the *Siberian* coasts' (Petermann 1853, 11; emphasis in the original) but only during winter and spring. Petermann deduced from these assumptions that Franklin and his crew must have accessed the Open Polar Sea and must still be alive. Therefore, a rescue mission should not depart during the summer months (as other missions before) but during winter or spring, and it should not sail north-west to the Canadian Arctic (as other missions before) but north-east, where at the Siberian coast access to the Polar basin would be easier. Petermann came to these conclusions in a particular way. Unlike many contemporary commentators of the fate of the Franklin Expedition, Petermann himself had never sailed to the Polar regions. Instead, he had assembled 'facts . . . derived as they are from high authorities' (Petermann 1852b, 13) – in particular, reports of the explorations of the Dutch captain Willem Barents in the late sixteenth century and the Baltic German navigator Baron Ferdinand von Wrangel in the 1820s – and merged them with theories about ice-drift, currents and temperature. As it is summarized in the introduction to Petermann's letter in *The Athenaeum*, this approach is solely based on 'physical data' and 'scientific reasoning' (Petermann 1852c, 82).

However, at least for the meantime, Petermann's plan for a Polar expedition was not realized. No ships were sent out. Instead, Petermann left London in 1854 and moved to Gotha, a minor capital in Germany, where he started to work for the publishing house of *Justus Perthes*. In the following decades, *Justus Perthes* developed into the leading German-language press when it comes to the mapping of non-European territories. As I will advance in this chapter, it rapidly turned into what Bruno Latour describes as a 'center of calculation' (Latour 1987). Petermann, in turn, became not only one of the most-renowned cartographers of his time, but also an 'organizer of discoveries', the prototype of an 'armchair geographer' or, as one biographer puts it, a 'spider in the world-wide grid web of cartography' (Felsch 2010, 141), whose main interest was to fill the 'blank spaces' on maps, in particular when it came to Central Africa and the Polar regions. As we will see, the 'search for Franklin' remained an important underlying *leitmotif* in these endeavours. By reconstructing the role of the *Justus Perthes* press and the work of August Petermann, this chapter seeks to reflect upon important epistemological conditions of possibility of the German imperial and colonial discourse in the nineteenth century.[2] In particular, I am interested in how an Enlightenment-driven, seemingly innocent cartography of exploration in the

Humboldtian tradition created, often unintentionally, some of the epistemological conditions of possibility for later imperial and colonial imaginations in Germany. Here, my main focus is on the use (and production) of 'blank spaces' (or 'silences') on maps. This cartographic technique creates, inter alia, the 'promise of free and apparently virgin land – an empty space for Europeans to partition and fill' (Harley 1988b, 70). As we have seen earlier, this was very much Petermann's own imagination of the Arctic region. Blank spaces, however, should not be perceived as 'passive' spaces of non-knowledge but rather seen as actively produced by incorporating certain sources (or 'authorities') and silencing others. Before investigating this, it is important to address two points.

First, in line with the overall theme of this volume, the chapter enquires into the intimate relationship between mapping and the making of European imperial projects. As, for example, Mark Neocleous notes, maps have a 'predisposition towards colonialism and imperialism' (Neocleous 2003, 419) and, as J. B. Harley claims, they even served as 'weapons of imperialism' (Harley 1988a, 282). More precisely, maps have not only been mirrors and records of European expansionism but became core devices and instruments in the creation and imagination of these imperial and colonial projects; rather than operating as their 'cameras', they should be understood as their 'engines'.[3] This echoes, of course, the idea of the 'performativity' of maps and mapping, introduced by Harley some three decades ago (Harley 1989) and since then well established in the history of cartography and beyond. Therefore, it is important for those studying current and past developments in world politics to be aware of, as Jeppe Strandsbjerg has put it, the 'cartographic reality of space' of one's own object of study as the 'spatial reality underwriting state territory, globalization and the conduct of international relations is assembled through cartographic practices historically' (Strandsbjerg 2010, 4).

Second, these imperial projects have developed differently across Europe. This is particularly so when we look at the example of German cartography and its connection to imperialism. In contrast to the empires of the first wave of European expansionism, Portugal and Spain (Lobo-Guerrero, this volume), or later, France and Britain (Le Douarin and Goettlich, this volume), Germany became an imperial power relatively late as German 'unification', under Prussian leadership, occurred only in 1871 and was seen by many as 'incomplete' as the German-speaking parts of the Austro-Hungarian Empire were not included in the German Empire (*Deutsches Reich*). As such, the German *Reich* was part of a number of – connected – 'positioning games' (Çapan and dos Reis 2019): first, it was in search of its own place in Europe, involving not only discussions on whether or not to include the German-speaking parts of the Austro-Hungarian Empire but also the Netherlands or parts of Central and Eastern Europe in a larger sphere of German influence – as it happened in particular in discussions in the context of the concept of *Mitteleuropa* (Central Europe); second, it was in search of its own geopolitical take, which revolved around notions such as *Weltpolitik* (world politics) or *Lebensraum* (living space); and third, it was in search of colonial spaces outside of Europe.[4] In other words, empire-building and nation-building are closely intertwined.

In order to develop my argument, this chapter is organized as follows. First, I present Latour's notion of 'centers of calculation' and introduce three such centres on different scales, namely the town of Gotha as a scientific centre in the scattered environment of mid-nineteenth-century Germany, the *Justus Perthes* publishing house as a hybrid between commercial firm and scientific enterprise and August Petermann and his journal *Petermanns Geographische Mitteilungen* (Petermann's Geographical Messages). Second, I discuss the idea of blank spaces on maps by embedding it in broader transformations of spatial imaginaries as well as tying it to a Humboldtian ideal of cartography. Third, I retrace two projects of explorations – the 'German Inner-Africa expedition' (1860–1863) and the first two 'German North Pole expeditions' (1866–1870) – which were organized by Petermann and the *Justus Perthes* publishing house. I conclude by further problematizing the link between mapping and empire-making by highlighting the role of centres of calculation in the distribution of geographical knowledge and the production of imperial spaces.

## ON CENTRES OF CALCULATION AND EARLY SCIENTIFIC MANAGEMENT OF CARTOGRAPHY

Drawing upon some of the recent literature in the post-representational tradition of cartography, this chapter argues that maps and mapping were historically often embedded in what Bruno Latour describes as 'centers of calculation' (Latour 1987; cf. Turnbull 2000, chap. 3; Pickles 2004, chap. 3; Strandsbjerg 2010, 58–62; Jöns 2011; Edney 2019, 94). According to Turnbull (1996, 22), the *Casa da Índia* in Lisbon and the *Casa de la Contratación* in Seville developed during the sixteenth century into centres of calculation, serving as main sites for the accumulation and distribution of geographical knowledge and thereby essentially enabling the expansion of the Portuguese and Spanish empires. Similarly, in the late-eighteenth and particularly during the nineteenth century, large private publishing houses such as *Hachette* in France, *Murray* in Britain and *Perthes* in Germany 'played a primary role in the shaping of geographical knowledge' as they were the 'first agencies for the production of scholarly geography in those countries before the institutionalization of geography in universities' (Ferretti 2019, 23).

Latour advanced the notion of 'centers of calculation' in his seminal study *Science in Action: How to Follow Scientists and Engineers through Society*, published in 1987. According to Latour, knowledge, which is the building block of the modern sciences, 'cannot be defined without understanding what *gaining* knowledge means' (Latour 1987, 220; emphasis in the original). Neither can it be grasped by opposing it to concepts such as 'belief' or 'ignorance', nor does it 'sit' in the 'mind' of scientists. Instead, knowledge is produced, mobilized, combined and stabilized in and through networks, including human and non-human resources. Thus, to study knowledge properly one has to consider 'a whole cycle of accumulation: how to bring things back to a place for someone to see it for the first time so that others might be sent to bring other things back. How to be familiar with things, people and events, which are *distant*' (Latour 1987, 220; emphasis in the original). These circular processes are tied to centres of calculation, where human and non-human resources are 'combined and make possible a type of calculation' (Latour 1999, 304).

In order to function, these centres are organized (and govern at a distance) through 'immutable mobiles' (Latour 1987, 1990). For Latour, immutable mobiles have three characteristics: first, they have to be mobile 'so that they can be brought back'; second, they have to be kept stable 'so that they can be moved back and forth without additional distortion, corruption or decay'; and finally, they have to be combinable 'so that whatever stuff they are made of, they can be cumulated, aggregated, or shuffled like a pack of cards' (Latour 1987, 223). In other words, centres of calculation and immutable mobiles are closely linked to questions of connectivity. Maps are prime examples of immutable mobiles as they, in the words of David Turnbull, 'allow for enhanced connectivity' (Turnbull 2000, 92). Maps are small enough that they can be brought to the centre but also taken to the field; they can easily be standardized and commensurated by introducing a common metric; based on this, they are easily 'readable' when 'map literacy' (Jacob 2006) among all members of the network (including experts and laypersons) is high, something which became the case increasingly during the nineteenth century; and they can permanently be adapted, reworked and superimposed.

However, Latour's conceptualization of maps as immutable mobiles has recently given rise to some criticism. For example, Matthew Edney argued that maps should be considered *mutable*, that is, 'active and dynamic', rather than immutable mobiles as 'people are always undertaking mappy acts: making maps, circulating them, using them, ignoring them'; and, even 'the storage and destruction of maps are dynamic processes', which signifies that in the end also 'archives and libraries are not just places of storage but are sites of further knowledge production' (Edney 2019, 48). One promising avenue to unpack this tension between mutability and immutability (as well as mobility and immobility) has been suggested by John Law and Annemarie Mol in their discussion of the link between scientific and technological objects, for example, a map, a vessel for exploration or an instrument to survey a territory, and (the making of) spatialities. According to Law and Mol (2001, 619–20), these objects might have different characteristics *at the same time*. A map, for example, can be an *immutable immobile* in a first instance. As such, it might be situated within a local context where it is drawn on the working desk of a map-maker. But when it starts moving to other locations, it can turn into an *immutable mobile* in the Latourian sense. This means that it circulates within the space of a network, where it is kept mostly stable. In this sense, it might travel as a supplement of a journal to readers or be used as a standardized object to survey a territory. Yet, maps move not only within the space of this network as they enact, simultaneously, a specific understanding of spatiality – modern European maps, for example, share the same notion of (Euclidean/Cartesian) geometry. Moreover, a map can become a *mutable mobile*. To speak of it as a mutable mobile emphasizes the fluidity rather than the stability of the object. Readers might interpret it in a different way, or 'newly discovered' territories might be mapped during an exploration. Finally, a map can be a *mutable immobile*, when, for example, readers write to the editor of a journal or the most recent information from field work arrives at the centre of calculation, where it is added and edited to the initial map and where then, 'paradoxically, the global is already included in the local' (Law and Mol 2001, 619).

This signifies that mapping needs to be grasped as a dynamic process of circulation and translation, where both circulation and translation are understood as contested, non-linear, contingent and transformative endeavours (cf. Çapan, dos Reis, and Grasten 2021) – and where both circulation and translation can always fail (see Callon 1984). Such a process-focused understanding of mapping was, at least to some degree, already shared by Petermann in 1866: 'If our first and best explorer-travellers touch one and the same area, the same thing on the map becomes a true *perpetuum mobile*, as with each traveller the map gets a more or less different depiction, and it is often even impossible to judge which is the more correct one' (Petermann 1866, 588–89).

Moreover, the notion of centres of calculation raises two important points for the conceptualization of empire in this chapter. First, mirroring one of the commonplaces of actor-network theory (ANT), namely that society cannot explain but needs to be explained in the first place (Latour 2005; see also dos Reis 2019, 155), empires cannot explain but are in need of explanation in the first place. To reconstruct the work of and within centres of calculations helps, then, to understand how empires are invented, fabricated, formed, articulated, mobilized and stabilized. Empires are always empires in the making, they are never fixed. As a corollary, there cannot be a trans-historically and inter-imperially valid fit-it-all concept of empire, but it should be understood rather as a 'language game' connected through 'family resemblances' in the Wittgensteinan sense (Wittgenstein 1953). Second, centres of calculation might be located remotely and unremarkably far away from imperial metropoles. As Latour points out, they might be 'a small provincial town, or an obscure laboratory, or any puny little company in a garage, that were first as weak as any other place [and] become centers dominating at a distance many other places' (Latour 1987, 223). We can find centres of calculation on different scales. These centres of calculation are empires of science. If we take the nexus between power and knowledge seriously, however, empires of science might produce the science of empire. In this chapter, I focus not only on one centre of calculation, however, but on three – intertwined and interwoven – centres operating on different scales, namely the 'small provincial town' of Gotha, the 'puny little company' of *Justus Perthes* and August Petermann as an 'armchair geographer' and, with the help of his journal, 'organizer of discoveries'.

When Petermann joined *Justus Perthes* in 1854, Gotha was a minor capital located in central Germany. It is important to remember that at this time Germany did not constitute a nation-state yet but was composed of the German Confederation (*Deutscher Bund*), an association of thirty-nine mainly German-speaking states, which was established at the Congress of Vienna in 1815 in the aftermath of the Napoleonic Wars and replaced the former Holy Roman Empire. As the patriotic and liberal revolution of 1848 failed, it was not until 1871 that the German Empire (*Deutsches Reich*) was founded, which became a German nation-state under Prussian leadership and was created without the German-speaking parts of Austria-Hungary – disappointing many who had hoped for a 'greater German' (*großdeutsch*) solution including the latter. Moreover, as the German Empire was created rather late, there were for a long time no official state-run German colonies. It was only in the 1880s that the *Reich* began to hold official colonies. Nevertheless, the far-right of the German Empire started to claim in the 1890s a German colonial pre-history in Eastern Europe dating back to the Teutonic Order of the Middle Ages (Çapan and dos Reis 2019). Apart from these claims, there had been a variety of sporadic mercantilist colonial enterprises, such as, for example, the Welser between 1528 and 1556 in South America. This Augsburg-based family of merchants had lent money to the Spanish emperor Charles V and received in return colonial rights over a territory in Venezuela, which the Welser used for exploitation and as a trading post. Another example is the private initiative of the 'Texas Society' (*Texasverein*) in the 1840s, which was an attempt by aristocratic army officers to buy land in Texas to establish a German colony. However, this endeavour had to be abandoned after the annexation of Texas into the United States in 1845. In general, these were privately run and rather scattered enterprises, which lacked any organization and support from a central German government. Therefore, it 'is important to recognize', as Sebastian Conrad summarizes, 'that the active phase of German colonialism, from 1880 onwards, did not develop in linear fashion, out of such episodes' (Conrad 2012, 16). Nevertheless, as we will see, colonial imaginaries developed already during the mid-nineteenth century. These were also linked to ideas of German nation-building.

The German Confederation was divided into smaller states, mostly duchies, which did not form a nation-state or empire but a confederation of sovereign states. These states were often in competition with each other. In particular, the rivalry between the Kingdom of Prussia and the Austrian Empire complicated further integration. Even though Gotha was a small town, it was the capital of the northern part of the Duchy of Saxe-Coburg and Gotha. The current Duke was Ernst II, a liberal monarch, who had supported the 1848 revolution. His younger brother was Prince Albert, the husband of the British monarch Queen Victoria. Already at the turn of the nineteenth century, Ernst II's predecessor had developed Gotha into a centre of the natural sciences – the 'Weimar of the natural sciences' (Felsch 2010, 136) – including an observatory and one of the largest libraries in Germany (cf. Brogiato 2008). As Schelhaas summarizes, Gotha was 'since the eighteenth century a scientific center of international significance, a creative space for the production, collection and communication of scientific knowledge' (Schelhaas 2009, 229). This scientific environment facilitated a variety of entrepreneurial projects. For example, Ernst-Wilhelm Arnoldi founded the first German insurance company in the 1820s, which specialized in fire and life insurances.

It was in this environment that the *Justus Perthes* publishing house was established in September 1785 by Johann Georg Justus Perthes (see Smits 2004, 23–26; Demhardt 2015a). A larger success was, around 1800 onwards, from the publication of the famous *Almanach de Gotha*, or, *Gothaischer Hofkalender*, a directory of Europe's nobility, published on a yearly basis in German and French, which developed during the nineteenth century into, what could be called today, a 'logbook of governmentality' for European rulers as the *Almanach* assembled not only genealogical material about European dynasties and nobility but also began to include gradually a collection of detailed statistical data covering all countries of the world. From 1815 onwards *Justus Perthes* started to specialize in scientific maps and atlases, which led to the breakthrough of the press. In line with this new branch of its business, it adjusted its official name to *Justus Perthes Geographische Anstalt* (Justus Perthes's Geographical Institute).

The specialization in cartographic material was made possible through an important transformation in the production of geographical knowledge in continental Europe after the Napoleonic Wars. While geographical knowledge was, for centuries, often under a (quasi-)monopoly of the state and, here, particularly the military, the cartographic publishing market for private companies started to expand at the turn of the nineteenth century. For example, the King of Prussia, Frederick II, lifted the ban on the publication of cartographic products in 1783 (Felsch 2010, 37). As a consequence of this transformation, centres of geographical knowledge production were no longer located in the state or military, and as universities established chairs of geography only slowly during the nineteenth century, private companies became main hubs for geographical knowledge. In order to understand how geographical knowledge was shaped during this period, it is thus important to analyse the role and the 'geographies of knowledge' of large publishing houses and their editorial networks. Companies such as *Hachette*, *Murray* or *Perthes* did not limit themselves to the publication of existing geographical knowledge but created a market for private explorations, discoveries and travel literature. For example, *Perthes* would become a '"Central Bureau" for surveying the world' ('*"Zentralbüro" für die Vermessung der Welt*'; Felsch 2010, 138). These private mapping agencies turned geography into a public and popular topic as they were able to communicate and disseminate this kind of knowledge to a growing readership in the expanding bourgeoisie. Thereby, maps started to become a mass product and to circulate among a broader audience, making them affordable beyond the political, military and professional elites. In turn, however, this led to the commodification of geographical knowledge as these publishing houses still had to operate on the basis of economic needs (see also Lo Presti's chapter in this volume).

A good illustration of the working processes at *Justus Perthes* is provided by the *Stielers Hand-Atlas*, one of the first cartographic publications of *Justus Perthes*. This world atlas was initially edited by Adolf Stieler (1775–1836), a self-taught cartographer. The first edition was published in various instalments between 1817 and 1823. The *Stielers Hand-Atlas* became a major success. It ran eventually through eleven editions and has been translated into many languages, becoming, for example, the first significant atlas for a major public in Italian (Boria 2007, 66–69). It 'inaugurated what became known as the Gotha School' of cartography, which, as Demhardt summarizes, was 'characterized by an exclusive reliance on verified data, the courage to concede uncertainty rather than print questionable details, and the meticulous documentation of all sources' (Demhardt 2015a, 721). One of the main features of this atlas was the inclusion of large 'blank spaces' of the 'unknown parts' of the world – yet, as we will see in the following, they did *not* always rely on verified data. By combining different instalments of different editions of the *Stielers Hand-Atlas* the reader could participate in the 'discovery' and 'exploration' of these parts. An imaginary of 'cartographic progress' (Edney 1993) became visible in the shrinking of 'blank spaces'. This was made possible through the standardization of scale for most of the cartographic publications at the *Perthes* firm, which increased the combinability of different (editions of) maps and atlases.

The main success of *Justus Perthes* was, however, the publication of the flagship journal *Petermanns Geographische Mitteilungen*. As the title indicates, it was a journal created by and around August Petermann. Petermann started this geographical journal in 1855, one year after he had left London and joined *Justus Perthes* in Gotha. Within a short period of time, the journal developed into one of the world's leading periodicals for the scientific study of geography – a status it was able to obtain from the second part of the nineteenth to the first part of the twentieth century (cf. Smits 2004; Lentz and Ormeling 2008; Demhardt 2015b). The success of the *Mitteilungen* had several reasons. Firstly, the journal was issued on an approximately monthly basis. Thereby it was possible to publish the latest research results and permanently update news from ongoing explorations. Information about explorations, for example, were often released in the fashion of a serialized novel. This provided the reader with the impression of not only having access to the most recent information but also of being directly involved in the progress of geography, which was understood as an 'unveiling of the world' (Schelhaas 2009, 230). Secondly, as Smits argues, the 'greatest strength' (Smits 2004, 37) of the journal was its emphasis on maps, and at least a couple of coloured maps were included in every number. As Petermann explained in the journal's inaugural editorial, 'Our *"Mitteilungen"* should differ from all similar journals in that carefully edited and neatly executed maps are used as the end result to summarize the latest geographic research and graphically illustrate' (Petermann 1855b, 2). A decade later, Petermann added that 'the end result and the final goal of all geographical research, exploration and surveying is, first of all, the depiction of the surface of the earth: the map. The map is the basis of geography. The map shows us in the best, most precise and most exact way what we know about our earth' (Petermann 1866, 581).

From a commercial point of view, maps helped to reach a broad readership among the interested public as they can be considered as means of communication, which are relatively easy to access in an 'age hungry of adventure, but not yet totally scientifically literate' (Smits 2004, 37). In addition, the maps in the *Mitteilungen* were often taken from other cartographic products from *Justus Perthes*, which facilitated the promotion, for example, of the newest edition of the *Stielers Hand-Atlas* to possible customers. Thirdly, Petermann operated as a kind of 'scientific manager'. He brought a large network of contacts, which he had established in Britain, to Gotha and made frequent use of this for the journal, for example, by acquiring authors or presenting novel material. As we saw in the introduction, Petermann had been an active member of the *Royal Geographical Society*, where he was in contact with a number of most renowned explorers of his time. Prior to this, he had also worked with Alexander Keith Johnston in Edinburgh on a translation of

Heinrich Berghaus's *Physikalischer Atlas* (*Physical Atlas*) from German to English. The German original of this atlas was commissioned and published by *Justus Perthes* as the official 'cartographic translation' of Alexander von Humboldt's late magnum opus *Kosmos*. Based on this variety of contacts, the *Mitteilungen* published in its first years, for example, letters from Alexander von Humboldt to Petermann and it held exclusive publishing rights (at least for the German market) for travelogues and the most recent information of some well-known explorers of that period such as Eduard Vogel, Heinrich Barth or David Livingstone. And, finally, Petermann started organizing his own explorations through the journal. These journeys were intended to 'discover' the last 'unknown territories' on earth, which were often depicted as blank spaces on maps, and concerned mainly two regions: in the 1850s and in the first half of the 1860s the inner regions of Africa, and from the mid-1860s onwards Petermann turned to his earlier interest in the North Pole. For this reason, Petermann has been named the founder of both 'German Africa cartography' (Demhardt 2000) and 'German Polar research' (Krause 1993, 7). Before I reconstruct two expeditions, which were initiated by Petermann, namely the 'German Expedition to Inner-Africa' and the 'German North Pole Expedition', I discuss in the next section the role of 'blank spaces' for mapping.

## BLANK SPACES, SILENCES AND GERMAN IMPERIAL ASPIRATIONS

How was it possible to think of blank spaces on maps? What are the underlying epistemological operations at stake that make such spatial thinking possible? And, where is this operated? I argue that two epistemological shifts, which occurred over a long period and ended only in the nineteenth century, were of particular importance. The first shift concerns the emergence of the notion of globality. The idea that the planet has the form of a globe is far from natural and needs to be understood rather as the product of a long transformation in the way space has been imagined (see Bartelson 2010; Ramaswamy 2017). Importantly, the notion of globality is, as, for instance, Latour points out, deeply embedded in modern European thinking, and it brings Latour to the conclusion that if 'there is one thing to provincialise, in addition to Europe, it is the idea of a natural globe' (Latour 2016, 308; cf. dos Reis 2019). From the moment onwards from which the planet has been conceived as a globe, it became possible for Europeans to speculate about regions which they had not fully explored yet – but where they now 'knew' that there must be 'something'. In the case of Africa, for example, Europeans had, after the first wave of European expansion, a more or less accurate picture of the coastal lines of the African continent – and could start to imagine its interior. Second, and related to this, is the emergence of the idea of empty and extended space, an idea which is usually attributed to Leibniz and (or) Descartes.[5] Now, it became possible, for instance, to divide space, whereby maps started to play a pivotal role in this process as they could depict abstract spaces where the struggle over 'empty space' (imagined as 'no man's land') could take place. Importantly, such operations do not take place *in abstracto*, but are often fabricated in centres of calculations and mobilized through devices such as maps. This means that centres of calculations are not only located (and situated) in space (and time) but produce space (and time) as concrete reality (Latour 1987, 228–32; Strandsbjerg 2010, chap. 3). Similarly, maps and other devices are not just '*observations* of the global' but on top of that always '*operations* of the global' (Staeheli 2012, 233; emphasis added).

Petermann's fascination for the 'blank spaces' on maps, which he shared with most cartographers of his time, became already visible in the short episode at the outset of this chapter. The northern polar region, which was one of the biggest 'unknown' swathes on nineteenth-century maps, was in Petermann's theory not a hostile environment but consisted of a navigable Open Polar Sea, rich in animals and plants. According to Petermann, the situation was similar in other regions of the world, and it was the task of the cartographer to uncover this:

> In fact, our geographical knowledge of the territories of the earth is far less than it is generally assumed.... We see on our maps the whole of Europe, the whole of Asia, the whole of North America and the whole of South America, including rivers and mountains, places and roads, all of it cleanly engraved in copper and the boundaries of states and peoples sharply defined by coloured lines. Even the African and Australian *terrae incognitae* are shrinking progressively, and there are only some white spots, maybe 'desert areas' where there seems to be 'nothing'. In reality, however, everything we see on these maps is only the first step, the beginning of more accurate knowledge of our earth's surface.... Where we suspected absolutely nothing, where we felt completely satisfied, for example, with the monotonously dotted sand desert on the map and where we were happy with the notion of a sea of vast sand, there was only one single traveller needed ... to create a different image of this part of the Sahara: instead of areas of a sandy lowland without life, as we have seen on earlier maps, we find now ... an extensive hydrographic network of periodic rivers and rainwater basin, with a vast number of caravan routes, villages and fountains, which, even though they are not populated by farmers, have a widespread nomadic life.
> (Petermann 1866, 582–83; emphasis added)

As it was the case with several other themes in the context of the postrepresentational tradition in cartography, it was the historiographer of cartography John Brian Harley, who drew, in his eclectic style, our attention to the important role of blank spaces on maps. For Harley, 'There is no such thing as an empty space on a map' (Harley 1988b, 71). Instead, Harley argues that 'blank spaces' or ('silences', as he prefers to call them in a Foucauldian vernacular) are 'positive statements' and not 'merely passive gaps in the flow of language': they are 'active human performances' (Harley 1988b, 58). In European medieval maps, blank spaces were used, as Hiatt explains, to depict 'the land that was rather a product of hypothesis rather than exploration'; in later periods these blank spaces were replaced with longer texts or 'pseudo-topography' such as 'speculative mountain ranges, vegetation and rivers'; the technique of blank spaces was reintroduced in 1749 in a map of Africa by the cartographer Jean Baptiste Bourguignon d'Anville, and, finally, by the 'mid-nineteenth century the blank interior of Africa – marked, if at all, with captions such as "unexplored", "unknown interior", "unexplored by Europeans" – was a fairly standard feature of maps of the continent' (Hiatt 2002, 230, 244, 245). By this time, blank spaces figured prominently as well in maps of Australia and the Polar regions.[6]

In general, the technique of using blank spaces was central for European imperial mapping and imagination. While, as Matthew Edney stresses, the cartographic discourse around the 'state' was mainly driven by the idea that its 'participants inhabit, or at least own, the lands being mapped', the discourse on 'empire', in turn, is 'constructed through cartographic discourse that represent a territory for the benefit of one group but that exclude the inhabitants of the territories represented. "Imperial mapping" is thus an ironic act', Edney continues, 'postulating as it does a double audience: the population in the mapped territories remains ignorant while another population is actively enabled and empowered to know the mapped territories' (Edney 2009, 13). In other words, maps produce hierarchies of knowledge. While, for example, European sources (or, 'authorities' as they were called) are regarded as reliable and scientific, local geographies, cosmologies and maps are often silenced. This does not mean that European map-makers and travellers did not rely on indigenous information – quite the opposite was the case. But this kind of information was always in need of translation by Europeans in order to become trustworthy, valid and authoritative (Jones and Voigt 2012, 18). Moreover, in line with (and reinforcing) the 'empiricist' (or 'scientific') world view of this time, blank spaces produce the image that those parts on a map, which are filled with, for example, topographical details, are composed of objective and scientific knowledge. They become validated because non-knowledge seems to be excluded. What is depicted must be true and everything that seems to be speculative becomes 'unknown' territory marked as 'blank' or 'empty'; either something is known, or it is unknown; no third possibility is given (*tertium non datur*). Ironically, this grounding in 'scientific data' and mostly Western 'authorities' often produced highly problematic 'facts'. We have seen this at the outset of the chapter when reliance on

Inuit sources would have helped to clarify the fate of the Franklin Expedition from early onwards. The most familiar example is, however, the Mountains of the Kong, which figured prominently in many nineteenth-century maps of Africa – including the *Stielers Hand-Atlas* – as a great mountain chain in Western Africa, but which never existed outside of the imagination of European map-makers (Bassett and Porter 1991).

Finally, 'maps anticipated empire' (Harley 1988a, 282; see also Bassett 1994, 326). It became possible, through blank spaces, to claim or promote land before it was effectively occupied and the 'promise of free and apparently virgin land – an empty space for Europeans to partition and fill –' (Harley 1988b, 70) is created. Thereby, the landscape becomes 'de-socialized' and even 'dehumanized' (Bassett 1994, 326; Harley 1988a, 303). According to Pickles, such an imaginary can be found prominently in Alexander von Humboldt's geographical work on South America, as 'von Humboldt mapped the contact zones of the "new world" by erasing local peoples and their histories and inscribing maps and geographies of primal nature in their place' (Pickles 2004, 119).

Petermann, as many of his contemporaries, shared this Humboldtian imaginary. As Petermann writes in the first editorial of the *Mitteilungen*:

> Without rest and against all diseases and dangers, humans wander to the unexplored interior of long known continents; without fear of hostile nature they uncover the secrets of the permanently iced ends of the globe; they have a desire to measure the highest peaks of the sky-striving mountains, and with their meter-long plumb bob they have to capture the ground of the sea, where it is the deepest. The phenomena of the air, the flood tide, the interior of the earth they have to explore and reduce to its most simple laws of nature; they have to announce the spots where one could find the yellow metal, which rules the world, as they have to lay grid-lines over the whole earth to depict the natural spots of the for them indispensable plants and animals. This is the empire of today's Geographical Science, the wonderfully large world of human knowledge, of which our fathers couldn't ever have an imagine.
> (Petermann 1855b, 1)

According to Petermann, this 'empire of today's Geographical Science' stands in the tradition of Alexander von Humboldt, who '300 years after Columbus, as a second Columbus, . . . discovered the New World again' (Petermann 1855b, 1). Although conceptualized as a journal covering all regions of the world – carrying in its initial phase the slogan *Ubique Terrarum* (everywhere in the world) – the 'discovery' of two regions stand out in the first decades of the *Mitteilungen*. On the one hand, and mainly in the 1850s and 1860s, the journal focused on the exploration of Central Africa; on the other hand, the Polar regions, and here first and foremost the North Pole, started to play an important role from the mid-1860s onwards.

## SEARCHING FOR THE GERMAN 'FRANKLIN' – THE 'GERMAN INNER-AFRICA EXPEDITION', 1860–1863

Already the first article of the *Mitteilungen* gives a good impression of the central role which the exploration of the last 'blank spaces' in Central Africa played during the first years of the journal. It is a report of Heinrich Barth's expedition to this region, more precisely from Kuka to Timbuktu, the latter described as the 'most famous city of Inner-Africa' (Petermann 1855a, 3). The report includes several letters of Barth, which are written as travelogues. These travelogues are then further contextualized by Petermann. The expedition was organized on British initiative and started in 1849. It was led by James Richardson, a missionary and abolitionist. The aim was to travel from the northern coast of Africa through the Sahara to Sudan. Petermann, who lived in London at the time, was able to include, with Heinrich Barth and Adolf Overweg, two German explorers in the mission. As both Richardson and Overweg died in the first years of the expedition, Barth became its new leader. Barth continued to travel to Timbuktu. Toward the end of Petermann's article, the reader is informed that Barth, after travelling through 'countries never before visited by Europeans' (Petermann 1855a, 13) and after successfully arriving in Timbuktu, was then missing and presumed dead.

In the meantime, Eduard Vogel, another German explorer, was sent, again on British initiative, to join the expedition. Vogel's mission was to compensate for the loss of Richardson and Overweg, and clarify Barth's fate. As it turned out quickly, Barth was still alive, and the two met briefly at Lake Chad, from where Barth travelled back to Europe. Vogel decided to stay in the region and explore the Wadai Empire (located in present-day Chad). Since 1856, however, there was no news about Vogel, with some reports claiming that he had been murdered in Wadai, while others assuming that he was still alive but held captured in its capital Wara. There were even some voices in Germany who believed that he might have abandoned the British expedition out of German patriotic sentiments. Vogel's fate started to concern the German public and, as Franklin for the British, Vogel became the ideal-typical figure of the missing (or 'lost') explorer (Kuhn and Struck 2019). In 1862, the national liberal German newspaper *Die Gartenlaube* (Garden Arbor) even presented Vogel as 'our Franklin' (*Die Gartenlaube* 1862, 72). It was under these circumstances that a search mission for Vogel was launched, the *Deutsche Expedition nach Inner-Afrika* ('German Inner-Africa Expedition'), which was initiated, advertised and organized largely by Petermann. As it was the case with Barth, Petermann had been in contact with Vogel through the Royal Geographical Society in London and had been publishing Vogel's travelogues in the *Mitteilungen* since 1855.

Petermann started to work on a plan for the German Inner-Africa Expedition in 1860. From the very beginning, Petermann designed the expedition not only as a search mission for Vogel but saw it also – as the name '*German Inner-Africa Expeditions*' already indicates – as an opportunity to unite those voices which wanted to overcome the particularism of the German Confederation and advocated instead a unified German nation-state.

Broadly speaking, Petermann initiated the mission on two intersecting levels. The first level concerns the creation of a committee. In July 1860, the *Comité für die Expedition nach Inner-Afrika* ('Committee for the Expedition to Inner-Africa'), or shorter the *Wadai-Comité* ('Wadai-Committee'), was established in Gotha, with Ernst II, Duke of Saxe-Coburg-Gotha, as its president, Justus Perthes, director of the publishing house of the same name, as its treasurer and Petermann as its secretary. Among others, Heinrich Barth figured as a founding member. In August 1860, the committee published an exposé for an 'Expedition to Inner-Africa', in which it presented a detailed plan for the endeavour. Theodor von Heuglin, an ornithologist and explorer, who had previously served for seven years as Austrian consul in Khartoum, was selected as its leader. According to the *Exposé*, the mission should 'clarify' Vogel's fate and 'complete' Vogel's work as a researcher. The latter was mainly understood as exploring the last blank spaces of the Wadai Empire. As the *Comité* summarizes in the *Exposé*, 'As far as all credible reports received until 1860 reveal, with the exception of Vogel on his journey to Wadai, no European has ever entered this great *terra incognita* at any point' (Wadai-Comité 1860a, 7; emphasis in the original). The lack of knowledge about the Wadai Empire stands however in contrast to the possible role that it could play in geopolitical terms as it 'is a rich land, with a wide variety of different peoples, and as it is located in the center of Africa it links its West and East, North and South' (Wadai-Comité 1860a, 8). Overall, the *Exposé* frames the enterprise as a 'patriotic task' to which everyone could contribute by signing up for a subscription. In December 1860, that is, four months after publishing the *Exposé*, the *Comité* issued detailed instructions for the journey, consisting of fifteen paragraphs (Wadai-Comité 1860b). These paragraphs covered, among other things, the purpose of the journey, namely 'to clarify the fate of Vogel, save his research papers and complete his scientific mission' (§2); the route of the journey, namely to 'spend all power and energy' to reach Wadai as fast as possible (§9); the financial resources of the mission of up to 15,000 Thaler (§5); but also the obligation to send 'from time to time . . . completed diaries, albums, maps, itineraries as well as astronomical, meteorological and physical observations to the Comité' (§12); and a clarification of the copyright of these notes and materials (§15). The instructions were accompanied by a small booklet with instructions from various scientists and experts, as well as by a map of Africa (figure 5.1). This map depicts Africa with large blank

122                                  Chapter 5

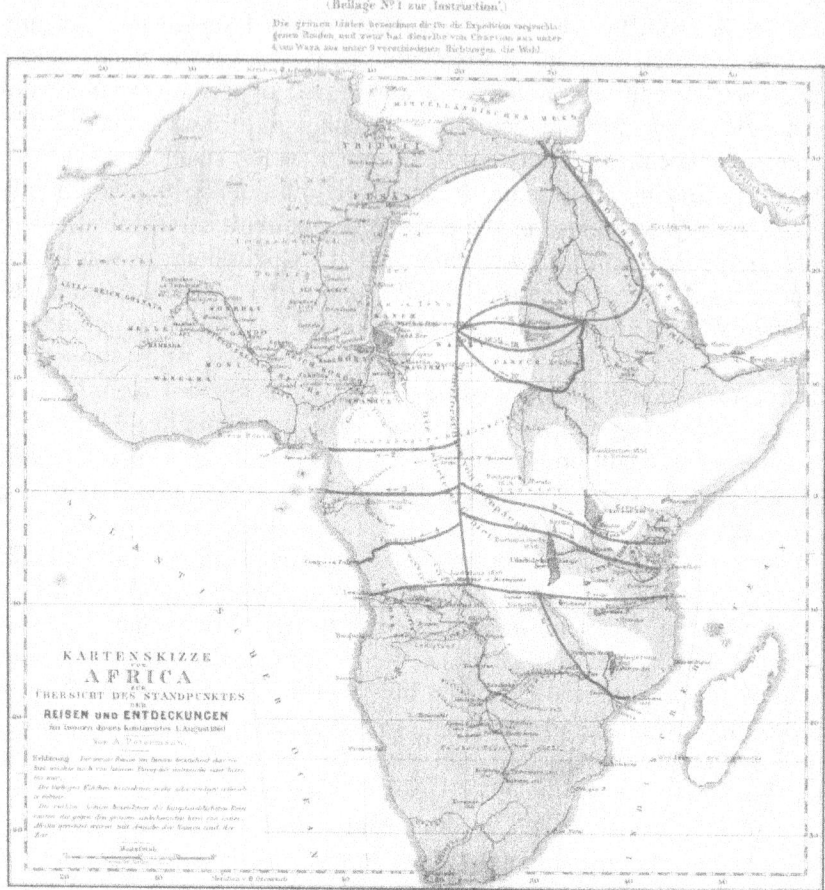

**Figure 5.1.** Map of Africa including itineraries for the 'German Expedition to Inner Africa', Justus Perthes Gotha 1861.

areas in its centre and includes possible travel routes for the expedition. The expedition is supposed to start in Alexandria and travel along the Red Sea to Khartoum. From there the map includes four different routes (I–IV) to the 'unknown' land of the Wadai Empire and its capital Wara, as well as nine options (1–9) for the way back. A similar map was included in the earlier *Exposé* – the only difference was that it did not include the itineraries.

On a second level, Petermann used the *Mitteilungen* to promote the search mission. As previously mentioned, the journal had published Vogel's travelogues in the mid-1850s. It stopped, however, giving much attention to the topic in the upcoming years. This changed again in 1860 when it began to speculate first in a couple of short notes about Vogel's fate and later announced the plan of the *Wadai-Comité* for the 'German Inner-Africa Expedition' under the lead of Theodor von Heuglin. As the *Mitteilungen* informed its readers: 'Loud and urgent goes a call for humanness and honour to the German Nation in the name of Eduard Vogel, the traveller who has disappeared in the distant interior of Africa while serving German science' (Anonymous 1860, 318). The fact that this was supposed to be a distinctively 'German' expedition was further highlighted: 'What has been started by German travellers, what had cost German sacrifice, must be completed by German travellers' (Anonymous 1860, 318). Moreover, the 'general participation of the audience is requested' (Anonymous 1860, 318): by donating for the enterprise, every patriotic German could become part of the exploration. Petermann continued the campaign for the mission in the following issues of the journal with more articles introducing and advertising it. This included the publication of parts of the *Exposé* of the *Wadai-Comité* and further initiatives for fund-raising. With regard to the latter, the *Mitteilungen* started to list the exact financial contribution of each monarch of the German-speaking countries – including those who had not donated. In the end, twenty-one out of thirty-three monarchs, who had been contacted – including Prince Albert, the husband of the English Queen Victoria and brother of Ernst II of Saxe-Coburg and Gotha – contributed financially to the 'German Inner-Africa Expedition'. In a similar way, the journal listed the donations of scientific institutions, such as the Leopoldina, and of several private individuals from all parts of the German Confederation. The fund-raising campaign was accompanied by reports that Vogel might be alive after all. And, finally, the *Mitteilungen* published travelogues of Heuglin's previous explorations in order to prove his scientific expertise. To make it short, Petermann used a number of channels to promote the 'German Inner-Africa Expedition', and to provide it with sufficient financial means. Moreover, the reader was given the impression of becoming part of a greater patriotic joint venture.

In the end, the fundraising campaign was a huge success, and Heuglin and the other members of the expedition arrived in Alexandria in March 1861. Heuglin, however, would have preferred a later date of arrival to prepare the scientific part of the mission more carefully. Yet, the *Wadai-Comité* was not willing to take this concern into account as patriotic voices in the German public pushed for an early departure as they were convinced that Vogel was still alive. After arrival, Heuglin and the other members of the expedition started to send various letters and notes to Gotha. This material contained mostly topographical, ethnographical, zoological and botanical information. The *Mitteilungen* compiled the arriving information into various reports, often accompanied by carefully arranged maps, which were supposed to show the progress of the expedition. Additional material was published in supplementary volumes. During the first months, the 'German Inner-Africa Expedition' took the route as planned, including stops, among others, in Cairo and Suez along the Red Sea. However, the mission made much slower progress than initially expected, and as the *Comité* was to find out in August 1861, it was not only delayed, but Heuglin had decided to take a different route in the meantime. Instead of travelling from the coast to Khartoum and then directly to Wadai as set in the instructions of the mission, the expedition was taking a detour through Abyssinia. Knowing the region well, Heuglin had realized that Wadai was not accessible because of the outbreak of local conflicts; apart from that, it was also too hot during the summer months to travel up-country. Nevertheless, the *Comité* could not accept the deviation from the planned route, as pressure from the public remained high. As a consequence, it announced its disapproval of the independent change of the route in a letter to the expedition, which was sent on 12 August 1861. Yet, Heuglin did not react to this request and kept sending letters with zoological and botanical observations to Gotha. In short, the *Comité*'s attempts to 'govern at a distance' did not work anymore.

In December 1861, the *Comité* decided to send a second mission to Wadai, which was led by the former military officer Moritz von Beurmann. However, it was only in March 1862, after several months without publishing substantial articles on the 'German Inner-Africa Expedition', that the *Mitteilungen* started to inform its readers about the current state of the mission. The *Mitteilungen* announced that the *Comité* had revoked Heuglin as the leader of the 'German Inner-Africa Expedition' because he had 'acted against the instructions [*instruktionswidrig*]', and had asked Heuglin additionally to send back 'the equipment, provisions, etc' (Anonymous 1862, 98, 99). The *Mitteilungen* reported further that another member of the expedition, Werner Munzinger, was appointed its new leader. Munzinger was instructed to travel directly from Khartoum, where he had arrived already, to Wadai; at the same time, Beurmann headed into the same direction by taking a northern route through the Sahara; and, in the meantime, Heuglin had reached Khartoum as well, where he was accompanied by Hermann Steudner, another member of the initial mission. In other words, the 'German Inner-Africa Expedition' had split into three different expeditions. However, none of them was successful in the end. Munzinger decided to return to Europe after he had received reliable information from a former servant of Vogel, who confirmed that Vogel had been murdered in 1856. Moreover it still seemed to be too dangerous to enter the Wadai Empire. Moritz von Beurmann, however, tried to advance to Wadai and was killed in this attempt in April 1863. Finally, Heuglin and Steudner decided to join the expedition of the Dutch baroness Alexine Tinné to explore the White Nile in Sudan. When Steudner died of Malaria in 1863, Heuglin returned to Europe where he arrived in 1864.

In the aftermath of the 'German Inner-Africa Expedition', Petermann tried to turn the obvious failure of the mission into a partial success. First, Petermann emphasized the *patriotic* achievement of the journey. When Beurmann died, the *Mitteilungen* published an obituary, which also included Overweg, Vogel and Steudner. Despite the fact that Overweg and Vogel were part of the British exploration led by Richardson, and that only Steudner and Beurmann were members of the 'German Inner-Africa Expedition', all four were 'intimately connected' because they 'worked on the same task and [. . .] are all buried deep inside the African continent, victims of climate and barbarism, they are martyrs of German science' (Anonymous 1864, 27). The article is accompanied by a map of the itineraries depicting the routes of the 'four martyrs of German science' (figure 5.2). Second, Petermann foregrounded the *scientific* value of the journey, in particular its contribution to filling the last 'blank spaces' of the map of Africa. In this context, Petermann published a large map of Eastern Africa to summarize the results of the expedition. The map came in several instalments, which were added to supplementary volumes of the *Mitteilungen*. This large map could also be combined with maps previously published in the *Mitteilungen* or other cartographic products at

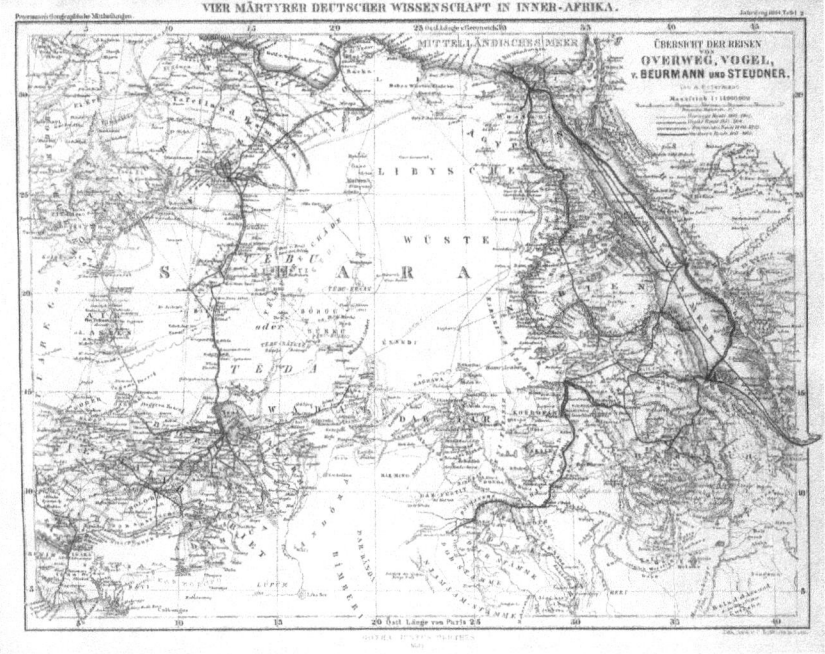

Figure 5.2. Map of 'Four Martyrs of German Science in Inner-Africa' in *Petermanns Geographische Mitteilungen*, Justus Perthes Gotha 1864.

*Justus Perthes*. Such a collage of different maps is included, for example, in a register volume published in 1865. Its map of Africa is intended as a 'summary' of the maps published during the first decade of the *Mitteilungen* on the continent (figure 5.3). Third, Petermann praised the mission as a foundation for future European *imperial* ambitions. For Petermann, the 'German Inner-Africa Expedition' has shown that areas it travelled 'deserve a special interest; they are not deadly African swamps or sandy deserts that would deserve to be visited only every 100 years by a geographical traveller, but areas that have a history and a purpose, . . . and which are an El Dorado when it comes to their nature' (Petermann 1864, ii). Despite these 'favorable natural conditions, these areas are a kind of "no man's land" to which any European power could extend its hand' (Petermann 1864, ii).

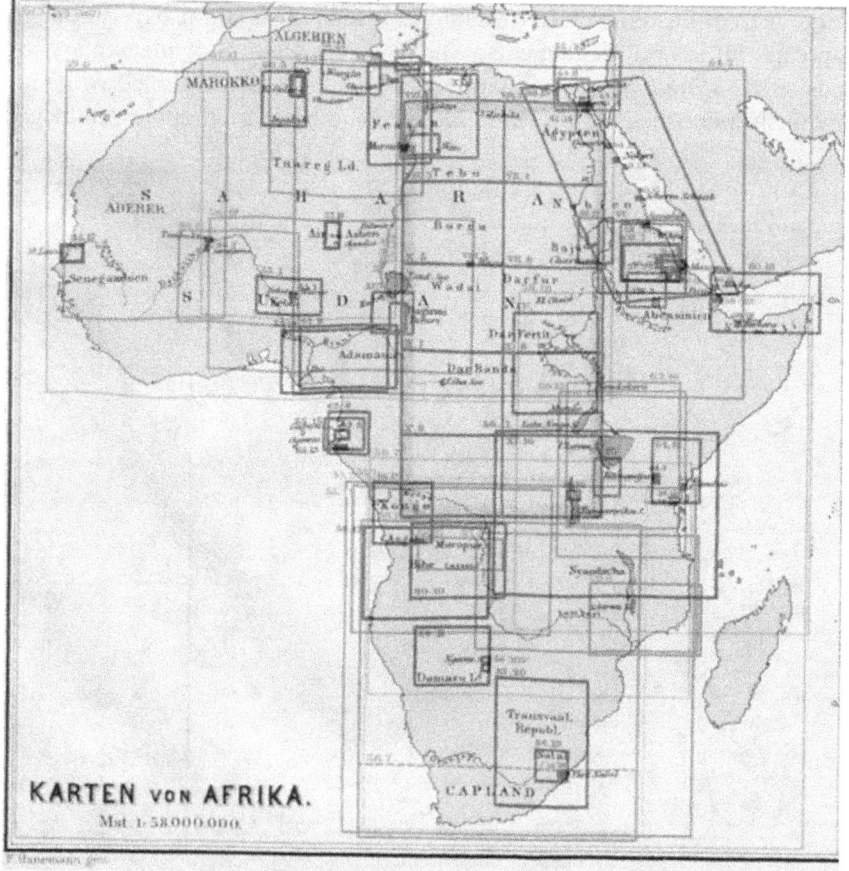

Figure 5.3. Map of Africa in Register Volume of *Petermanns Geographische Mitteilungen*, Justus Perthes Gotha 1865.

## AN IMAGINED EMPIRE IN THE NORTH – THE 'GERMAN NORTH POLE EXPEDITIONS', 1866–1870

From 1865 onwards, that is, two years after the end of the 'German Inner-Africa Mission', Petermann started to return quite abruptly to his old passion of the hypothesized ice-free Open Polar Sea and the exploration of the North Pole, this time with the support of the *Justus Perthes* press. As we will see, Petermann was able – due to the infrastructure provided by the publishing house – to launch several initiatives, including two large polar expeditions. Importantly, these initiatives need to be situated in the context of two synchronous and connected developments, namely the process of German nation-building and empire-building.

Initially, however, Petermann's revived interest in the Open Polar Sea was not triggered by patriotic feelings but by an emerging debate in Britain about the possibility of sending a new expedition to the North Pole. When the tragic outcome of the Franklin Expedition became evident in the mid-1850s, the British government had not made any new attempt to explore the Arctic. It was only in the spring of 1865 when a new effort was considered. Petermann was still a corresponding member of the Royal Geographical Society and, as such, started to interfere in the debate. He presented his plan for a polar mission, which very much resembled the one he had drafted fifteen years earlier to launch a search mission in order to find the *Erebus* and the *Terror*, in a talk to the Royal Geographical Society and in several letters to its president. Some of the material was then published in the *Mitteilungen*. Petermann explained the importance of launching a new polar mission in one of the letters: 'Now that most mysteries of the interior of Africa and Australia have come to light, the exploration of the geography of the central polar regions as well as the task to reach the poles remain the most significant geographical problems to be solved, and it is my conviction that the English nation, before all others, would be able to achieve this great triumph which would offer it the crown of the discoveries of our planet' (Petermann 1865b, 99). Petermann was still convinced that there must exist an Open Polar Sea, and according to his plan, the British initiative would arrive at it through a route between Spitzbergen and Nowaja Semlja from where it would reach, finally, the North Pole – all of this a 'steamboat would travel within two to three months from the Thames to the North Pole and back' (Petermann 1865b, 104). Moreover, Petermann published in the same year several articles and reports in the *Mitteilungen* and in one supplementary volume on 'the Arctic Central Region' in order to prove the existence of the Open Polar Sea. These publications were often accompanied by large coloured maps, which depicted the two poles as 'blank spaces' (e.g. figures 5.4 and 5.5).

In the end, however, a British initiative did not materialize in this form, and Petermann started to work on an alternative German polar mission from

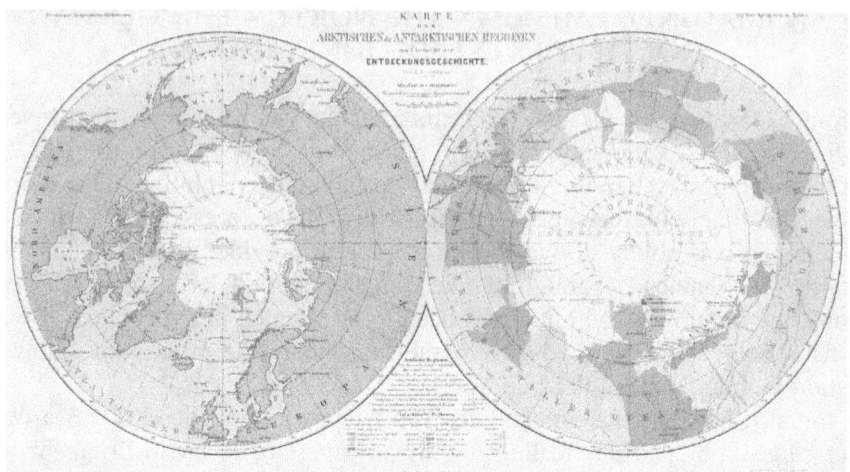

Figure 5.4. The History of the Discovery of the Arctic and Antarctic Regions in Supplementary Volume to *Petermanns Geographische Mitteilungen*, Justus Perthes Gotha 1865.

spring 1865 onwards. The whole endeavour started, however, with a minor accident as a small reconnaissance expedition, which Petermann had organized in the summer of 1865 to explore the region between Spitzbergen and Nowaja Semlja, failed due to problems with the ship's engine after only nine hours while being still in German waters. Nevertheless, Petermann continued the project and started to look for governmental support. German initiatives had a disadvantage in this regard when compared to France or Britain. The German Confederation was politically fragmented and lacked a central government or navy to support explorations in financial or organizational terms. This was the reason why Petermann turned directly to the governments of the two most powerful principalities of the German Confederation, Prussia and Austria. To secure Prussian support Petermann met in November 1865 with the Prussian Prime Minister Otto von Bismarck and the Prussian Minister of War and Navy Albrecht von Roon. At the same time, intermediaries reached out to the Austrian government. At first, both governments appeared very interested in supporting a joint German expedition to the North Pole for which they intended to use a ship under both Prussian and Austrian flags. This made the *Mitteilungen* announce that one of the main purposes of the endeavour was 'to act *together*, . . . to leave the particularistic envy and jealousy of the governments behind, and to join forces in the desire to honour the German name' (Petermann 1865a, 443; emphasis in the original). In other words, Petermann hoped that a German expedition to the North Pole would help to overcome the scattered regionalism (*Kleinstaaterei*) of the German Confederation and lead to a Greater German (*großdeutsch*) nation, which would include both Prussia and Austria.

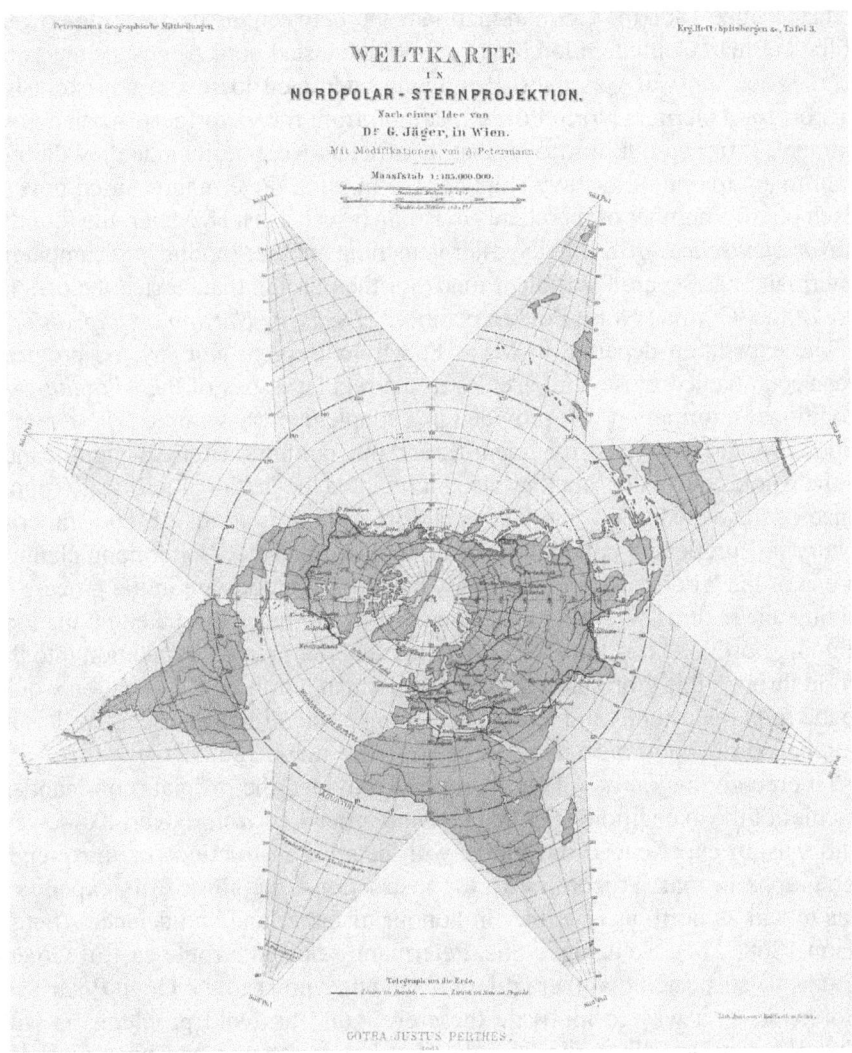

Figure 5.5. World Map with the North Pole in Its Centre in Supplementary Volume to *Petermanns Geographische Mitteilungen*, Justus Perthes Gotha 1865.

The *Mitteilungen* did, however, not only continue to publish articles addressing the 'honour of the German nation', but it started, as it had done earlier with the 'German Inner-Africa Expedition', to launch a large fundraising campaign. This was necessary as the sum of the expedition was estimated at 200,000 Thaler, a considerably high amount by the standards of the time. Unfortunately for Petermann, the joint initiative of Prussia and Austria did not happen in the end as in June 1866 the German-German War between the two leading powers of the German Confederation broke out, which lasted until August of the same year. When the war was over, Petermann attempted to secure the exclusive support for a German North Pole expedition from the victorious Prussian government. It turned out, however, that its officials were hesitant as they did not want to equip one of its navy ships for the mission. Petermann started now to reach out to a number of merchants in Bremen such as H. H. Meier, the founder of *Norddeutsche Lloyd*. Finally, after launching another fundraising campaign, Petermann had secured sufficient funds for the mission that carried the official title of the 'German North Pole Expedition' (*Deutsche Nordpolar-Expedition*).

The expedition departed in May 1868 from Bergen, Norway. Its progress was accompanied by several articles in the regular issues of the *Mitteilungen*. Additional information was provided in a supplementary volume. These publications did not only stress the scientific and the 'cultural-historical' significance of the whole endeavour, but they also highlighted the 'national-political' importance of the expedition – the latter understood both in terms of inter-imperial rivalry in Europe and national unification in Germany. As Petermann claimed in one of his articles, 'other less highly developed nations are in the process of getting ahead of us. We can already see that even France has taken up the idea of going north . . .; it is time for us now to carry our national reputation into the world through this glorious enterprise. A German North Pole expedition would be the right opportunity to increase the German scientific impulse as well as its national spirit and to raise its self-esteem' (Petermann 1868, 210).

To prepare the journey, Petermann had provided the official 'commander-in-chief of the expedition' (*Oberbefehlshaber der Expedition*) Karl Koldewey, who was an experienced navigator, with detailed instructions of thirty-eight paragraphs in total. According to the instructions, the aim of the expedition was to sail as north as possible 'in honour of fatherland and science' (Petermann 1868, 214). To achieve this, Petermann selected a route east of Greenland as he suspected that there might be an entry point to the Open Polar Sea. Moreover, as a way to motivate the crew – and to avoid problems as with Theodor von Heuglin earlier – a detailed bonus scheme had been included in the instructions, according to which an extra pay would be given for every degree of longitude with a maximal amount of 5,000 Thaler if the mission would reach the North Pole (at 90°N). Although the instructions were written in an authoritative tone, Koldewey did not comply entirely to them as he refused to rename the ship of the expedition from *Greenland* to *Germania* – as demanded by Petermann. Even though the name of the ship was actually another, Petermann still opened the supplementary volume to the 'German North-Pole Expedition' with a frontispiece of a ship named *Germania* (figure 5.6). While the expedition was able to collect valuable scientific information about currents and temperatures in the polar region, it did not pass 81°

*Empires of Science, Science of Empires*

Figure 5.6. The Ship *Germania* during the German North Pole Expedition in Supplementary Volume to *Petermanns Geographische Mitteilungen*, Justus Perthes Gotha 1868.

North in the end. Despite these mixed results, the crew was celebrated 'enthusiastically' (Krause 1993, 20) upon arrival in Germany, and Petermann was able to collect more than enough financial resources for a second expedition.

The financial situation was so comfortable that a ship with a steam engine was built for the expedition only. The name of the ship was finally *Germania*, and it was accompanied by a smaller vessel called *Hansa*. The two ships left Bremerhaven in June 1869 for the 'Second German North Pole Expedition' (*Zweite Deutsche Nordpolar-Expedition*). The departure was a major event in which both the Prussian King Wilhelm I and Prime Minister Otto von Bismarck participated. Again, Petermann provided the crew with extensive instructions. This time the main goal was to finally answer the 'polar question', that is, to clarify whether an ice-free sea exists in the Arctic (Petermann 1870, 224). Moreover, it was planned that the two ships spend the winter as north as possible and freeze in the Arctic ice. When arriving in the polar region, the ships lost contact with each other, however, and the *Hansa* had to be abandoned. Its crew survived on an ice floe for almost 200 days and drifted around 600 kilometres southwards before reaching safe land again. As planned, the *Germania* became icebound and stayed for the winter in the polar region, where it was able to collect numerous scientific data. As the ship could not reach the pole and had to come back at 77°N, the polar question had to remain unsolved for now. When arriving in Bremerhaven in September 1870, there was no enthusiastic reception this time – as the Franco-Prussian War had broken out. After winning the war, Prussia founded the German *Reich* a few months later, in January 1871. Wilhelm I became the first German Emperor and Bismarck the Chancellor. A third German polar mission was not demanded anymore.

Yet, Petermann's attempt to find the Open Polar Sea would have one final twist. In 1874, Julius Payer, an Austro-Hungarian officer, polar explorer and cartographer who had participated in the 'Second German North-Polar Expedition' of 1869–1870, and who had joined the Austro-Hungarian North-Pole Expedition (1872–1874), advanced far north with a sledge ride. North of the Franz Josef Land, an archipelago which he had just named in honour of the Austro-Hungarian Emperor, he found a vast, seemingly endless sea and named the most distant point, which he could see, Petermann Land. Petermann himself was, of course, enthusiastic about this news, as it seemed to prove the theory of an Open Polar Sea. However, he should not receive final confirmation during his lifetime. Petermann died in 1878. It was only in 1892 that the Norwegian Fram Expedition, which would come later as close to the North Pole as no other before, and which was led by Fridtjof Nansen, who would receive three decades later the Nobel Peace Prize for his humanitarian work for refugees in the aftermath of World War I, found out that Payer's Open Polar Sea was only a larger opening in the ice and that Petermann Land was a phantom island, a reflection in the Nordic air.

## CONCLUSION

This chapter has studied an important episode in German imperial mapping in the two decades preceding the proclamation of the German Empire in 1871 as it reconstructed the work of August Petermann, one of the leading cartographers of his time, and the role he played at *Justus Perthes* cartographic press in Gotha. For Petermann, as for many contemporaries, the geographical exploration of territories outside of Europe was intertwined with imaginaries of German empire-making and nation-building: imperial expansion was always seen as a catalyst to create cohesion in the scattered political landscape of the German Confederation. Petermann focused in particular on the exploration of the last blank spaces on maps. Blank spaces figured prominently in European cartographic products of the nineteenth century as they indicated unexplored and unknown territories. To fill these blank spaces became an aspiration for geographers such as Petermann, who was able to organize, with the infrastructural support of the *Justus Perthes* press, major expeditions to two of the last 'blank spaces' of his time, namely the 'German Inner-Africa Expedition' (1860–1863) and the first two 'German North Pole Expeditions' (1866–1870).

By drawing on what Latour called centres of calculation, the chapter reconstructed attempts to fill the blank spaces on maps. Small towns with a scientific community such as Gotha, private publishing houses such as *Justus Perthes* and individual cartographers such as Petermann became such centres of calculation. Although these centres of geographical knowledge production were not located in the imperial metropole and organized by the state, they became nevertheless important sites in the creation of new forms of connectivity. They were able to connect such distinct regions as the North Pole and Central Africa and thereby created, mobilized and stabilized new networks. The circulation of objects as (im)mutable (im)mobiles plays a central role in these processes. Maps were highly successful devices in these processes as they could be combined, complemented and amplified when new information came in; but they could also be brought to the 'field' outside of Europe in order to guide explorers in their endeavours. Importantly, however, centres of calculations are not just located in space and time but produce – through the circulate of ideas, people and objects – space and time as concrete reality.

However, while Latour, and many following him, often turned to projects where connectivity was rather smooth and successful, some voices started to call for more attention to episodes of failure and disconnectivity.[7] In the context of mapping, this resonates with Dodge, Perkins and Kitchen's call to put greater emphasis on 'moments of mapping failure' (Dodge, Perkins, and Kitchen 2009, 234–35). As we have seen, failure has always been inherent in Petermann's projects. In the case of the 'German Inner-Africa Expedition', Petermann was not able to govern at a distance when Theodor von Heuglin, the expedition's leader on the ground, decided to take a different route, as set in the initial instructions; moreover, many members died during the expedition. In the case of the two 'German North Pole Expeditions', these expeditions never reached the North Pole and they never found the hypothesized Open Polar Sea. To foreground these episodes of failure, improves our understanding of (imperial) mapping better and helps us to leave the idea of a smooth, teleological and progressive imaginary of mapping behind. Rather, mapping can be conceptualized as a messy, contested and contingent process, often full of failure.

## NOTES

1. The shipwrecks of the *Erebus* and *Terror* were discovered only in 2014 and 2016, respectively (*The Guardian* 2019). There seems to persist some fascination with this topic until the present day. For example, *Amazon Prime* produced in 2018 a new series on this failed endeavour, called *The Terror*.

2. On the relevance of early colonial fantasies in Germany, see Zantop (1997).

3. I borrow this formulation from Donald MacKenzie and his conceptualization of financial models (e.g. MacKenzie 2006).

4. For example, around 1900, German far-right circles of the ethnic-nationalistic *völkische Bewegung* created the idea of *Deutschtum* ('Germandom') to connect German emigration outside of Europe with the 'colonisation' of Eastern and Central Europe in order to create an imaginary of a larger German Empire. For a reconstruction of this episode of German geopolitical thinking, which focuses mainly on the use of maps and statistics, see Çapan and dos Reis (2019).

5. Alternative (and complementary) reconstructions of this spatial imaginary could emphasize either the role of the mathematical operation of zero (cf. Rotman 1996) or the void (cf. Shapin and Schaffer 1985).

6. For a comparison of the use of blank spaces in British cartography of Africa and Australia, see Kennedy (2013).

7. An important exception is Latour (1996). See also Callon (1984).

# REFERENCES

Anonymous. 1860. 'Th. von Heuglin's Expedition nach Wadai'. *Petermanns Geographische Mitteilungen* 6: 318.

———. 1862. 'Die Deutschen Expeditionen nach Wadai: Achter Bericht: Stand des Unternehmens am 1. März 1862'. *Petermanns Geographische Mitteilungen* 8: 98–102.

———. 1864. 'Moriz v. Beurmann's Tod nebst Übersicht seiner Reise (1861–1863) so wie derjenigen von Overweg (1850–1852), Vogel (1853–1856) und Steudner (1861–1863)'. *Petermanns Geographische Mitteilungen* 10: 25–30.

Bartelson, Jens. 2010. 'The Social Construction of Globality'. *International Political Sociology* 4 (3): 219–35.

Bassett, Thomas J. 1994. 'Cartography and Empire Building in Nineteenth-Century West Africa'. *Geographical Review* 84 (3): 316–35.

Bassett, Thomas J., and Philip W. Porter. 1991. '"From the Best Authorities": The Mountains of Kong in the Cartography of West Africa'. *The Journal of African History* 32 (3): 367–413.

Boria, Edoardo. 2007. *Cartografia e Potere: Segni e Rappresentazioni negli Atlanti Italiani del Novecento*. Torino: UTET.

Brogiato, Heinz Peter. 2008. 'Gotha als Wissens-Raum'. In *Die Verräumlichung des Welt-Bildes: Petermanns Geographische Mitteilungen zwischen 'explorativer Geographie' und der 'Vermessenheit' europäischer Raumphantasien*, edited by Sebastian Lentz and Ferjan Ormeling, 16–29. Stuttgart: Franz Steiner.

Callon, Michel. 1984. 'Some Elements of a Sociology of Translation: Domestication of the Scallops and the Fishermen of St Brieuc Bay'. *The Sociological Review* 32 (1 suppl): 196–233.

Çapan, Zeynep Gülşah, and Filipe dos Reis. 2019. '"Making Up Germans": Colonialism, Cartography and Imaginaries of "Germandom"'. In *Imaginaries of Connectivity: The Creation of Novel Spaces of Governance*, edited by Luis Lobo-Guerrero, Suvi Alt, and Maarten Meijer, 127–52. London: Rowman & Littlefield.

Çapan, Zeynep Gülşah, Filipe dos Reis, and Maj Grasten, eds. 2021. *The Politics of Translation in International Relations*. Houndmills: Palgrave MacMillan.
Conrad, Sebastian. 2012. *German Colonialism: A Short History*. Cambridge: Cambridge University Press.
Demhardt, Imre Josef. 2000. *Die Entschleierung Afrikas: Deutsche Kartenbeiträge von August Petermann bis zum kolonialkartographischen Institut*. Gotha: Klett-Perthes.
―――. 2015a. 'Justus Perthes (Germany)'. In *The History of Cartography*, , vol. 6, edited by Mark Monmonier, 720–25. Chicago: The University of Chicago Press.
―――. 2015b. 'Petermanns Geographische Mitteilungen'. In *The History of Cartography*, vol. 6, edited by Mark Monmonier, 1095–99. Chicago: The Chicago University Press.
*Die Gartenlaube*. 1862. 'Die Deutsche Expedition nach Mittelafrika und ihre Gegner', 5: 72–74.
Dodge, Martin, Chris Perkins, and Rob Kitchin. 2009. 'Mapping Modes, Methods and Moments: A Manifesto for Map Studies'. In *Rethinking Maps*, edited by Dodge, Martin, Chris Perkins, and Rob Kitchin, 220–43. London: Routledge.
dos Reis, Filipe. 2019. 'Wir sind nie global gewesen. Latour, die Internationalen Beziehungen und die (Geo)Politik der Diplomatie'. In *Der große Leviathan und die Welt der Ameisen. Zum Staatsverständnis Bruno Latours und der Akteur-Netzwerk-Theorie*, edited by Hagen Schölzel, 155–74. Baden-Baden: Nomos.
Edney, Matthew H. 1993. 'Cartography without "Progress": Reinterpreting the Nature and Historical Development of Mapmaking'. *Cartographica: The International Journal for Geographic Information and Geovisualization* 30 (2 & 3): 54–68.
―――. 2009. 'The Irony of Imperial Mapping'. In *The Imperial Map*, edited by James R. Akerman, 11–45. Chicago: The University of Chicago Press.
―――. 2019. *Cartography: The Ideal and Its History*. Chicago: The University of Chicago Press.
Felsch, Philipp. 2010. *Wie August Petermann den Nordpol erfand*. München: Luchterhand.
Ferretti, Federico. 2019. 'Networking Print Cultures: Reclus' Nouvelle Géographie Universelle at the Hachette Publishing House'. *Journal of Historical Geography* 63: 23–33.
*The Guardian*. 2019. '"Frozen in Time" Wreck Sheds New Light on Franklin's Ill-Fated 1845 Arctic Quest', *The Guardian*. 28 August 2019. www.theguardian.com/world/2019/aug/28/hms-terror-sir-john-franklin-evidence-recovered-arctic-ocean.
Harley, John Brian. 1988a. 'Maps, Knowledge and Power'. In *The Iconography of Landscapes*, edited by Denis Cosgrove and Stephen Daniels, 277–312. Cambridge: Cambridge University Press.
―――. 1988b. 'Silences and Secrecy: The Hidden Agenda of Cartography in Early Modern Europe'. *Imago Mundi* 40 (1): 57–76.
―――. 1989. 'Deconstructing the Map'. *Cartographica* 26 (2): 1–20.
Hiatt, Alfred. 2002. 'Blank Spaces on the Earth'. *The Yale Journal of Criticism* 15 (2): 223–50.
Hill, Jen. 2008. *White Horizon: The Arctic in the Nineteenth-Century British Imagination*. Albany: SUNY Press.

Jacob, Christian. 2006. *The Sovereign Map: Theoretical Approaches in Cartography throughout History*. Chicago: The University of Chicago Press.

Jones, Adam, and Isabel Voigt. 2012. '"Just a First Sketchy Makeshift": German Travellers and Their Cartographic Encounters in Africa, 1850–1914'. *History in Africa* 39: 9–39.

Jöns, Heike. 2011. 'Centre of Calculation'. In *The SAGE Handbook of Geographical Knowledge*, edited by John A. Agnew and David N. Livingstone, 158–70. Los Angeles: SAGE.

Kennedy, Dane Keith. 2013. *The Last Blank Spaces: Exploring Africa and Australia*. Cambridge, MA: Harvard University Press.

Krause, Reinhard A. 1993. 'Hintergründe der deutschen Polarforschung von den Anfängen bis heute'. *Deutsches Schiffahrtsarchiv* 16: 7–70.

Kuhn, Kristina, and Wolfgang Struck. 2019. *Aus der Welt gefallen: Die Geographie der Verschollenen*. Paderborn: Wilhelm Fink.

Latour, Bruno. 1987. *Science in Action: How to Follow Scientists and Engineers through Society*. Cambridge, MA: Harvard University Press.

———. 1990. 'Drawing Things Together'. In *Representation in Scientific Practice*, edited by Michael Lynch and Steve Woolgar, 19–68. Cambridge, MA: MIT Press.

———. 1996. *Aramis: On the Love to Technology*. Cambridge, MA: Harvard University Press.

———. 1999. *Pandora's Hope: Essays on the Reality of Science Studies*. Cambridge, MA: Harvard University Press.

———. 2005. *Reassembling the Social: An Introduction to Actor-Network-Theory*. Oxford: Oxford University Press.

———. 2016. '*Onus Orbis Terrarum*: About a Possible Shift in the Definition of Sovereignty'. *Millennium* 44 (3): 305–20.

Law, John, and Annemarie Mol. 2001. Situating Technoscience: An Inquiry into Spatialities. *Environment and Planning D: Society and Space* 19 (5): 609–21.

Lentz, Sebastian, and Ferjan Ormeling, eds. 2008. *Die Verräumlichung des Welt-Bildes: Petermanns geographische Mitteilungen zwischen 'explorativer Geographie' und der 'Vermessenheit' europäischer Raumphantasien*. Stuttgart: Franz Steiner.

MacKenzie, Donald A. 2006. *An Engine, Not a Camera: How Financial Models Shape Markets*. Cambridge, MA: MIT Press.

Neocleous, Mark. 2003. 'Off the Map: On Violence and Cartography'. *European Journal of Social Theory* 6 (4): 409–25.

Petermann, August. 1852a. 'Notes on the Distribution of Animals Available as Food in the Arctic Regions'. *Journal of the Royal Geographical Society of London* 22: 118–27.

———. 1852b. *The Search for Franklin: A Suggestion Submitted to the British Public*. London: Longman, Brown, Green, and Longmans.

———. 1852c. 'The Arctic Expeditions'. *The Athenaeum*, 17 January 1852, 82–83.

———. 1853. 'Sir John Franklin, the Sea of Spitzbergen, and Whale-Fisheries in the Arctic Regions'. *Journal of the Royal Geographical Society of London* 23: 129–36.

———. 1855a. 'Die Expedition Nach Central-Afrika: I. Dr. H. Barth's Reise von Kuka nach Timbuktu [November 1852 bis September 1853]'. *Petermanns Geographische Mitteilungen* 1: 3–14.

———. 1855b. 'Vorwort'. *Petermanns Geographische Mitteilungen* 1: 1–2.
———. 1864. 'Vorwort'. *Petermanns Geographische Mitteilungen* Supplement 13: i–ii.
———. 1865a. 'Aphorismen über die projektierte Deutsche Nordfahrt'. *Petermanns Geographische Mitteilungen* 11: 442–45.
———. 1865b. 'Die projektierte Englische Expedition nach dem Nordpol'. *Petermanns Geographische Mitteilungen* 11: 95–104.
———. 1866. 'Notizen über den kartographischen Standpunkt der Erde'. *Geographisches Jahrbuch* 1: 581–600.
———. 1868. 'Die Deutsche Nordpol-Expedition, 1868'. *Petermanns Geographische Mitteilungen* 14: 207–28.
———. 1870. 'Instruktion für die zweite Deutsche Nordpolar-Expedition, 1869 bis 1870'. *Petermanns Geographische Mitteilungen* 16: 254–63.
Pickles, John. 2004. *A History of Spaces: Cartographic Reason, Mapping, and the Geo-Coded World*. London: Routledge.
Ramaswamy, Sumathi. 2017. *Terrestial Lessons: The Conquest of the World as Globe*. Chicago: The University of Chicago Press.
Rotman, Brian. 1996. *Signifying Nothing: The Semiotics of Zero*. Stanford: Stanford University Press.
Schelhaas, Bruno. 2009. 'Das "Wiederkehren des Fragezeichens in der Karte". Gothaer Kartenproduktion im 19 Jahrhundert'. *Geographische Zeitschrift* 97 (4): 227–42.
Shapin, Steven, and Simon Schaffer. 1985. *Leviathan and the Air-Pump: Hobbes, Boyle, and the Experimental Life*. Princeton: Princeton University Press.
Smits, Jan. 2004. *Petermann's Maps: Carto-Bibliography of the Maps in Petermanns Geographische Mitteilungen 1855–1945*.'t Goy-Houten: Hes & de Graaf.
Staeheli, Urs. 2012. 'Listing the Global: Dis/Connectivity beyond Representation?' *Distinktion: Scandinavian Journal of Social Theory* 13 (3): 233–46.
Strandsbjerg, Jeppe. 2010. *Territory, Globalization and International Relations: The Cartographic Reality of Space*. Houndmills: Palgrave Macmillan.
Turnbull, David. 1996. 'Cartography and Science in Early Modern Europe: Mapping the Construction of Knowledge Spaces'. *Imago Mundi* 48 (1): 5–24.
———. 2000. *Masons, Tricksters and Cartographers Comparative Studies in the Sociology of Scientific and Indigenous Knowledge*. London: Routledge.
Wadai-Comité. 1860a. 'Th. v. Heuglin's Expedition nach Inner-Afrika, zur Aufhellung der Schicksale Dr. Eduard Vogel's und zur Vollendung seines Forschungswerks'. Gotha.
———. 1860b. 'Instruktionen für die Expedition nach Inner-Afrika zur Aufhellung der Schicksale Dr. Eduard Vogel's und zur Vollendung seines Forschungswerks'. Gotha.
Wittgenstein, Ludwig. 1953. *Philosophical Investigations*, translated by G. E. M. Anscombe. New York: Macmillan.
Zantop, Susanne. 1997. *Colonial Fantasies: Conquest, Family, and Nations in Precolonial Germany, 1770–1870*. Durham: Duke University Press.

*Chapter 6*

# Representing France's Syrian 'Colony without a Flag'

## Imperial Cartographic Strategies at the Margin of the Peace Conference

Louis Le Douarin

On 30th June 2014, the terrorist organization Islamic State in the Levant issued a video staging the destruction of the berm that materialized the border between Syria and Iraq. Operating bulldozers and waving the organization's black flag, armed men shouted to the camera, 'We killed Sykes-Picot', thus claiming the restauration of an ancient, traditional and 'Islamic' political geography and the disappearance of exogenous borders, imposed by colonial powers.[1] The fighters referred to the infamous 1916 secret treaty between the United Kingdom and France over the future of the Middle East. The agreement kept the name of two diplomats involved in the final negotiations, Mark Sykes, an ambitious young diplomat who had travelled in the Middle East and acted as an advisor on the region for Asquith's and Lloyd George's governments, and François Georges-Picot, former French consul in Beirut and a member of the French colonial party (Cloarec 2010; Barr 2012). The aim of the agreement was to prevent tensions from emerging between the two allies regarding the partition of the Ottoman Empire's territories. During World War I, the alliance between Istanbul and Berlin had indeed opened a new front in the Eastern Mediterranean and at the end of 1915, it seemed clear that the British wished to expand the conflict from Egypt into Palestine, with the help of Arab rebels. The eventuality of the disappearance of Ottoman sovereignty in the Arab provinces of the empire – what is now Syria, Lebanon, Israel and the West Bank, Jordan and parts of Turkey and Saudi Arabia – introduced new perspectives where French and British, but also local national, aspirations opposed. As a compromise, the 1916 agreement proposed a division of the region in several 'zones'. Direct control would be granted to France in coastal Syria and Cilicia, and to the United Kingdom in

Lower Mesopotamia and in the Bay of Acre in Palestine. The rest of Palestine would be put under international administration, while the Syrian hinterland would form a new independent Arab state divided into two zones of European influence: French in the north and British in the south.[2]

The 'Sykes-Picot agreement' has become a cliché of the history of the Middle East. In 2014, the jihadists were only reproducing a discourse shared by a number of scholars and journalists, in which 'Sykes-Picot' incarnates how the West has conquered and reshaped the region to its will. This narrative has prevailed and is still taught without nuance, although the borders of the territories put under European mandate in 1919 did not follow most of the lines drawn on the 1916 map, but resulted from complex negotiations between a great number of European, but also local, actors (Pursley 2015; Patel 2016).[3] For this reason, the map attached to the agreement has itself come to epitomize the violence of colonial arbitrariness, illustrating how European diplomats arbitrarily drew lines on 'an empty map', without taking pre-existing social realities into consideration.[4] This critical approach focusing on the cartographic dimension of this famous partition echoes the post-colonial denunciation of the role geography and cartography played in the implementation of imperial domination, as the study and representation of space prepared and helped the exploration, conquest and administration of overseas territories by Europe. A critical history of cartography has thus applied the seminal teachings of Brian Harley to the Middle East, denouncing the 'power' of maps as essential instruments in how Europeans 'carved up' the region and designed new colonial states (Harley 1988; Culcasi 2011; Foliard 2017). The Sykes-Picot map, however, is not the only layer in the complex history of the relation between cartography and the shaping of the modern Middle East. The end of the First World War and the construction of a new world order coincided with a considerable cartographic production. For the first time, the 1919 negotiations and treaties put maps at the centre of diplomatic relations: original maps were produced, and new techniques were developed by all parties to defend conflicting territorial claims (Crampton 2006; Branch 2014). Emboldened by the spirit of the 'Wilsonian moment' and by the promises made by the Allies, Kurd, Armenian, Lebanese and Zionist nationalist movements for instance rushed in front of the Peace Conference, with maps attached to their memoranda, giving place to well-known cartographic confrontations (Foliard 2016). Although all national demands were not taken into account, the power of these maps was considerable, as some of them gave a spatial shape to emerging national claims, further impacting the future of the region.

However, national delegations were not the only actors involved in this cartographic combat. In 1919, French capitalists and merchants with economic interests in the Ottoman Empire, along with French diplomats, army officers and scholars, engaged in a large political campaign to defend their interests in the region. The aim of this chapter is to look at the cartographic dimension of this campaign, questioning a new layer of the relation between cartography and the shaping of the Middle East. The cartographic production of colonial lobbies, although small and not coordinated, functioned as an alternative both to the inter-imperial Sykes-Picot narrative and to the narratives of the different national delegations. Two maps are at the centre of this study. The first one, drawn in 1914 by cartographer René Bolzé represented French interests in the Ottoman Empire before the war. This map was used by colonial milieus in 1919 to illustrate their demands to the French government and public. The second, an ethnographic map, was drawn in 1919 by geographer Augustin Bernard, in preparation for the Peace Conference. Because they offer a far more revealing account of the nature of the French 'imperial' gaze on Syria than the famous Sykes-Picot map, these maps, I believe, reflect more accurately how these territories were understood and transformed after the war. First of all, they illustrate an epistemic shift in the representation of the region. With these thematic maps, the colonial lobby adapted to the growing importance of economic and ethnographic expertise that had a strong impact on cartography at the time of the Peace Conference. Moreover, the two maps were infused with a particular French imperial geographical imaginary of the Levant.[5] The 'rediscovery' of the region, its exploration, its mapping and the development of French economic and cultural influence during the long 19th century had indeed fashioned an idea of a deep connection between France and the eastern Mediterranean, which would in turn legitimate the incorporation of this territory into the existing empire.

Produced in specific and sometimes marginal contexts, the two maps circulated among colonial networks, were adapted and transformed to fit different and at times conflicting political strategies. Studying maps in this relational context allows us to consider them as collective and changing objects, going beyond the representational understanding of the role of cartography in history (Kitchin, Gleeson, and Dodge 2013). The chapter thus focuses not only on the two original maps but on larger multi-layered and evolving cartographic strategies, involving earlier sketches and sometimes non-explicit reuses of the two maps. The focus on a complex network of actors, involved in colonial matters both in France and in the Levant, also questions the way we understand the functioning of imperial structures themselves. Historical geographers of empire have insisted on the *reticular* dimension of imperial spatialities:[6] circulations inside the empire, social and material networks, were not only attributes of the empire or tools serving the imperial mind, but they constituted the core of the empire, its structure (Lester 2006). France's network in the Levant thus incarnated its informal, yet very real, empire in the region.

Both maps and empire must therefore be considered as collective and reticular processes, which force us to question the relation between the two, and the way we understand the performative value of cartography in imperial and colonial context. The chapter looks at two different forms of interrelated connectivities that characterize the relation between cartography and empire: on the one hand, the colonial networks of merchants, officers and diplomats that produced and circulated the maps; and, on the other, the imaginaries of connection between France and the Levant displayed on the map through lines and other graphic devices. These two social and discursive 'connections' were articulated inside deeply interrelated cartographic and imperial strategies. Maps gave a spatial shape to the material and immaterial networks, which formed the very structure of France's reticular empire in the Eastern Mediterranean. This study therefore further illustrates how maps are not only tools in the hand of the imperial mind, but that cartography and imperialism are actually two codependent and coconstructed historical phenomena, which both illustrate a similar evolution in the way modern Europeans came to understand the rest of the world and act on it (Edney 2009; Branch 2014). The imperial and cartographic gazes characterize what Ingold has labelled the 'occupant knowledge', which allowed states and institutions to consider and picture space from a distance, drawing black lines across blank spaces to convey men and resources between imperial capitals and remote provinces (Ingold 2016, 89–90).

In what follows, I start by briefly situating my analysis in a larger historiographical debate on the role of cartography in the formation of Middle Eastern 'geo-bodies' in the nineteenth century. I then present the two thematic maps and the way they were used in complex cartographic strategies put in place by a network of French actors with material or academic interests in Syria. In 1919, these networks campaigned for their vision of a 'French Syria', adapting their maps to new imperial and international rationales based on ethnography and economy. In the last section, I contextualize these maps, drawing on older geographical debates in order to show how they relied on deeply rooted geographical imaginaries of connection, between France and the Levant.

## PRE-1919 EUROPEAN CARTOGRAPHY AND THE 'GEO-BODIES' OF SYRIA

In his seminal history of the cartography of Siam, Thongchai Winichakul has shown how European and European-influenced cartography played a central part in the emergence of colonial and national geographical imaginaries. His concept of 'geo-body' refers to the territories that were shaped by colonial powers' use of modern cartographic techniques, overriding preceding spatialities. A 'man-made territorial definition', the concept of geo-body implies long-lasting effects on space and on the people, as such representations were generally in turn adopted and used by indigenous national movements to illustrate their territorial claims (Winichakul 1994). Although the Middle East was not directly under European control in the 19th century, growing European presence in the region had profoundly impacted its spatial organization. Directly, by forcing international settlements on Istanbul for internal issues, as they did in 1862 in Lebanon, but also indirectly, by influencing the reorganization of the entire region's administrative geography by the Ottoman state. The 'rediscovery' of the Holy Land put maps at the centre of conflicting imperial strategies combining political and economic interests to a fascination for the 'cradle of civilization' (Ben-Arieh 1979). Napoleon's invasion of Egypt and parts of Palestine in 1798 had indeed opened a new era of explorations during which European military and scholars applied modern cartographic techniques to the region. European cartography, circulating inside and outside the Ottoman empire, played a central role in the evolution of how the region was represented and divided into different entities on the eve of the Great War. Asher Kaufman has thus insisted on how these French and British pre-mandate 'colonial cartographies' contributed to the formation of national 'geo-bodies' in the region (Kaufman 2015). Two large-scale semi-topographical maps in particular were decisive in the process: the 1862 *Carte du Liban*, drawn in the aftermath of the 1860–1861 French Syria campaign, and the *Map of Western Palestine* of the Palestine Exploration Fund.[7] The Lebanon map, after becoming the cornerstone of France's cartographic projects in the region, was picked up by father Henri Lammens, professor at the Jesuit Saint-Joseph University in Beirut. Father Lammens then introduced the map to his students, some of whom became active in the Lebanese nationalist movement. At the time of the world conflict, the 1862 map was therefore used as an embodiment of the 'geo-body' of the nation, serving as a nationalist argument to legitimate extended territorial claims. Similarly, the PEF's map of Palestine became a reference which contributed to fixing the identity and shape of both ancient and modern 'Palestine', eventually influencing how the Ottoman administration itself pictured the land (Kaufman 2015, 231).

The territories depicted in these two maps did not, however, take a physical shape before 1920, and their borders were not 'drawn' on the ground until the European mandates were created. As always, when questioning the performative power of maps, great heed must be paid to avoid the teleological narrative according to which territories created in 1920 had already been depicted on maps drawn fifty to sixty years earlier. If the two maps presented by Kaufman did play a role in the formation of new mandatory states, Palestine and Greater Lebanon, they only did so because they were intertwined with political strategies that eventually succeeded. Before, but also after, 1920, other alternative geographical imaginaries, in line with other groups of actors and other strategies, had also emerged and coexisted with that of 'Lebanon' and 'Palestine'. The region as a whole in particular was framed in Europe under the name 'Syria', a term encompassing all the territories of the Eastern Mediterranean between Alexandretta and the Red Sea, and as far as the Euphrates and the desert in the east. The rediscovery of the Greek-Roman name itself was due to French orientalist Volney who visited the region and published his travelogue in 1787 (Kiwan 1997). Volney's description of Syria as a large and coherent whole, with an Ancient and glorious past that could be restored after centuries of decay, was instrumental in shaping the new spatial imaginary for the region. After circulating in European salons, his definition of Syria circulated in the East where it was used by authors as a synonym for *bilad esh-Sham*, the 'region' or 'country' of Damascus (*ash-Sham*), a phrase that could both refer to the immediate surrounding of the city or the larger area under its political influence (Kiwan 1997). In 1867, the name 'Syria' was even adopted in the official Ottoman nomenclature for a new province created around Damascus. It was then adopted by local nationalists who claimed independence or administrative autonomy for a region that stretched between Anatolia and Egypt.

The geo-body of this large 'Syria', like those of Lebanon and Palestine with which it overlapped, was thus formed in the 19th century in the context of strong European influence and of cultural circulation between European scholars and diplomats on one hand, and Ottoman elites and local movements on the other. But Syria did not take shape on the ground in 1920, unlike Lebanon and Palestine, which were carved out of it. Kaufman finds an explanation for this in cartography: 'The absence of an authoritative map of Syria' at the time of the Peace Conference proved that, contrary to Lebanon and Palestine, Syria lacked a 'comprehensive cartographic depiction of its geo-body' to illustrate the claims of this advocates (Kaufman 2015, 232–34). In 1919, however, French advocates of 'Syria' defended their territorial claims. They opposed the Sykes-Picot agreement, for it denied France its right over the whole of Syria 'in its natural boundaries' and used the term 'Greater Syria' or 'integral Syria' to oppose an unnatural 'partition'. Inside and outside the Peace Conference, French and pro-French Syrians networks produced different maps to give form to their claims, shaping and diffusing the 'geo-body' of a French Syria.

## COLONIAL NETWORKS AND THE CAMPAIGN FOR FRENCH SYRIA: INTERTWINED CARTOGRAPHIC STRATEGIES

In the second half of the 19th century, French influence in the Ottoman Empire dramatically increased. It relied on cultural and missionary institutions subsidized by the French state and on financial investments in several sectors. Between 1895 and 1914, French investments came to represent 67% of all foreign investments in the Empire. Before any formal domination was implemented in the region, this influence was encapsulated in France by the phrase *France du Levant*, the Levant France, a complex network of capitalists, merchants, diplomats and French-speaking protégés that spread all along the eastern coast of the Mediterranean. Developed in part as a substitute for direct colonial rule and settlement colonization, which had become difficult to support and finance at the turn of the century, the concept was meant to glorify the French civilizing mission and the constitution of imperial power through influence (Cloarec 1996). This diasporic community of French and Syrian men circulated between Marseilles, Lyons, Paris and the Levant, connecting the Mediterranean shore through a dense social and economic web, shaping France's 'informal' imperial space in the Levant. This informal Levantine empire, made of connections and circulations, reacted strongly to the possibility of the Ottoman Empire's collapse, as a new ruler could put an end to French activities. The *France du Levant* in the East and the 'colonial party' in the mainland thus organized to defend themselves against other imperial claims, national aspirations but also other French leaders that did not want to see Syria added to the map of the imperial empire.

The argumentation they built was in line with the challenges of the time, responding to new national and international agendas. Statistics, economic geography and ethnographic mapping had all matured in the previous century but were granted a new importance at the end of the global conflict, as the organization of a new 'international' world order granted experts and expertise a central position. The Peace Conference, the growing support for national aspirations and the progressive reconsideration of imperial rule indeed fostered the use of these new ways of understanding and representing space and human communities. In the next section, I look at how French colonial networks organized into a specific epistemic community and developed cartographic strategies adapted to these new rationales, in order to find new ways to justify imperial expansion in Syria.

## RENÉ BOLZÉ'S MAP: DISPLAYING THE FRANCE DU LEVANT IN FRONT OF THE COLONIAL LOBBY

On the 4th of January 1919, geographer Henri Froidevaux ended his lengthy presentation to the *Congrès français de la Syrie* by displaying and analysing a beautiful and colourful thematic map, representing 'French interests in the Levant' (figure 6.1). A Professor at the *Institut catholique de Paris*, Henri Froidevaux was closely tied to conservative and colonial groups. He

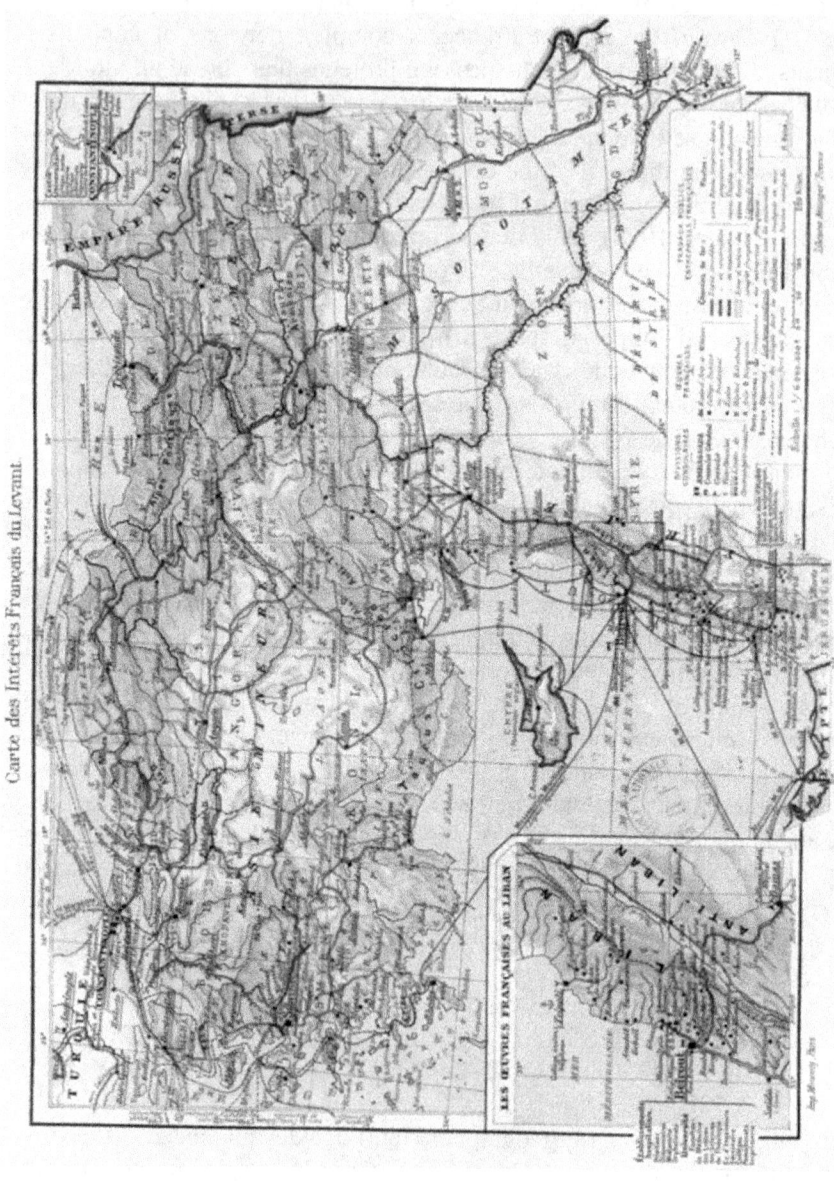

**Figure 6.1.** Bolzé, René. 1920. «Carte des intérêts français au Liban». Published in Congrès français de la Syrie, Congrès français de la syrie et Chambre de commerce de Marseille, 1919. Fascicule 2. Paris; Marseille: E. Champion. Courtesy of the Bibliothèque nationale de France.

was specialized in the history of French India, was Secretary General of the *Office colonial* and, for just a few months, was director of *L'Asie française*, journal of the main lobby federating the members of the 'Syrian party' (Andrew et Kanya-Forstner 1971). In January 1919, with the rest of the *Asie française*, Froidevaux joined the chambers of commerce of Marseilles and Lyons, the two cities most interested in preserving French interests in the Levant, to organize the *Congrès français de la Syrie*. The French Congress for Syria was organized at the very beginning of the year 1919, just a few days before the opening of the Peace Conference in Paris (18 January 1919), and at a moment when the future of France's role in Syria was still to be defined. A small contingent had indeed joined when Allenby's troops had entered Palestine, but the British were still occupying the region, along with the Arabs led by Prince Faisal, who had participated in the charge against Damascus.

The conference was organized in Marseilles, which was a French margin, but a central colonial hub. There, the colonial party staged its response to what appeared to be the French government's official position: agreement to the partition of Syria and the creation of an Arab state in the hinterland, ruled by Faisal.[8] The ultimate and decisive step in the campaign for a French Syria, the Congress's aim was to 'shine a true light on the historic and, even more, actual rights of France over Syria' and promote the inclusion of all of Syria inside the colonial empire (Froidevaux 1919a).[9] What place did cartography take in this Syrian campaign? As mentioned before, the 19th century saw a considerable cartographic production centred on Syria and Mesopotamia. But pseudo-topographic maps and traverse surveys of little use to the colonial lobby. As businessmen, the primary argument of the men in Marseilles was economic. At the opening ceremony of the Congress, the director of the Chamber of Commerce stated that the aim of the meeting was to shed light on France's right over Syria, doing it 'not only from a traditional point of view, but from a triple scientific, economic and intellectual point of view, by showing past, present and possible [French] action, and our country's interests' (Froidevaux 1919a).

The Marseilles Congress was representative of a larger evolution in France in the theorization of empire and its role in the economy. As France was exhausted by the costs of war, the economic imperative progressively replaced glory and the civilizing mission in legitimizing imperial expansion. As historian Jackson noted, the economic argument was central in Marseilles, and the quest for the 'permanent postwar mobilization of imperial resources was matched by the development of new international languages and metrics within which to capture such potential' (Jackson 2013). The merchants of Marseilles and Lyons had learnt and mastered this language in order to demonstrate the need for France to be granted exclusive influence over Syria. By the summer of 1915, the Marseilles Chamber of commerce had already sent a lengthy note to the Minister of Foreign affairs on the 'economic value of integral Syria'.[10] A similar phrasing would be used four years later when the mission sent by the Marseilles Congress to Syria presented its final report under the name 'What Is Syria worth?' (Huvelin 1919).

The 1919 campaign needed thematic and statistical maps in order to show, and prove, that France had an economic past, present and future, in Syria and that Syria would provide enough resources to France to justify the implementation of French rule. However, they lacked the information to do so. In 1919 Paul Huvelin started his statistical and economic report over the 'worthiness' of Syria by presenting how difficult it was to gather good data on the region. The colonial party therefore relied on the data compiled by Vital Cuinet more than twenty years before. Cuinet was a French geographer who had served as a member of the Ottoman public debt administration and had access to official Ottoman data, which he partly published in an exhaustive review of the administrative and economic geography of Syria (Cuinet 1896).[11] This need for, and lack of, data impacted cartographic choices and the first maps produced by the lobby were very basic. The 1915 note on the 'economic value of integral Syria' was for instance accompanied by a first sketch, based on a map published the same year by Salim Cressaty, a 'Levantine French' advocating Greater Syria under French tutelage. The sketches only drew a list of railway lines according to the country holding the concession and its length.[12]

Cartography was then explicitly discussed in 1919 in Marseilles. Froidevaux's own lecture, which focused on the role played by the *Société de géographie* in the exploration of Syria in the 19th century, included an extended presentation of the history of European surveys in the region. It was complemented by a presentation by another French Levantine, Abdullah Thomeh, of his own cartographic work.[13] A former student at the Jesuit University of Beirut, Thomeh had produced several thematic maps in French and Arabic. In 1891, he had published in Paris, with a certain F. Bianconi, *ingénieur-géographe*, the most complete economic map of the region. The 'Commercial map of Syria and of the island of Cyprus', consisted in a pseudo-topographic map (1:200, 000) representing administrative borders, along with railroads, roads, shipping lines, submarine cables, mines and quarries, wells and sources, and an indication in red of the main production of each area. But despite the absence of any other detailed thematic maps in 1919, and although it was included in the final 528-page-long bibliography that was published with the proceeding of the Marseilles congress, Thomeh's work was not directly used during the Congress.[14]

The main cartographic piece of the Congress was presented by Froidevaux, in the second part of his lecture. The map, entitled *Carte des intérêts français du Levant* was drawn in 1914 by René Bolzé, a cartographer already known for his work in several great atlases. It was originally meant to be part of the *Atlas de la plus grande France*, directed by the famous geographer Onésime

Reclus. Composing a massive work for the glory of the French colonial empire, Reclus did not want it to be limited to the formal French colonies and wished to also picture the 'colonies without flags', namely the 'countries where France possessed the most interests of all nature' (Froidevaux 1919b). Initiated in 1913, Bolzé's work was therefore meant to map the *France du Levant*, showing three aspects: 'consular organizations'; 'French institutions', missionary and educational; and 'public works done by French companies'. Bolzé retrieved the data and maps he needed from the very actors of these networks. He went to the library and map rooms of the *Société de géographie de Paris*, one of the major centres for the promotion of imperial expansion since the late 1860s (Lejeune 1993), and then directly contacted the Parisian head-quarters of both the religious organizations and the private companies involved in the region.

After the death of Onésime Reclus in 1916, the Attinger publishing house had refused to include Bolzé's map in the *Atlas*, but the collapse of the Ottoman Empire offered a new life to Bolzé's work, now in the hands of Froidevaux. An 'excellent and valuable overview, so conscientious and so useful', the map was put forward as the perfect example of the Congress's general argument: not only did France have historical rights over parts of the Ottoman Empire, but its recent political, cultural and economic activity granted it contemporary, 'actual', rights. Bolzé's map thus constituted in the eyes of Froidevaux the perfect tool for the members of the Congress to assimilate and to circulate: 'By allowing us to see at a single glance [the importance of French interests], Mr. R. Bolzé has produced a very commendable work that is at the same time very useful, worthy of your approval and of your encouragement' (Froidevaux 1919b, 216). A thematic map relying on economic data, Bolzé's map answered the economic rationale at play in Marseilles. After his speech, Froidevaux and other members of the audience even asked for more statistical information, namely graphs showing the share of French trade in each port of Syria, to be added to the map.

The Marseilles Congress did not have its mind on the whole of Asiatic Turkey represented on the map. One argument defended in Marseilles was actually that a French Syria would compensate for the loss of the rest of the *France du Levant*, meaning all its economic and cultural interests on the Anatolian coast. In Marseilles, Bolzé's map therefore served a double purpose: it reminded them what the Republic was about to lose, and at the same time illustrated the Congress's claims by showing where these interests were concentrated the most. Turning Bolzé's map into an argument for *Syrie intégrale*, Henri Froidevaux concluded:

> As we look at the map, we are immediately stricken by the fact that, nowhere else in Turkey in Asia French activity is more nor best visible. Surely it is also

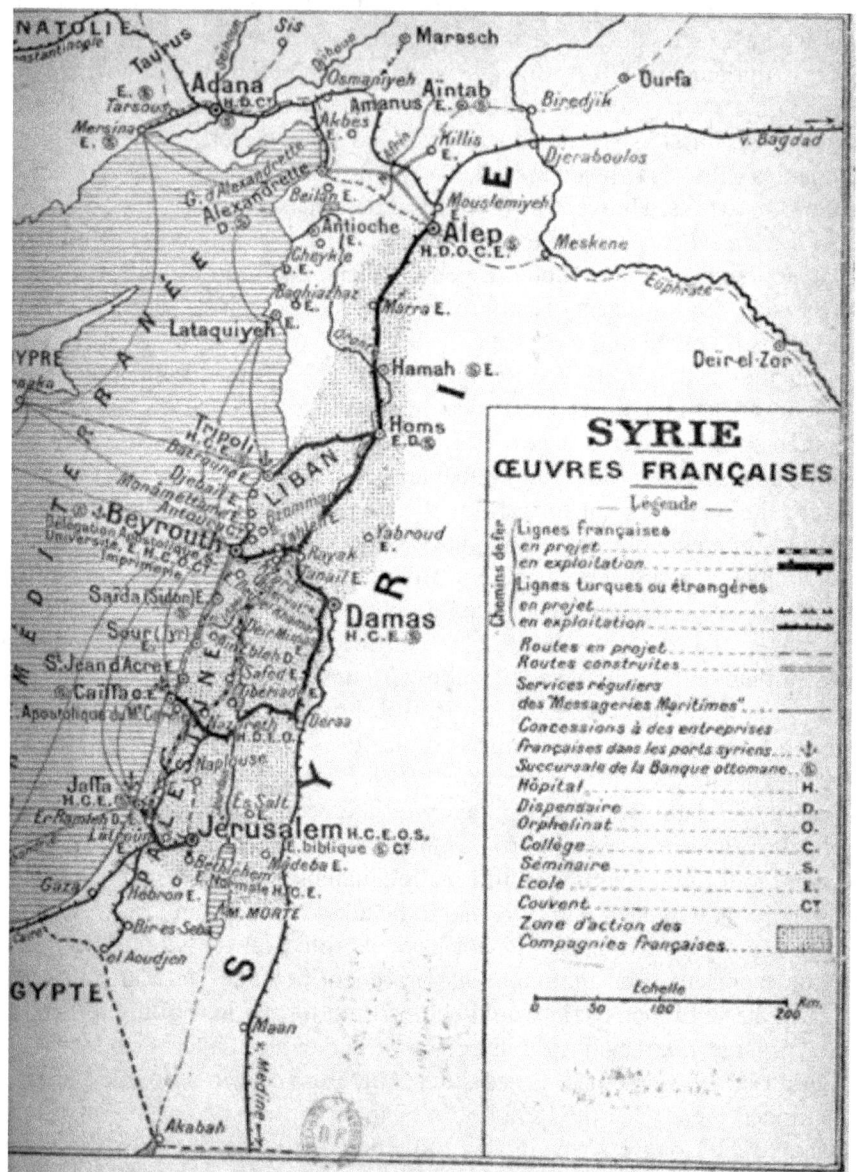

**Figure 6.2.** 'Syrie. Œuvres françaises' in Comité central syrien. La Syrie devant la Conférence. Paris, 1919. Courtesy of the Bibliothèque nationale de France.

important . . . in that part of Anatolia where we own the rail lines, from Smyrna to Afiou-Kara-Jissar and in Panderma; but how even more important, and more firmly rooted it is in Syria! . . . Importance of French activity in Syria in various forms, that is the first fact that emerges from the examination of M. Bolzé's map. Here is the second: the supremacy of French influence in that country.

(Froidevaux 1919b, 217)

Circulated among political and economic circles with the substantial volume of the Congress's proceedings, Bolzé's map became a major and colourful piece added to the campaign for French Syria. The map even indirectly integrated one of the memoranda presented the same year at the Peace Conference, the memoir of the *Comité central syrien* (Comité central syrien 1919). This committee had been created in 1917 by Shukri Ghanim and Georges Samna, two Syrians living in Paris who had been defending Syrian autonomy and had progressively associated themselves with major figures of the colonial party. The Quai d'Orsay saw the *Comité* as an instrument of its future action in Syria, to counter other pro-British, panarabist or anti-French associations (Cloarec 2010, 343). One of the three maps attached to the 1919 memorandum was an economic map showing French activity in Syria (figure 6.2). Although Bolzé's map was not explicitly referred to, its influence transpired since the information given, and the legend were almost identical. The only information removed was the limits and seats of consular divisions and the borders of Ottoman provinces, illustrating in this case the need to free Syria from its former administrative geography.

## AUGUSTIN BERNARD, AN EXPERT ON THE MARGINS OF THE PEACE CONFERENCE

If René Bolzé's map and its use show the greater place taken by economic expertise and the related thematic cartography in the campaign for French Syria, the advocates of French influence delivered other readings of the territory. At the same time that Henri Foidevaux was presenting the map in Marseilles, another French geographer, Augustin Bernard, published an article on 'Syria and the Syrians' in the January issue of the *Annales géographiques* and later that same year, his map on the 'Populations of Syria' was released (Bernard 1919a; 1919b). A lecturer and then professor of Geography of Africa in Algiers from 1894 to 1902, Bernard held the chair of Geography and Colonization of North Africa at the Sorbonne from 1902. This position made him the lead specialist of that region, and one of the most influential colonial geographers. In November 1917, he joined the *Comité d'études*, a group of scholars gathered by conservative deputy Charles Benoist to produce a number of documents that could be used by the government to study the different territorial issues that would follow the world conflict. The documents included precise reports, maps and statistical data, with geographers playing a central role (Ginsburger 2010).

If the expansion of the colonial empire was not the first preoccupation of the *Comité*, the future of German colonies and the partition of the Ottoman Empire did raise the question of France's possible claims. In 1916, the colonial party, through its deputies and the *Asie française*, had already summoned some of the most influential geographers of the time in a commission on the 'purposes' of the war, held at the *Société de géographie*. While Bernard only participated at the time in the talks about Africa, one sub-section focused on Asia and Oceania (Cloarec 2010, 278–79).[15] The sub-commission discussions on the future of Syria were led by Robert de Caix, lead member of the *Asie française* and predecessor of Froidevaux as director of its journal. The sub-commission also included Emmanuel de Martonne, central figure in French geography, founder of the *Institut de géographie* and son-in-law of Paul Vidal de la Blache, founder of the rising new French school of geography. In 1917, the *Comité d'Études* had a more official dimension but reunited some of the same experts and was co-directed by Vidal de la Blache himself. Bernard entered the committee a few months after its creation. His main achievement there was the redaction of the *Comité*'s only report on Syria, entitled *Les populations de la Syrie*, that was supported by the coloured map with the same name (figure 6.3).

The map was presented as an expert map that resembled those produced at the same time for Eastern Europe and the Balkans and were famously used in the long negotiations that led to the fragmentation of the continent and the creation of new Nation-States. Between the time of their origin in Europe in the late 1830s until the Peace Conference, ethnographic maps had acquired a strong scientific authority, mirroring the growing interests in ethnography and the rise of nationalisms throughout the continent. Such documents had already been used in diplomatic treaties in the second half of the 19th century, but in 1919, the promotion of the Wilsonian principles and the progress made in cartography granted these maps a crucial place in the delegations' argumentations (Palsky 2002). For the data, Bernard relied on Vital Cuinet, who presented, for each district of the Ottoman Empire, the religious distribution of the population. But like his colleagues from the Marseilles Congress, the geographer mostly complained about the lack of recent information, which diminished the scientific value of his work (Bernard 1919b, 858).

In terms of graphic representation, the cartographer directly followed the principles de Martonne had formulated for his ethnographic map of Romania (Bernard 1919b, 857; Palsky 2002). In order not to grant too much importance to a group spread over a large space but without a homogenous occupation of

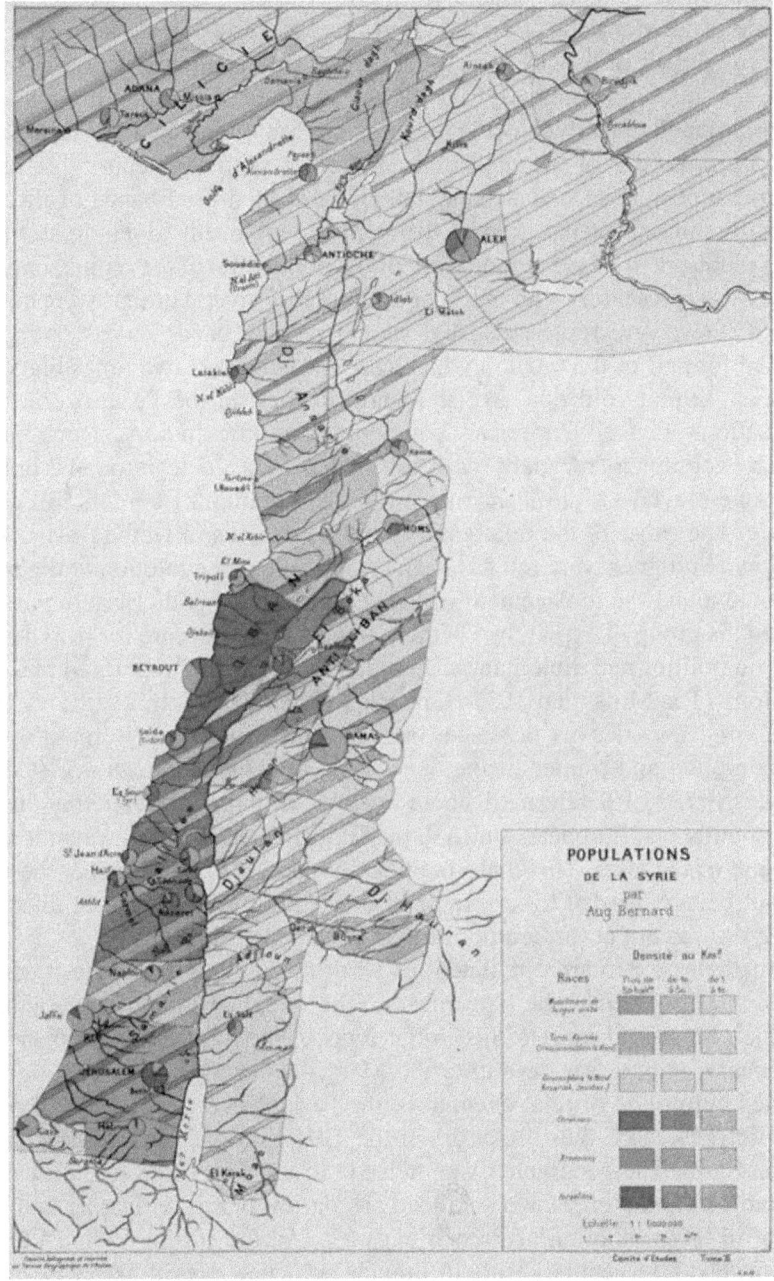

**Figure 6.3.** Bernard, Augustin, "Populations de la Syrie" in Comité d'études. 1919. Travaux du comité d'études. Tome 2. Questions européennes. Atlas. Paris: Service géographique de l'Armée.

it, he had added a density factor to the classic ethnographic colour filling. Following de Martonne, Bernard used three shades of the same colour to represent classes of density (one to ten, ten to fifty and more than fifty inhabitants per square kilometres). Likewise, to counterbalance the importance of the rural population which occupied large sparsely populated territories, both maps introduced proportional circles for cities with segments representing ethnic composition. De Martonne and Bernard then used bands of different width, to show the repartition of different groups inside given areas: if one group represented 75 percent or more of the population of the region, only this group was represented, with one opaque colour; if several groups were equally present, they were represented by several narrow bands unless one group counted for half of the total, in which case the band was two times bigger.

French experts did not have the same impact on the Peace Conference negotiations as their American counterparts of the Inquiry. None of the French geographers officially worked for the French delegation and only de Martonne played a significant role in the delimitation of borders in Eastern Europe. The cause of the relative disgrace or oblivion in which the works of the *Comité* progressively fell has been attributed to the evolution of the political context and the replacement of Prime Minister Aristide Briand, who had created the group of expert, by Clémenceau, who did not care for it, and relied more on politics and diplomacy than maps and scientific reports to make his decisions (Ter Minassian 1997; Ginsburger 2010, 692). In 1918 and 1919, the *Comité*'s work was published and an atlas, including Bernard's map, was compiled and printed at the *Service géographique de l'armée* (Comité d'études 1918; 1919). Bernard's note was placed in the last section of the second volume, on 'European and Asiatic Turkey', and the map was put at the very end of the atlas. This marginal position, added to the fact that the work had not been entrusted to an expert of the region but to Bernard, illustrates that Syria was not at the centre of the *Comité*'s attention.

Nonetheless, Bernard circulated his work through other channels, namely the *Annales géographiques*, spearhead of the 'vidalian' school of geography, in which he reused most of his initial report. The article was published on 15 January, only a few days after the Marseilles Congress for French Syria and just before the official opening of the Paris Peace Conference. Through his article, Bernard thus took part in the 1919 colonial party campaign for French Syria. The geographer was indeed closely connected to political and economic colonial elites and as a lead scholar on North Africa, he had been central in the promotion of French expansion in the region (Deprest 2009). He was also a fervent advocate of French influence, and in his 1919 article, he clearly stated his support for a French rule in Syria:

> France, now that she has triumphed in the terrible struggle that was threatening the very existence of our country, has recovered the freedom of mind that

was needed to deal with Oriental matters. . . . Our country, which for centuries has been committed to maintaining [Turkey] alive and to protecting her against herself, is, as everybody agrees, able to claim a part in her succession. This part, which is vested to her [France] by both her traditions and interests and her agreements with the Allies, is Syria.

(Bernard 1919a, 33).

Bernard was involved in some of the same networks as Henri Froidevaux, with whom he shared a mentor, colonial geographer Marcel Dubois. Bernard himself was expected to speak at the Marseilles congress, and present a 'bibliography for Syria', although his presence cannot be verified as his lecture was not published in the final proceedings of the conference.[16] Emmanuel de Martonne also appeared in the programme of the *Congrès français de la Syrie*. Although his commitments in Paris did not allow him to come to Marseilles, he did however send a paper to the Chamber of Commerce that was published in the proceedings. *L'Unité géographique de la Syrie* was based on a previous lecture he had given in 1916 at the *Société de géographie,* at one of the meetings of the Asia-Oceania sub-commission, to complete and provide geographic arguments to Robert de Caix's speech on the necessity for France to take possession of Syria (Martonne 1919), illustrating the continuity of de Martonne's involvement in the Syrian party's campaign for Syria through the war.[17]

Bernard's map, like his original report to the *Comité*, was therefore not directly conceived to be displayed in a lobbyist conference like the Marseilles congress. Contrary to Bolzé's map, his was rather an 'expert' document, only supposed to help the delegations of the Peace Conference in making their decisions. The work of the *Comité d'études* remained confidential, as only delegates of the Conference and other high-level diplomats and officers had access to the volumes and atlas. However, Bernard's connections and the organization of the public campaign for French Syria gave the documents a new importance, notably through the publication of the *Annales* article in January 1919. A few months after the publication of the map, Henri Froidevaux also published an 'ethnographic map' to illustrate one of his own articles in the *Asie française* (figure 6.5) (Froidevaux 1920). Bernard was not named, but the filiation is clear. Although a simplification of the original work, the monochrome map had the same framing and the same regional entities. It was also done by Georges Huré, who had drawn five maps for Bernard's monograph on Morocco a few years earlier (Bernard 1913).

The campaign for French Syria therefore took place at a time when older conceptions of empire and world order were being challenged and reshuffled. The choice of economic and ethnographic cartography illustrates how cartographic strategies evolved and adapted to this shift. The level of intertextuality and the evolution of maps through circulation from sketches to large coloured maps also show a collective process where maps are the products of constant negotiations. The number of different actors involved, and the role played by Syrian map-producers, like Salim Cressaty or Abdullah Thomeh, show that these cartographic strategies moved between Beirut, Marseilles, Paris and other places. In order to defend and shape the structure of France's imperial presence in Syria, these groups functioned as a transnational epistemic community with shared interests and that relied on one another.[18] In what follows, I show that the French informal Syrian empire, structured by these enmeshed human networks, also relied on deeply rooted geographical imaginaries of connection, which brought Syria closer to France.

## BINDING SYRIA TO FRANCE: MATERIAL AND GRAPHIC NETWORKS OF THE FRENCH EMPIRE

In his famous history of lines, anthropologist Tim Ingold uses a cartographic metaphor to state that 'imperial powers have sought to occupy the inhabited world, throwing a network of connections across what appeared, in their eyes, to be not a tissue of trails but a blank surface' (Ingold 2016, 89–90). Ingold proposes that modern cartography and empire express a shared, modern, conception of space, the 'occupant knowledge', as opposed to that of the 'inhabitant'. Imperial ships, armies and companies moved not *in* space, but *across* it, connecting sites of settlement and extraction, and dismissing what laid in-between. The development of European capitalist interests in the Levant in the late 19th century brought the 'occupant's' eye to the region. The time was one of transcontinental networks, grand infrastructure projects and the globalization of financial markets. The linkage of the Orient to Europe was done through the construction of kilometres of roads, railroads, cables and the opening of shipping lines. Interconnection meant European domination and, in 1881, the Ottoman finances were put under joint European supervision. At the turn of the century, the region was put on the world map, but that map was drawn by European imperial powers. Two astronomical observatories were built by the American Protestant mission in Beirut and by French Jesuits in Ksara, producing the first modern astronomical determinations of latitude and longitude, therefore symbolically attaching Beirut to the global grid, centred on Paris and London.

These connections and the power struggle they implied were key in building an imaginary of proximity in time and space between France and the Levant, and Syria in particular. Cartography was central in giving shape and coherence to these intricate and sometimes discontinuous or immaterial networks that made France's Levantine empire. The materiality of distance remained indeed the main obstacle to imperial domination as European conceptions of empire as a unified, coherent whole were contradicted by its actual fragmentation. The representation of networks of transportation and commercial exchanges on maps offered both a graphical solution to this discontinuity and an expression of 'occupant knowledge'. Lines and arrows were used to attach patches of lands to the mainland and to each other, presenting the empire as a reticular yet continuous space. In the 19th century, imaginaries and representations of connectivity had therefore matured in intellectual circles, progressively attaching Syria to France. In this section, I propose to briefly examine these geographical imaginaries of connection by looking at how they operated at different scales and how they echoed in Bolzé and Bernard's maps, only to serve specific imperial strategies in a particular political context.

## BRIDGING CONTINENTS: SYRIA AS A GLOBAL RAIL HUB

In 1884, geographer Élisée Reclus, brother of Onésime, published the ninth volume of his *Nouvelle géographie universelle* on *Asie antérieure*. In Reclus's historical theory of space inherited in part from Carl Ritter, the Near-East held a special place in the organization of the world, as a bridge between continents, and a central position in the path of civilization, between its origins in the East and its flowering in the West. This role was determined by the region's geographical position between East and West but also by its 'geographical form', 'that accounts well for the area's advantages as center of civilization. Not only is it located more or less at the geometrical center of the group of land that forms the Ancient World, but it offers at the same time the easiest passage between the three continents and the great maritime sides' (Reclus 1884, 2–5). Placed at the centre of this regional mass, Syria held an even more central position: 'No crossing point is more important in the Mediterranean than the road that goes from Jerusalem to Damascus' (Reclus 1884, 689). A bridge between the great centres of civilization, Egypt, Mesopotamia and Anatolia, Syria was presented as a corridor, a road rather than a space, that connected continents and therefore stood at the centre of the world.

Reclus's work deeply influenced geographers and other scholars that came after him. Henri Lammens, the Jesuit father in charge of educating the future leaders of Lebanese nationalism, referred to Reclus's volume on numerous occasions and started his famous textbook by celebrating 'Syria's lucky situation', a 'land located at the cross-roads of the three continents of the Ancient World'.[19] In his January 1919 article, Augustin Bernard also quoted Reclus and repeated what had become a commonplace: 'Syria is essentially a crossroad: it is its essential feature [sic]' (Bernard 1919a).[20] And in Marseilles, Syria was again presented as 'the natural passage between Egypt and the Tigris and Euphrates valleys' (Huart 1919). This image was directly echoed

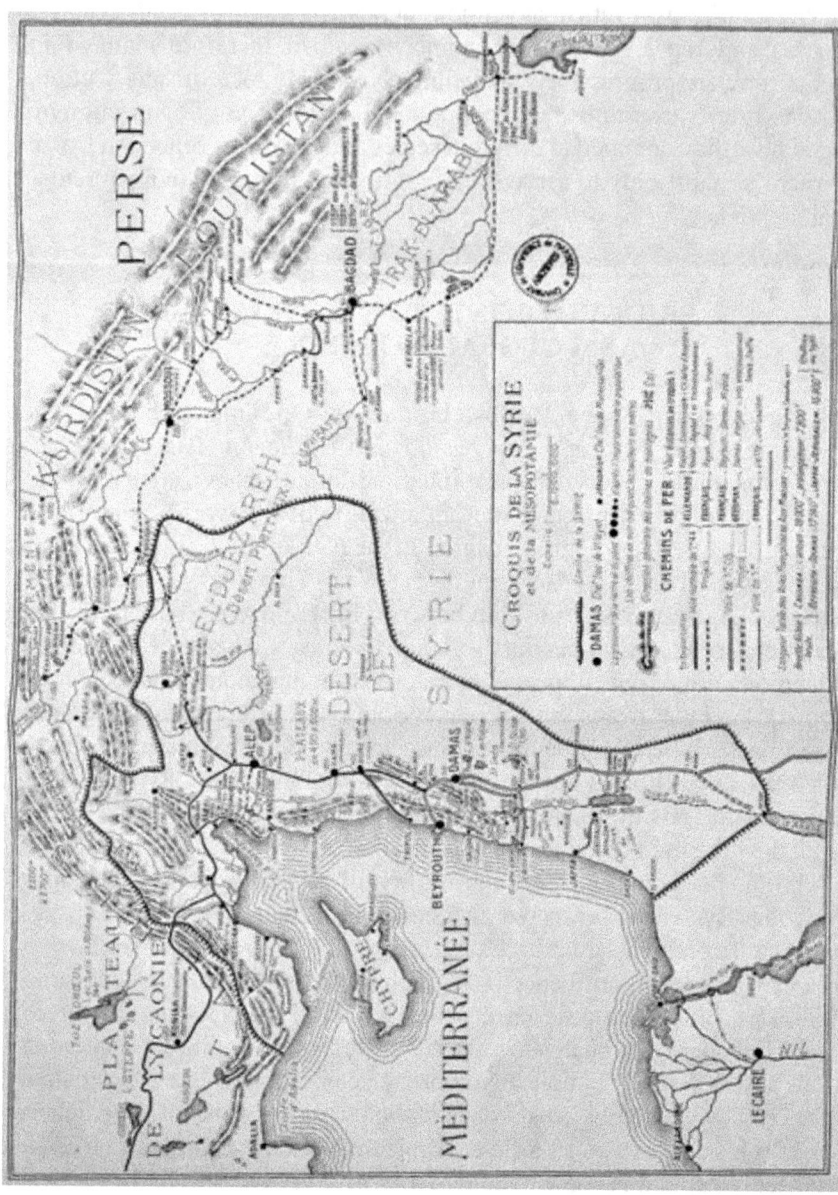

Figure 6.4. Sketch of Syria and Mesopotamia Attached to the Note on the economic Value of Syria Sent to the Ministry of Foreign Affairs by the Chamber of Commerce of Marseilles in July 1915, Archives of the Chamber of Commerce of Marseilles, MQ 5435. Courtesy of the Chambre de commerce de Marseille.

by the reality of the development of rail in the Ottoman Empire. Located between Europe and its Asian colonies, the region was indeed looked at by great powers as a transit zone, a bridge to Asia, and many different projects were designed to connect the Mediterranean to the Persian Gulf.[21] The opening of the Suez Canal in 1869 had already brought Asia closer to Europe, but in the 1880s, European companies backed by their governments engaged in an intense competition over rail in order to be granted concessions inside the Empire's territory. In 1893, the *Deutsche Bank* started financing a line that would connect Baghdad to the already German-built Anatolian network, to the Ottoman capital and to the whole of Europe (McMurray 2001). Confirming the primacy of German influence in Istanbul, the *Bagdadbahn* would create a direct land route between European capitals and Asia. As the natural 'road' from South to North and from West to East, Syria was deemed to be placed at the centre of the new networks that connected the modern world. In 1919, the geopolitics of rail were of course in all minds and the route of the *Bagdadbahn* determined the extension of the European zones of influence. Likewise, controlling the route between India and the Mediterranean was one of the reasons why Whitehall wanted Palestine to be administrated by Britain, in order to protect Suez from French influence.

At the end of the 19th century, interest for what the rail hub Syria was to become saw the emergence of a particular cartographic genre, with maps and sketches offering comparisons of operating and projected lines. From precise traverse survey maps to general sketches, these networks maps were maps of occupation. Drawing continuous or dotted black competing lines on a white background, they transformed the Syrian land into an object of desire, a technical space that could be rationalized and put to profit in the greater scheme of transcontinental connection (Christensen 2017). The 1913–1919 French maps produced by the colonial lobby directly inherited from these. The sketch map accompanying the first memorandum of the Marseilles Chamber of Commerce (figure 6.4) only represented operating and projected rail lines. Syria was therefore placed at the centre of the region's main rail route, from Anatolia to the Persian Gulf. By depicting a complex web of lines, rail and maritime lines, Bolzé's map also reproduced a representation of the region common to the readers of the time, showing dark lines connecting Alexandretta or Istanbul to Persia.

## A SYRIAN ISLAND IN A FRENCH MEDITERRANEAN

Bolzé's map was a vivid illustration of a symbolic appropriation of the Ottoman territory through cartography (figure 6.5). All the different elements gave a picture of a coherent French Levant structured by areas (1), lines (2) and nodes (3): the Ottoman space disappeared behind consular territories

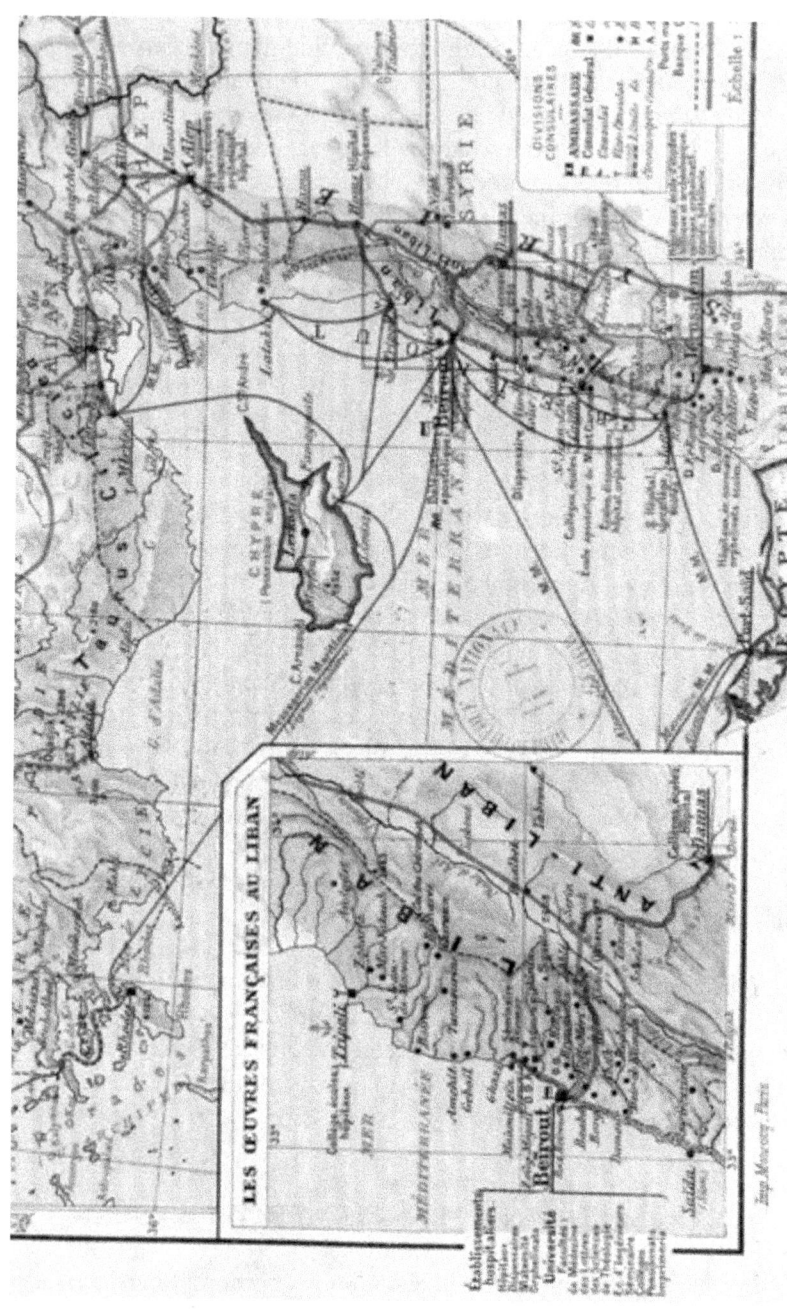

Figure 6.5. Bolzé, René. 1920. 'Carte des intérêts français au Liban'. Published in Congrès français de la Syrie, Congrès français de la syrie et Chambre de commerce de Marseille, 1919. Fascicule 2. Paris; Marseille: E. Champion. Courtesy of the Bibliothèque nationale de France.

and limits (1), represented through thick yellow lines mimicking state borders, and opaque, densely hatched, pink 'zones' of French economic action, crisscrossed by a dense network of numerous communication lines (2), and framed by a compact web of institutions (3): consulates, schools, orphanages etc. Provincial limits were cited last, and represented with a dotted line, a sign already used for consular divisions . . . Bolzé's map also clearly leaned west, with the left-hand side packed with dots, lines and colours, contrasting with the empty sand-yellow right-hand side.

The *France du Levant* was indeed a coastal one and Syria, like the rest of the Levant, belonged to a larger entity, central to the geographical conception of the evolution of the French empire: the Mediterranean Sea (Bourguet, Lepetit, and Nordman 1998). During the 19th century, the conception of the Mediterranean in French geography had evolved from the 'classical' definition of the sea as a natural boundary, to the identification of a common natural space, determined by botanic, geological and ultimately human features (Blais and Deprest 2012). Erasing the symbolic continental division between Europe and its neighbours, this idea was central to the process of symbolic and concrete appropriation of the meridional shore of the Mediterranean. The identification of Algeria not as African but as Mediterranean contributed to the intellectual legitimization of its colonization. French geographers transferred part of the geographical images produced on Algeria and other parts of the Mediterranean to Syria. Reclus for instance, presented it as a 'narrow zone of inhabited countries [sic]', that stretched on the oriental bank of the Mediterranean (Reclus 1884, 685), and in 1919, Bernard used a similar image:

> What strikes in the shape of Syria is the narrowness of this strip of territory, long by more than one thousand kilometers and large by just a hundred and fifty kilometers. Because of this, some have compared it to Italy, the desert replacing the Adriatic on one of its sides; one could also draw a parallel with Egypt, the Mediterranean having the same vital role as the Nile for the inhabitants of its valley.
> (Bernard 1919a, 35)

The two comparisons were of course not neutral, as Bernard, associating Syria with these centres of Ancient history, proceeded in 'anchoring' Syria in a shared history and in a coherent regional entity: Syria was yet another of the great peninsulas in this cradle of history. This geographical definition of Syria as a narrow strip of land surrounded by natural boundaries, sea and desert, thus accentuated its maritime nature and brought it closer to Europe. The Syrian 'peninsula', separated from its continent by the desert, was more Mediterranean than Asiatic, and was bound to enter the existing French Mediterranean empire.[22] In 1891 Abudullah Thomeh's 'commercial map' was one of those reproducing and picturing this image of insularity. In the map, Syria, drawn as a narrow coastal strip, densely populated and bustling with economic activity, was graphically detached from the continent, a white void in the east, while firmly tied to the west by the many lines representing navigation lines and maritime cables. Bolzé's map, picturing a dense and pink-filled area of French rail domination, separated from the empty interior and attached by a web of French strings also already connected the Syrian 'island' to the French empire. Filling the coast with vivid colours, Bernard's ethnographic map also left the interior entirely empty, without any colours and devoid of any graphic information (figure 6.3).

## CONNECTING SYRIA'S PARTS

The graphic accumulation of symbols of French presence in Syria in Bolzé's map shaped the form of the French sphere of influence, legitimizing, and almost naturalizing, French claims: it 'revealed', and proved, the density and the extension of French influence, making visible a concrete picture of French Syria. The choice to represent railroads not only through lines, but also through pink-filled regions of exclusive French activity was particularly powerful, as the 'zone' expanded along the Mediterranean coast, from Bethlehem to Aleppo, including Palestine. Henri Froidevaux's geographic definition of 'integral Syria, in other words the region that extends from the Cilician gates to the Dead Sea and from the Mediterranean Sea to the loop of the Euphrates' was thus confirmed by the map: Syria was a clearly delimited country and it was there that French interests had concentrated. Such argumentation illustrated the entanglement of geographical, economic and political debates around the definition of Syria. Following Volney, most authors accepted a geographical definition of Syria that went from the Taurus to the Red Sea and from the Mediterranean to the Euphrates, as Élisée Reclus did, but also most British scholars.[23] Unsurprisingly, therefore, we find Bernard, Froidevaux or de Martonne presenting the same definition in 1919.

Although commonly accepted, this geographical definition was, however, used in 1919 to defend political claims and to denounce the partition of Syria into different zones of influence or different states. Syria was a whole, and anyone trying to divide it would oppose nature's laws by threatening the existence of an amputated country. Like others before them, French geographers insisted on the orographic unity of the country, centred around two mountainous ranges separated by the Syrian trench (the Jordan, Bekaa and Orontes valleys). Likewise, the 'natural' border of the country was the desert, as it was for Algeria. In front of the colonial lobby in 1916, de Martonne had insisted on the climatic argument stating that 'the true boundary of Syria is the desert, which reaches the coast at Gaza'.[24] Putting the climatic limit at Gaza condemned the exclusion of Palestine and directly opposed the recently signed Sykes-Picot agreement, and British claims over Palestine. This issue of natural limits had already been a political matter a few decades before. In the 1880s, considering that Anatolia and Mesopotamia were lost respectively to Russia and Great Britain, captain Louis de Torcy led a mission to Syria and urged France to invest in Syria.[25] As the 1878 convention had granted Great Britain the right to defend Asia Minor, de Torcy took several pages to justify how he drew the border between that region and northern Syria. As in 1916–1919 with the eastern and southern desert border, delineating Syria equalled determining where British influence should stop.

However, the argument of geographical unity used to denounce partition and the British will to divide the country was almost always followed by the acknowledgment of fragmentation. Far from nullifying other imperial arguments, physical and social fragmentation even became a reason for French intervention. In 1884, Reclus had already noted that the region was 'divided in different countries by climate and historical evolution. . . . The great length of the territory, comparatively to its narrow width, has diminished its cohesion force; the populations, without a common center, living in basins separated by high mountains, have divided into different groups' (Reclus 1884, 685–86). Acknowledging the problem, de Torcy wished to solve it by building what he called a 'Syrian' rail network to connect separated yet complementary parts of the land, and unite major metropolises of the hinterland and fertile regions of the Orontes, Bekaa and Hauran, with the coast, thus offering new commercial opportunities. Built according to the topographic organization of the land, this modern and fast rail network would consequently rely on and reinforce the country's natural and historic homogeneity.

Echoing the emerging idea of the primacy of economic development (*mise en valeur*) idea at the end of the century, French capitalists did invest in Syrian rail and ports, eventually giving birth to a Syrian network similar to what de Torcy had imagined, with economic and social implications that certainly played a part in shaping a 'Syrian' geography (Lantz 2005). And although the rail had indeed contributed to 'connecting' the different parts of the Syrian body, it conversely helped define the extent of Syria and served as an argument for French colonial lobbyists to defend their interests. The cartographical representation of these Syrian networks was therefore central to the argumentation for the unity of the territory, the Deraa-Damas-Aleppo line, partly laid in the central Syrian trench, acting as the country's backbone, as shown in Bolzé's map and in the *Comité central syrien's* adaptation of it (figure 6.2). After geographical Syria had inspired the French network its shape, French rail became an argument in the territorial definition of a French Syria.

However, in 1919, the fragmentation argument remained. Like Reclus fifty years before him, Bernard believed that human fragmentation prevented the unification of the country. Syria's crossroad position, which had shaped its unique destiny, also made it a bottleneck where different peoples had come to meet and battle (Bernard 1919a, 38). But Reclus was a libertarian involved in the anarchist movement, and he used this fragmentation as the proof that geographical unity did not determine political unity. In 1919 however, fragmentation was on the contrary used as an argument for French intervention. Underlining the religious or ethnic diversity was first of all a direct response to national aspirations. Already in 1916, the perspective of the consolidation of an anti-French national Syrian movement helped by the British had led de Martonne to state that 'the ethnography of Syria offers such a mix of races and religions that it is impossible to speak of a Syrian nationality. . . . Syria for the Syrians is a senseless phrase'.[26] In 1919, France had managed to gather Francophile Syrians around her in the *Comité central syrien*, but a new threat had since then emerged with Arab nationalists who relied on the McMahon-Hussein promise to see the creation of an Arab state which included Syria.

This political and ideological context thus sheds a new light on Bernard's expert map. Like the other ethnographic maps presented at the Peace Conference, it presented a strong political bias, highlighting in this case the human fragmentation of the country in order to legitimate French oversight. As a comparison, in 1917, the main British ethnographic map available for the region filled the whole of Syria in blue and called its people 'Arab', with an East-West division between nomadic and settled.[27] But in contrast, Bernard chose to multiply different categories, which accentuated an impression of 'ethnic' chaos, with almost no fully filled, homogeneous, region. What he called 'races' actually implied a mix of religious (Muslim, Christian, Druze . . .), linguistic (Arabic-speaking or not) and ethnic (Kurdish, Turk . . .) affiliation, enhancing the idea of an intricate mess. A canvas of coloured stripes, the map directly echoed Bernard's text where he talked of the 'vivid colors of a carpet'.

Picturing a fragmented Syria meant that a Syrian unitary nation-state could not exist at this point in time. However, Bernard did not oppose the idea of a Syrian nation as did de Martonne. A supporter of Lyautey's actions in Morocco and of the 'associationist' approach to colonial rule, Bernard was strongly connected to the Republican colonialists who supported a form of indirect rule and opposed settler colonization. He was also a strong advocate of the secular state and of the French conception of the nation. As such, he opposed Pan-Islamism but also British-backed Zionism, for being incoherent because they relied on religion (Bernard 1919b, 854–55). In his text, he transposed the French Republican ideal to Syria, where a modern state would eventually make religious differences disappear into the national *creuset* (crucible), as the country seemed 'ready to understand the fundamental occidental idea: the secularization of civil society'. The vivid colours of the different communities would thus be interwoven like in his map, shaping the nation's fabric. This conception also favoured the choice of France as a legal guardian and a mediator between communities: 'no other power is best prepared to this task than France where the Edict of Nantes and the Revolution took place, which first among all nations allowed Protestants and Jews inside the nation' (Bernard 1919a, 49). If France was to rule over Syria, for Bernard, this rule had therefore to be indirect, and to include all communities. Before they could merge into one nation, these groups had to be respected, which is why he proposed a fragmented political organization, building on what the map had revealed:

> One can imagine that, with time, three nuclei would eventually form: the North and East of Syria, with Alep and Damascus, mainly Muslim; the Center, with Beirut, the Lebanon and the Haouran, mostly Christian or Druze, the South, with Haifa and Jerusalem, presenting a relatively high portion of Israelite elements: all autonomous republics that would compose the United States of Syria.
> (Bernard 1919a, 48).

This Republican vision of what Syria should become also meant that Bernard advocated the defence of all communities on equal grounds. In this, he opposed the more traditional stance of the most catholic part of the colonial party, who wished to build France's influence only on its historical protectorate over Eastern Christians. Officers and scholars involved in the administration and study of Algeria and West Africa had indeed stressed that a Syrian strategy which played France's Lebanese Maronites protected favourites against Muslim Syrians could damage France's image in other parts of the Empire. In 1918, Bernard entered the *Commission interministérielle des affaires musulmanes* and was actively involved in the debates on the Republic's 'Muslim' strategy. Picturing France as an 'Arab' or 'Muslim' power also acted as an argument in favour of a French Syria, building on the memory of previous attempts to promote the emergence of an 'Arab kingdom' under French protection (Laurens 1990). As the only European power to have an experience in a similar geographical and human region, France was the natural choice for Syria, and Syria would complete the Mediterranean and Muslim empire. However, although he wanted to picture the 'racial' diversity of the country, Bernard still used an intense red to represent the non-Armenian Christian population. The Maronite country, which was likewise conveniently located at the centre of the map, was also the only fully filled area on the map. This granted a special place to the western slopes of the Lebanese range, inhabited by a majority of Christian Maronites. This detail brings some nuance to Bernard's inclusive and secular stance as, like most of his contemporaries, he saw in the Christian Maronites a useful ally to the French, a territorially and socially coherent core, around which the new Syrian nation-state could be built under French supervision.[28]

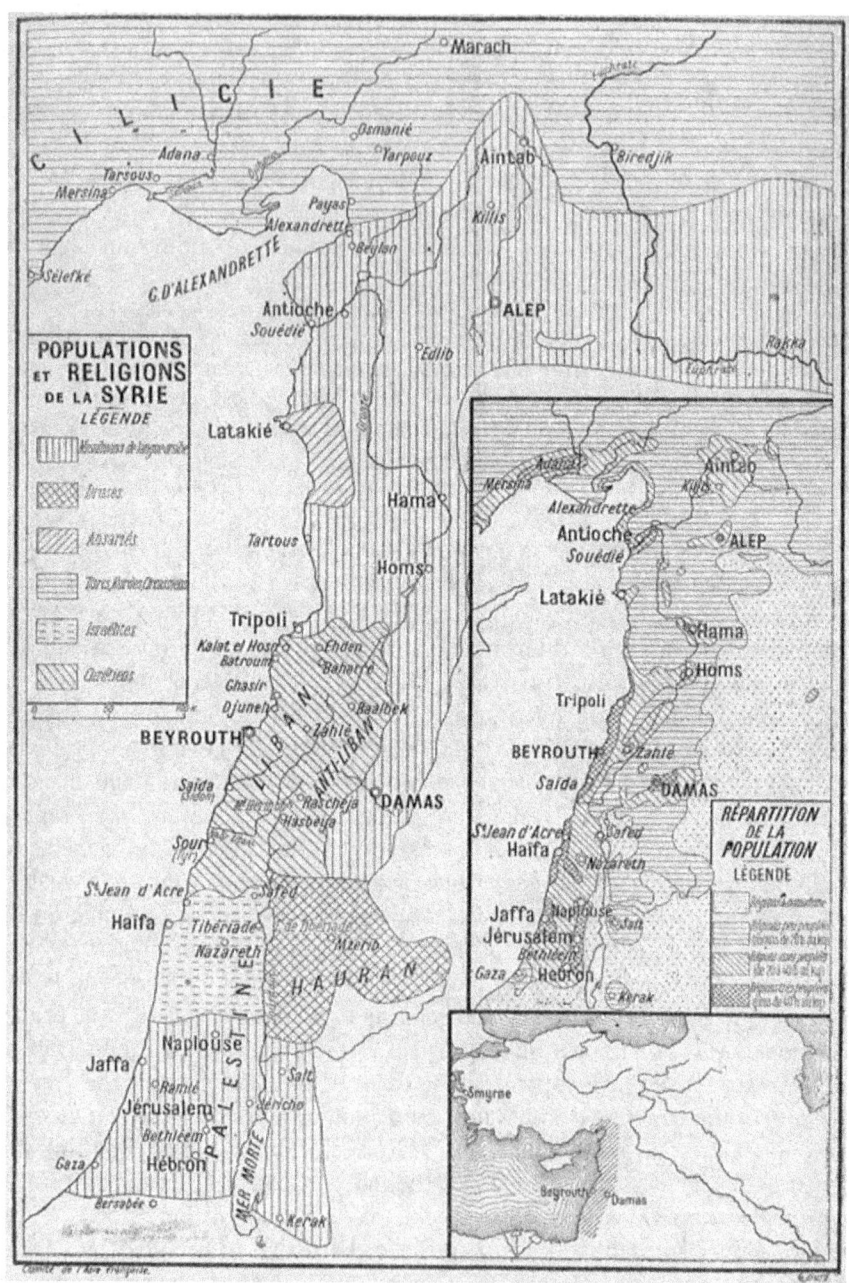

Figure 6.6. Map of the Populations and religions of Syria, in Froidevaux, Henri. 'Les difficultés de la France en Syrie. Leurs causes'» *L'Asie Française* 20, n0. 179 (février 1920): 43–47. Courtesy of the Bibliothèque nationale de France.

As mentioned, Bernard's original map was then reused by his colleagues George Huré and Henri Froidevaux in February 1920 to illustrate an article in the *Asie française* (Froidevaux 1920). At that time, France's rule was organizing in Syria after the British withdrawal, but was facing many difficulties, holding back the Turks in the North and the Arab nationalists in the East. Once again, Froidevaux claimed that Syria's main problem, and the major obstacle to France's rule, was ethnic fragmentation: 'a simple glance at an ethnographic map of the region is enough to make one understand what a true mosaic of peoples inhabits Syria'. However, Bernard's original complex and nuanced map was grossly simplified: the density classes were removed, and each region was given a unique filling, replacing the interwoven stripes of Bernard's carpet with a juxtaposition of homogenous blocks (figure 6.6).

Froidevaux's aim here was to give fragmentation a political meaning, illustrating the thesis supported by his former colleague of the *Comité de l'Asie française* Robert de Caix, who had since become the general secretary to the French-High Commissioner in the Levant. De Caix proposed a 'cantonal' organization of Syria, a division of the territory into a number of small but homogenous territories. This solution resembled Augustin Bernard's United States of Syria, but from the beginning Bernard also warned that different populations would still be found in the same regions, and especially in cities. For Bernard, a differentiated administration was a means to national unity that would absorb fragmentation in time. But Froidevaux and de Caix naturalized these divisions and used them to justify and enhance their power. The new map had to show and prove the existence of a 'cantonal' Syria, explaining why Huré simplified the regional distribution of religious groups and removed the proportional circles for cities that Bernard had precisely drawn to express that urban centres would never present a uniform 'ethnic' composition.

## CONCLUSION: CIRCULATING MAPS AND CONFLICTING STRATEGIES

The history of the two thematic maps presented in this chapter offers interesting insights on the role cartography played during the partition of the Middle East in the beginning of the 20th century and, more generally, on the history of the relation between cartography and imperial space-making. France's informal empire in Syria before 1919 was structured on a transnational network of merchants, capitalists and scholars moving between Paris, Lyons, Marseilles and the coastal cities of the Levant. As we demonstrated, this reticular empire made of circulations was articulated with deeply rooted, century-long geographical imaginaries of connectivity. These two related forms of social and discursive 'connectivities' materially and conceptually attached Syria to France and its existing empire. The events of 1916–1920 pushed these networks and their imaginaries to the forefront, where they were put in discourses and maps but also reorganized and modified.

Rather than two static pictures used in political debates, the two maps discussed in this chapter appear as a series of interconnected and evolving objects integrated in complex cartographic strategies. Henri Froidevaux's reuse of Augustin Bernard's map shows that the same material was used to support conflicting strategies. In this case, the life of his ethnographic map illustrates how the way Syria's social fragmentation was intellectually dealt with time and according to political positions. In 1884, the anarchist Reclus exposed that the Syrian nation did not exist and that they 'knew unity only through commune servitude' (Reclus 1884, 686). In 1919, Bernard, as a republican colonial geographer, wrote that 'a mediator must put himself between different populations . . . and teach them mutual respect' (Bernard 1919a, 49). A year later, Robert de Caix, the colonial administrator who tried to secure French domination in Syria and Lebanon, stated that Syria should be like 'a stained-glass window bound together by French lead', promoting a classical divide and rule policy.[29]

Through their use of cartography in the 1919 campaign for French Syria, colonial actors adapted to the political and epistemic challenges of the period. By producing economic and ethnographic thematic maps, they were first trying to answer a shift in the perception of empire. To fit in the new *international* order, European influence had to present itself as indirect, respectful of national aspirations all the while profitable for both the metropolis and the overseas territory. More generally, colonial actors adjusted their language to that of their time, adapting to the increasing role maps and economic and statistical expertise had taken in the settlement of territorial negotiations. They did so by producing their own ethnographical and economic maps, on the margins of the Peace Conference. Both these evolutions were echoed in the following period. The Mandate regime was indeed designed to both satisfy European claims and prepare national independences. It also accentuated the role given to experts and expertise in the administration of overseas territory (Dakhli 2010; Bourmaud, Neveu, and Verdeil 2017) and allowed for the emergence of a new international oversight on imperial matters (Pedersen 2015). However, both before and after 1919, this shift in discourses often acted as a camouflage for colonial domination and the establishment of a direct, violent and arbitrary order.

The two maps I presented did not have a directly visible impact on the new territories created, as opposed to other national delegation or inter-imperial agreement maps. However, the cartographic strategies analysed in the chapter contributed to granting a tangible shape to a certain image of Syria.

With the creation of the French Levant States, the cartographic definition of 'Syria' fundamentally changed: from a long and narrow strip of land facing west, it became a continental and arid triangular bloc. But if, as Kaufman recalls, the borders of what eventually became the state of Syria were indeed drawn by default, once Palestine, Transjordan, Lebanon and Turkey had been delineated, in 1919, the 'geo-body' of a greater Syria very much existed and even prevailed over others. It was framed by 'natural' borders, the desert and the sea, and organized along two parallel ranges and structured around a coherent (French) rail network. Although this geo-body did not become in turn an actual state, it was appropriated and adapted by Pan-Syrian nationalist narratives, which continue to this day to condemn its partition into smaller entities. Moreover, the representation of Syria at play in the two maps we studied echoes the way this same region is still represented in history books and in the media, questioning the permanence of colonial imaginaries, and the way maps impact how we understand the world. A patchwork of intricate yet mismatching spots of vivid colours *showing* to the novice reader the animosity between, for instance, Sunnis and Shias; a desert crisscrossed by darks lines connecting oil producers and consumers, *illustrating* the inextricable geopolitics of pipes, the scene is still set in a closed arena made of sand, bounded by seas and steep mountains, on the way between Europe and Asia.

## NOTES

1. The video is shown and put into context in this BBC article: *BBC News*. 2014. 'Isis Rebels Declare "Islamic State"', 30 June 2014, sect. Middle East. https://www.bbc.com/news/world-middle-east-28082962.

2. The initial March 1916 agreement was later amended, in order to include the other European Allies. New agreements were signed in October 1916 with Russia and in August 1917 with Italy.

3. The mandate regime created by the League of Nations was applied to the 'colonies and territories' that were no longer ruled by their previous sovereign but were inhabited by peoples not yet 'able to stand by themselves' (article 22 of the Covenant of the League of Nations). The states of Greater Lebanon, Aleppo, Damascus and of the Druze were proclaimed in September 1920. The Alexandretta Sanjak was detached from the State of Aleppo in 1923 and in 1924. The State of the Alawites was created on the coast north of Lebanon. In 1925 the States of Damascus and Aleppo merged with the State of Syria. The British Mandate was proclaimed in April 1920, and Palestine and the Transjordan Emirate were separated in 1923.

4. The phrase comes from a famous passage by David Fromkin (Fromkin 1989, 17). Several maps were attached to the different versions of the written agreement. The most famous one is a copy of the Royal Geographical Society 1910

'Map of eastern Turkey in Asia, Syria and western Persia' with the different zones delineated and colour filed. It was signed by Sykes and Georges-Picot and attached by Cambon, French ambassador in London to Grey.

5. Building on Castoriadis, Derek Gregory has defined the phrase 'geographical imaginary' as a 'taken-for-granted spatial ordering of the world', 'a more or less unconscious and unreflective construction' (Gregory 2009, 282).

6. Spatiality is here intended as the 'mode(s) in which space is implicated in the constitution and conduct of life on Earth' (Gregory 2009, 715–16), implying that space, or part of it, is the product of social practices.

7. We refer here to the different 'modes of cartographic writing' used in the History of Cartography Project of the University of Chicago. A general or geographical map is a small-scale map with few details and generally intended for a large audience. A topographic map is a large-scale map based of geodetic measure and triangulation, usually produced by official, military or public institutions. By pseudo-topographical, I mean large- of intermediary-scale maps that pretend to be only based on thorough surveys and adopt the graphic characteristics of topographic maps but are mostly based on compilations and not on surveys. Thematic maps depict the spatial repartition of natural or social phenomena, using specific graphic devices (like choropleth maps, or proportional circles maps; Edney 2015).

8. In December 1918 Clémenceau had indeed agreed to the addition of Palestine and Mosul in Britain's share.

9. All quotations, originally in French, are translated by the author.

10. 'Note sur la valeur économique de la Syrie', Archives of the Chamber of Commerce of Marseilles, MQ 5435.

11. The Ottoman public debt administration was created in 1881 to collect the payments owed to European companies. It had control on many sectors of the Ottoman economy.

12. "*Croquis de la Syrie et de la mésopotamie*" in 'Note sur la valeur économique de la Syrie', Archives of the Chamber of Commerce of Marseilles, MQ 5435.

13. Thomeh was not physically present in Marseilles, and his presentation was read on the January 4 by another member of the Congress.

14. Froidevaux later wrote that although Thomeh's work was 'very worthy', his presentation lacked the 'scientific proof and specimens of maps that would have given it a great importance' (Froidevaux 1919a).

15. Bibliothèque Nationale de France (BNF), archives of the *Société de géographie* (SG), Colis 9, notices 2268 to 2291.

16. His name appears only in the December programme of the conference. Archives of the Chamber of Commerce of Marseilles, MQ 5435.

17. 'Conférence de Robert de Caix et Emmanuel de Martonne', BNF, archives of the *Société de géographie* (SG), Colis 9, notices 2269 bis.

18. On the role of the Syrian diaspora in the 1919 negotiations and on the way colonial lobbyist tries to use this other network of empire, see Arsan (2012) and Fahrenthold (2013).

19. Archives of the Jesuit Université Saint Joseph, Beyrouth, 4J3 'Henri Lammens, Géographie du Liban'. Reclus's words also transpired from another of Lammens's lecture from 1915 (Lammens 1915). See also Lammens's 1921 textbook.

20. Reclus is named in page 47 and the quote is from page 38.
21. The most famous being Francis Chesney's plan to build a rail-line between Alexandretta and the Euphrates.
22. For Reclus, the whole of *Asie antérieure*, surrounded by sea, was also 'almost insular' (Reclus 1884, 4).
23. See, for instance, the definition given in 1865 by the lead scholar in scriptural geography (Robinson 1865).
24. 'Conférence de Robert de Caix et Emmanuel de Martonne', BNF, archives of the *Société de géographie* (SG), Colis 9, notices 2269 bis.
25. Archives of the *Service historique de la défense*, Versailles, 'Rapport d'ensemble sur la mission du Capitaine Torcy en Syrie avril-juin 1880', GR7N1643.
26. 'Conférence de Robert de Caix et Emmanuel de Martonne', BNF, archives of the *Société de géographie* (SG), Colis 9, notices 2269 bis.
27. Royal Geographical Society, 1917. 'Map of Eastern Turkey in Asia, Syria and Western Persia (Ethnographical)'.
28. This idea was shared by a number of French and Syrian nationalists. Lammens, for instance, saw Lebanon as the cradle of civilization in the region and the core around which all the parts of new Syria would unite and thrive, as Prussia and Piedmont had been for Germany and Italy. As he wrote, 'Lebanon is to Syria what the Nile is to Egypt' quoted by Firro (2004, 15).
29. '*Ainsi organisée la Syrie devait, pendant un certain nombre d'années au moins être comme un vitrail dont le plomb serait français*'. Note to the Quai d'Orsay, 26 January 1920. Archives of the *Centre diplomatique de La Courneuve*, Syrie-Liban 1918–1929 vol. 22 fol 50–77.

## REFERENCES

### Printed Primary Sources

Bernard, Augustin. 1913. *Le Maroc: avec cinq cartes hors texte*. Paris: F. Alcan.
———. 1919a. 'La Syrie et les syriens'. *Annales de Géographie* 28 (151): 33–51.
———. 1919b. 'Populations de la Syrie'. In *Travaux du comité d'études. Tome 2. Questions européennes. Atlas*, edited by Comité d'études, 847–59. Paris: Service géographique de l'Armée.
Comité central syrien. 1919. *La Syrie devant la Conférence*. Paris (3 rue Lafitte):
Comité d'études. 1918. *Travaux du comité d'études. Tome 1. L'Alsace-Lorraine et la frontière du Nord-Est*. Paris: Imprimerie Nationale.
———. 1919. *Travaux du comité d'études. Tome 2. Questions européennes*. Paris: Imprimerie Nationale.
Cuinet, Vital. 1896. *Syrie, Liban et Palestine, géographie administrative, statistique, descriptive et raisonnée*. Paris: E. Leroux.
Froidevaux, Henri. 1919a. 'La géographie au Congrès français de la Syrie'. *La géographie* 32 (5): 309–20.
———. 1919b. 'Une carte des Intérêts français dans la Turquie d'Asie en 1914'. In *Congrès français de la Syrie: 3, 4 et 5 janvier 1919*, edited by Congrès français

de la Syrie, Paul Huvelin, and Chambre de commerce de Marseille, 211–17. Paris; Marseille: E. Champion; Secrétariat Chambre de Commerce.

———. 1920. 'Les difficultés de la France en Syrie. Leurs causes'. *L'Asie Française* 20 (179): 43–47.

Huart, Clément. 1919. 'Les frontières naturelles de la Syrie'. In *Congrès français de la Syrie: 3, 4 et 5 janvier 1919. Fascicule 2*, edited by Congrès français de la Syrie, Paul Huvelin, and Chambre de commerce de Marseille, 139–44. Paris; Marseille: E. Champion; Secrétariat Chambre de Commerce.

Huvelin, Paul. 1919. *Que Vaut la Syrie? Congrès français de la Syrie: 3, 4 et 5 janvier 1919. Fascicule 1*, edited by Congrès français de la Syrie and Chambre de commerce de Marseille. Paris; Marseille: E. Champion.

Lammens, Henri. 1915. *Lammens: la Syrie et sa mission historique: Conférence faite à la Société Sultanieh de géographie, le 23 Janvier 1915*. Le Caire: Al-Maaref.

———. 1921. *La Syrie: précis historique*. Beyrouth: Imprimerie Catholique.

Martonne, Emmanuel de. 1919. 'L'unité géographique de la Syrie'. In *Congrès français de la Syrie: 3, 4 et 5 janvier 1919. Fascicule 2*, edited by Chambre de commerce de Marseille, 226–29. Paris; Marseille: E. Champion; Secrétariat Chambre de Commerce.

Reclus, Élisée. 1884. *Nouvelle géographie universelle. Tome 9, l'Asie antérieure*. Paris: Hachette.

Robinson, Edward. 1865. *Physical Geography of the Holy Land*. London: J. Murray.

## Secondary Literature

Arsan, Andrew. 2012. ' "This Age Is the Age of Associations": Committees, Petitions, and the Roots of Interwar Middle Eastern Internationalism'. *Journal of Global History* 7 (2): 166–88.

Barr, James. 2012. *A Line in the Sand: Britain, France and the Struggle That Shaped the Middle East*. London: Simon & Schuster Ltd.

Ben-Arieh, Yehoshua. 1979. *The Rediscovery of the Holy Land in the Nineteenth Century*. Jerusalem: Magnes Press, Hebrew University and Israel Exploration Society; Detroit: Wayne State University Press.

Bourguet, Marie-Noëlle, Bernard Lepetit, and Daniel Nordman. 1998. *L'invention scientifique de la Méditerranée: Égypte, Morée, Algérie*. Paris: Éd. de l'École des hautes études en sciences sociales.

Bourmaud, Philippe, Norig Neveu, and Chantal Verdeil. 2017. 'Experts et expertises dans les mandats de la Société des Nations: figures, champs et outils À propos du colloque INALCO/Lyon 3/Ifpo'. Billet. *Les carnets de l'Ifpo* (blog). https://ifpo.hypotheses.org/7419.

Branch, Jordan. 2014. *The Cartographic State: Maps, Territory, and the Origins of Sovereignty*. Cambridge University Press.

Christensen, Peter H. 2017. *Germany and the Ottoman Railways: Art, Empire, and Infrastructure*. New Haven: Yale University Press.

Cloarec, Vincent. 1996. 'La France du Levant ou la spécificité impériale française au début du XX' siècle'. *Outre-Mers. Revue d'histoire* 83 (313): 3–32.

———. 2010. *La France et la question de Syrie, 1914–1918*. Paris, France: CNRS.
Crampton, Jeremy W. 2006. 'The Cartographic Calculation of Space: Race Mapping and the Balkans at the Paris Peace Conference of 1919'. *Social & Cultural Geography* 7 (5): 731–52.
Culcasi, Karen. 2011. *Cartographic Constructions of the Middle East*. Proquest, Umi Dissertation Publishing.
Dakhli, Leyla. 2010. 'L'expertise en terrain colonial: les orientalistes et le mandat français en Syrie et au Liban'. *Matériaux pour l'histoire de notre temps*, no. 3: 20–27.
Edney, Matthew H. 2009. 'The Irony of Imperial Mapping'. In *The Imperial Map: Cartography and the Mastery of Empire*, edited by James R Akerman, 11–45. Chicago: University of Chicago Press.
———. 2015. 'Modes of Cartographic Practice'. In *Cartography in the Twentieth Century*, edited by Mark Monmonier, 6: 978–80. The History of Cartography. Chicago: University Of Chicago Press.
Fahrenthold, Stacy. 2013. 'Transnational Modes and Media: The Syrian Press in the Mahjar and Emigrant Activism during World War I'. *Mashriq & Mahjar: Journal of Middle East Migration Studies* 1 (1): 30–54.
Firro, Kais M. 2004. 'Lebanese Nationalism versus Arabism: From Bulus Nujaym to Michel Chiha'. *Middle Eastern Studies* 40 (5): 1–27.
Foliard, Daniel. 2017. *Dislocating the Orient*. Chicago: University of Chicago Press.
Fromkin, David. 1989. *A Peace to End All Peace: The Fall of the Ottoman Empire and the Creation of the Modern Middle East*. New York: Avon Books.
Ginsburger, Nicolas. 2010. ' "La guerre, la plus terrible des érosions". Cultures de guerre et géographes universitaires, Allemagne-France-Etats-Unis (1914–1921)'. PhD diss., Université Paris Ouest Nanterre-La Défense.
Gregory, Derek, ed. 2009. *The Dictionary of Human Geography*. 5th ed. Malden, MA: Blackwell.
Harley, John Brian. 1988. 'Maps, Knowledge and Power'. In *The Iconography of Landscape: Essays on the Symbolic Representation, Design, and Use of Past Environments*, edited by Stephen Daniels and Denis E. Cosgrove, 277–312. Cambridge: Cambridge University Press
Ingold, Tim. 2016. *Lines: A Brief History*. New York: Routledge.
Jackson, Simon. 2013. 'What Is Syria Worth?'. *Monde(s)*, no. 4 (October): 83–103.
Kaufman, Asher. 2015. 'Colonial Cartography and the Making of Palestine, Lebanon and Syria'. In *The Routledge Handbook of the History of the Middle East Mandates*, edited by Cyrus Schayegh and Andrew Arsan, 225–43. London: Routledge.
Kitchin, Rob, Justin Gleeson, and Martin Dodge. 2013. 'Unfolding Mapping Practices: A New Epistemology for Cartography'. *Transactions of the Institute of British Geographers* 38 (3): 480–96.
Kiwan, Charif. 1997. 'Les traductions d'une dénomination nationale: la Syrie'. In *Construction des nationalités et immigration dans la France contemporaine*, edited by Eric Guichard et Gérard Noiriel. Paris: Presses de l'Ecole normale supérieure.
Laurens. 1990. *Le royaume impossible: La France et la genèse du monde arabe*. Paris: Armand Colin.

Lejeune, Dominique. 1993. *Les Sociétés de géographie en France et l'expansion coloniale au XIXe siècle*. Paris: Albin Michel.
Lester, Alan. 2006. 'Imperial Circuits and Networks: Geographies of the British Empire'. *History Compass* 4 (1): 124–41.
McMurray, Jonathan S. 2001. *Distant Ties: Germany, the Ottoman Empire, and the Construction of the Baghdad Railway*. Westport: Praeger.
Palsky, Gilles. 2002. 'Emmanuel de Martonne and the ethnographical cartography of central Europe (1917–1920)'. *Imago Mundi* 1 (54): 111–19.
Patel, David Siddhartha. 2016. 'Repartitioning the Sykes-Picot Middle East? Debunking Three Myths'. *Middle East Brief*, no. 103 (November): 10.
Pedersen, Susan. 2015. *The Guardians: The League of Nations and the Crisis of Empire*. Oxford: Oxford University Press.
Pursley, Sara. 2015. ' "Lines Drawn on an Empty Map": Iraq's Borders and the Legend of the Artificial State (Part 2)'. Jadaliyya.
Ter Minassian, Taline. 1997. 'Les géographes français et la délimitation des frontières balkaniques à la Conférence de la Paix en 1919'. *Revue d'histoire moderne et contemporaine* 44 (2): 252–86.
Winichakul, Thongchai. 1994. *Siam Mapped: A History of the Geo-Body of a Nation*. Honolulu: University of Hawaii Press.

*Chapter 7*

# The Cartographic Lives of the Italian Fascist Empire

Laura Lo Presti

## INTRODUCTION

Over the last decades, critical scholarship on historical cartography has explored the epistemological, ontological and political role of cartography in preparing for conquest; orienting oneself in the space travelled; and governing, controlling, and ordering the conquered space (i.e. Buisseret 1992, 2003; Edney 1997; Harley 2001). The relationship between mapping, navigation and conquest was, however, apparently overlooked by Italy. Italian colonialism started, in fact, *without a map*. Long before the advent of Fascism (1922–1943), the country, under a liberal regime ruled by a moderate centre-left party, attempted to satisfy its imperialistic aspirations by taking part in the Scramble for Africa (1880). However, critics usually emphasized the unpreparedness that the young nation (Italian unity was only reached in 1861) manifested when deciding to extend its dominion overseas (Segré 1979; Romano 2005; Labanca 2018). It is no coincidence that Lenin (1917), in his famous analysis of different imperialisms and the growing link between empire and the affirmation of global financial capitalism, referred to the 'beggar imperialism' of Italy. This military and economic unpreparedness also involved the lack of cartographic training. Colonel Tancredi Saletta, commissioned for the mission in Africa in 1885, was in fact aware of the expedition's final destination only on the eve of the landing, when the British Colonel Chermside reached the Italian contingent in Suakim to help Saletta invade Massawa – an important harbour of Eritrea, at that time under Egyptian influence. As Saletta wrote in his diary: 'I could see for the first time a map of Massawa and have an idea of the particularities of those coasts, from Colonel Chermside' (Palma 1999, 9; author's translation). On February 5, 1885, Colonel Saletta invaded Massawa with 1500 riflemen (*bersaglieri*), aiming to penetrate – once the country was conquered – the inner part of Sudan.

This lack of mapping training does, however, raise some doubts: Is it really possible to navigate a territory without anticipatory cartographic knowledge? Is it really imaginable to colonize space, and impose order and control, without mapping technologies? Although the Italian intrusion into African affairs may be judged as rambling and daring, it did not start in such a sudden and clumsy way. Years before, private companies such as the Rubattino purchased some areas of the Horn of Africa (1882) and limited themselves to commercial exchanges with local populations. Traders and merchants were inspired by Italian explorers and missionaries who, in previous decades, had partially surveyed several African territories and, in the process, had both constructed and extensively circulated (through travel diaries and paintings) the imagery of an exotic continent. The *elsewhere* was not configured as a precise and determined space, but was instead a broader imaginary, a visionary mental cartography within which all the stereotypes, sentiments, desires and discursive constructions related to African places and their populations had already converged before the start of the official colonizing mission. The colonial conquest, in truth, did not begin and did not end with either surveys or the military occupation of foreign territories, but was preceded and accompanied by an intense historical narrative, even a cartographic narratological impulse, aimed at justifying the imperialistic enterprise under the duty of a civilizing mission. This aspect would suggest that representation and communication, conceived of more broadly as acts of imagination, were able to overcome physical, economic and materialistic constraints by formulating and institutionalizing specific ideological fantasies and projections of the empire. In this respect, Ben-Ghiat and Fuller have suggested that 'although Italian colonialism was more restricted in geographical scope and duration than the French and the British empires, it had no less an impact on the development of metropolitan conceptions of race, national identity, and geographical imaginaries' (2005, 1).

The ideological fantasy of extra-territoriality weighed specifically on geography and anthropology, the expansionist sciences *par excellence*. Several Italian geographical societies, launched in the second half of the nineteenth century, rapidly became colonialist epistemic machines: they offered an indispensable informative and organizational support to the imperialistic initiatives of Italy and proved to be an important means for the construction of national identity, in whose furrow Fascism tried to plant itself.[1] In those circumstances, colonization was made possible by *spatial epistemics* that developed and worked less in navigational terms and more through a persuasive, communicative and performative media apparatus; in this way, geographical knowledge was particularly aimed at visually and discursively defining the leading role of Italy within the Mediterranean basin and the country's relationship with eastern and northern Africa.

Fifty years later, because of the accumulation and standardization of overseas geographical knowledge, the relationship between cartography and empire strengthened, and maps of conquests became more accessible to the larger public. Cartographic products were cheaper and more widespread, and map producers transformed from printing companies, often family-run, into larger publishing houses (e.g. DeAgostini and Touring Club Italiano). In addition, with the birth of the entertainment industry, imperial imagery spread through cinema, radio and magazines. During the Second Ethiopian War (1935–1936), conducted by Mussolini, there was, in fact, an enormous increase in the popular production of maps, and maps came to pervade the physical and imaginary places of the empire. With propagandistic aims, imperial cartographic imagery began to disseminate through many objects of everyday life: forty-six million cartographic colonial postcards were, for instance, produced by Istituto Geografico Militare, the public institution devoted to mapmaking (Boria 2007). Postcards were a very low-cost propagandistic tool, easily circulated between the colonies and the motherland and continuously customizable through written messages. In October 1935, General Baistrocchi, Undersecretary of the Ministry of War, positively commented on a military postcard showing a colour map of East Africa: 'it has been very well conceived for propaganda and cartographic and colonial vulgarization purposes' (Boria 2007, 137; author's translation).

Under the framework of this unprecedented 'cartographic vulgarization', maps illustrating the advancement of Fascist troops appeared on postcards, street walls, newspapers, report cards and boardgames – but also in radio broadcasting and movies, where the flickering, sonant and cinematic vibrancies of many maps in motion were often redundant in order to produce 'unthinking response' (Hornsey 2012). We might deduce that without the constant visualizing, touching, voicing and listening of different mapping practices – thus, without the enduring sensory circulation of the colonial and imperial cartography in various mundane settings – the empire could not have been imagined, enacted, sensed and even contested by ordinary citizens and political actors. Drawing on such a wide sensorium, I suggest that cartographic senses, conceived as both senses of knowledge (epistemology) and vehicles of imagination (aesthetics), were instrumental to the development of imperial politics. This notwithstanding, the chapter aims to address the complex relation between maps, mapping and the making of the Italian Fascist empire through a multi-sensory approach that places a novel emphasis on the practices of mundane consumption other than production of imperial maps. As Oliver (2011, 75) reminds us, 'it was the social relations of consumption . . . that helped colonize minds among the masses . . .'.

First, considering that 'thinking about the imaginary is much more mundane than it might appear,' as argued by Lobo-Guerrero, Alt, and Meijer in the first volume of this series (2019, 3), I give saliency to this mundane but nonetheless powerful cartographic usage of the empire by casting light on a wide range of quotidian cartographic objects – and their perishable lives – circulating during Fascism, positioning them as tools of empire's space-*sensing* as well as of space-*making*. Second, suggesting that the empire transforms from a concept into a practice only at the moment of its consumption, I attempt to develop the notion of connectivity as a multisensorial ritual – a performance of seeing, touching and dreaming the empire through maps that emerged in diverse, often ordinary, circumstances and uses – that materially connected citizens with an imaginary elsewhere, simultaneously reinforcing their bond with the motherland.

Unfolding both sensory and rational interactions with maps, a multisensorial and experiential account of cartography will offer new insights into the study of the empire, illuminating those cartographic acts that not only put a map into existence but also make a particular imagining of political order a real and palpable presence. Following the recent post-representational turn in map studies, an innovative literature (Dodge *et al.* 2009; Kitchin *et al.* 2013; Lo Presti 2019; Rossetto 2019; Wilmott 2020) is indeed starting to explore the everyday consumption and enactment of contemporary maps with composite methodologies and multisensory experiences. Suggestions emerging from this new terrain of investigation should be speculatively imported within studies of imperial maps, with the aim of exploring even the *humble* version of empire, thereby embracing more banal and hitherto neglected quotidian cartographic objects. Understanding the circulation and reception of maps of the Italian empire thus translates into the possibility of tracing such a *multisensory* history of imperial maps, exploring 'how conscious and unconscious sensory practices played important roles in defining European imperialism and/or organizing responses to it' (Hacke and Musselwhite 2018, 14). However, this assumption does not leave us without methodological risks. As Rossetto (2019, 44) recently asked: 'How can we investigate "emergent maps" and their open contexts of existence in the past?' And in the *sensory milieu* of Fascism's empire, how can we explore cartographic imperial imaginaries of connectivity in events that we cannot experience first-hand, and that we cannot always and easily reconstruct, if not from the (sometimes deteriorated) surfaces of dusty maps that might have not even entered the public archive?

Scrutinizing the cartographic lives of the Italian Fascism's Empire raises indeed the parallel question about what historical sources should be culled in order to understand the past. By shedding light on the visuality, materiality and sonority of mapping through the deployment of audio-visual records of maps, portrayals of maps, imperial map-like objects that are easily found at home or on the Internet, but less commonly in historical archives, this chapter takes just one possible route through this complex quandary, considering the tight line between intention and expectation, and between production and reception. In the effort to address maps as mundane, mobile and active spatial objects for the imagination of the empire, I will utilize distinct sections that explore the political materiality and temporality of urban maps, small-size map-objects and vocal and cinematic maps, all circulating within the broader construction of the Italian Empire. This approach is taken in order to understand the *communicative* spatial epistemics of cartographic artefacts as everyday incubators of various forms of imperialism and to reveal how a physical and imaginative connectivity with imperial fantasies was made possible and operative at several levels through the quotidian sensing of maps.

## EXPERIENCING THE EMPIRE OF CARTOGRAPHIC SENSES

In 1940, in an intervention submitted to the *Journal of Geography*, the German geographer Kemp noted that the maps associated with the empire of Italian Fascism figured 'largely in propaganda' and were used 'as murals, and . . . featured in the expositions which are now a yearly feature' (1940, 140). Celebrating the work of Mussolini as that of a geographer in-chief, Kemp concluded that 'like every other geographer, Mussolini loves maps'. Before taking power, Mussolini was indeed a geography schoolteacher, and thus aware of the powerful role that 'popular cartography' (Kosonen 2008) could play in inculcating the vision of the regime. The cartographic onslaught of the empire was even broader than the one described by Kemp. It was reproduced in books, magazines, movies and even operated through several cartographic informalities whose initial functions were clearly set by the regime, although many other maps, and especially map-like objects, tended to simply replicate an original model and then proliferate autonomously, giving rise to a continuous process of becoming and personalization. In this sense, many experiments of cultural politics were aimed at soliciting a genuine and vernacular identification with the Fascist utopia (Kim 2009), involving private actors, state organizations and the public in reciprocal, rather than explicitly top-down, cartographic initiatives.

In the following sections, I propose to address the *cartographic* cultural politics of Fascism as a dynamic, both material and temporal, process whose effects, feelings, power and meanings are to be found at the crossroads of production and reception, of encoding and decoding, of intentions and expectations (Jacob 2006). This way, the gluing forces of maps as connective imaginaries of the empire can be epistemically and ontologically examined with multiple entryways. Particularly in 'a world of disjunctive flows [which] produce problems that manifest themselves in intensely local forms but have contexts that are anything but local' (Pitts and Versluys 2015, 2), maps – as objects enacted by a geographical imperial consciousness – enfold us with a range of questions and interrogatives requiring fresh insights: How are spatial imaginations of the empire created and nurtured? How do they physically circulate beyond their initial epistemic circles? How are they negotiated, resisted, or consumed and reproduced by ordinary people? How do they wither, decay and perish, both materially and politically?

In order to answer these questions, maps will be considered dynamic, active and bonding agents of the empire that silently or more gregariously colonized many objects, materials and devices of everyday life in Italy. Despite this huge and heterogeneous cauldron of – often politicized – cartographic mundanity, I am aware that the attention of many historians and geographers has been typically stimulated by the grand narrative of military, colonial and propaganda cartographies.[2] When addressing the connection between cartographic imaginaries and the production of the Italian empire – and I would argue of any form of imperialism – critical cartographers, geographers, historians and international relations scholars appear, however, to have seldom discussed the particular form of cartographic connectivity to the empire expressed through the reception of maps, as opposed to their production. In this sense, critics have more rarely, both conceptually and empirically, examined the materiality, visuality and vocality of cartography, particularly that of the everyday maps circulating in the imperial urban context. This absence is even more specifically evident when it comes to the ways that cartographic imageries – produced *after* the imperial conquest – were adapted, reinterpreted and 're-sensed' in contexts different from colonial battlefields and surveys (Olivier 2011; Hornsey 2012). Previous analyses paid, in fact, attention to 'the most obvious users' of maps, like 'soldiers, sailors, farmers, archaeologists and administrators' (Buisseret 2003, 176). As Edney (2009) has also contended, historians of cartography have usually adopted the point of view of the mapmaker, often limiting themselves to textual deconstructions of the cartographic representations, somehow overlooking 'the perception of the map as an everyday image in the cultural sphere' (Batuman 2010, 223). In those terms, historians of imperial maps have refrained from telling the 'experiences' of maps, how those cartographies were (or could be) enacted, sensed, felt or contested by ordinary people. 'What could happen' – Brückner asks instead (2017, 8) – 'when the gap separating maps and people is filled with [an] account of map experiences, situational behaviour, and cultural expectations?'.

As we will explore in the following sections, a multisensorial and experiential approach toward mundane imperial maps provides an original angle from which to understand the politics of the empire in temporal and contingent terms. An examination, in particular, of the functions of senses, materials, colours and motion in a multifaceted array of cartographic objects results in a vision of maps as strongly grounded in time and, as 'mappings,' carrying a temporal dimension with them, which appears more evident throughout the many imaginations and fantasies nurtured within the Italian Fascist empire. In the course of the chapter, several nuances of such temporality, expressly anchored to materialities of maps, will emerge. In particular, I will address the temporal narratives plotted by mural marble maps, connecting the glories of the Old Roman Empire to the Fascist present in order to manipulate imperial future claims; I will pay attention to several routinized everyday cartographic experiences of the empire, in which a map, as an object of touch and emotion as well as of sight and reason, is continuously reinterpreted and the process of mapping never stops but is substantially geared to the legitimization of present imperial politics; and I will use the example of 'cinemaps,' that is, animated maps disseminated in newsreels and documentaries, to assess more explicitly the kinaesthetic functions of mapping as they show the ongoing progress of imperial conquests while inculcating excitement and trust among the masses for Fascism and its political leader. Overall, materials of which maps are made and places where they are displayed invite readers not only to explore a variety of performative engagements with imperial imaginations but also to grasp in time the assembling and aggregating forces, and following withering, of the empire itself.

## MAPS IN THE URBAN STREETSCAPE

Given the chance to walk around Rome along the Via dei Fori Imperiali, formerly known as the Via dell'Impero, one's curiosity might be captured by a series of mural maps depicting the expansion of the ancient Roman Empire. They are four large wall maps, commissioned by Mussolini in April 1934 and designed by Superintendent Antonio Muñoz. Placed on the external wall of the Basilica of Maxentius, these maps are marble, with a very minimal selection of materials and colours: cipollino for grey, travertine for white hues, and black Apuan marble for the dark areas (Minor 1999; Follo 2013). Against one's warm or cold skin – depending on the season – the marble narrates Rome's expansion within the Mediterranean region, starting from Rome's birth (753 BC), followed by the Punic Wars (146 BC), the celebration of empire at the death of Augustus (14 AD), and ending with its greatest expansion under Trajan (in 117 AD). The observer, however, might not be aware of the existence of a fifth map that illustrates Fascist imperial conquests, thus celebrating Italy's new colonialism as an extension of the

Roman Empire. The fifth map, added in October 1936 but removed after Mussolini's fall, was anticipated by a temporary installation, on the base of the column of Marcus Aurelius, of a panel that tracked military operations in African territory to keep people abreast of their progress (Follo 2013). Because the opening ceremony was spectacularly documented by Istituto Luce (the first public cinematographic institution founded by the Fascist regime in 1924), it is possible to grasp even today the theatrical emphasis that was put on the event.[3] 'Returning a map to its original setting and "listening" to the rhythms inscribed within it' – argues Honsey (2012, 675) – 'might enable us to uncover the specific spatial practices it once sought to produce'. In this respect, the newsreel re-elaborates the event, with recording choices and background music performing a clear propagandistic intent. A drape featuring the Italian national flag is gradually wrapped aside to make way for a mute map of the empire, with the territorial expansion of the country highlighted in white. Isolated from the other four maps, the last map succinctly visualizes the entire narrative of imperial conquests through a comparison of the accomplishments of ancient Romans and Fascism.

The principal purpose of large wall maps in the nineteenth and twentieth centuries was to display current or future territorial claims as the empire advanced. However, the project of Mussolini was more peculiarly that of instilling *nostalgia* for the greatness of the Roman Empire in the minds of Italians in order to stimulate their pride in a glorious past; make them the natural heirs of the new civilizing mission; and solicit a sense of revenge against foreign powers' expansionist aims. For this reason, mapping became the imperial machine's privileged device for both carrying Italians back into a glorious past and projecting them into the future. This tension between past and future also required different expertise. For instance, while historians were commissioned to realize historical atlases of ancient Rome, like the 1932 *Piccolo atlante dell'Impero Romano* (The Little Atlas of the Roman Empire) curated by the historian Plinio Fraccaro, geographers devoted their attention to geographic explorations that established the Italian primacy over new discoveries (Boria 2007). Map colours, especially through the contrast between white and black, became the vehicles of this palingenetic rhetoric because they 'served to remind viewers of the Fascist government's claim that it was bringing culture and civilization to even the darkest and most barren reaches of the empire' (Minor 1999, 149).

This semantic of colour reveals also an interesting ambiguity because white no longer corresponded to the 'pristine whiteness of the blank space' (Edney 2009, 33), the empty space of maps that worried cartographers and cosmologists of the past who hastened to fill it with strange and exotic creatures. By contrast, that empty space was now represented by black – this choice emphasizing the darkness that must be removed and illuminated by the advance of Fascist civilization. The great irony is that, although black was actually the distinctive colour of Fascism's ideology, at the imperial level it could have been dangerously confused with the 'wild' and 'obtuse' black of Africa. To dispel this ambiguity and confusion, Fascism's empire had now to bleach clear the visual narrative. Maps, therefore, became a dark palimpsest to be filled in by the pure and pristine desire for *spazio vitale* (vital space), theorized by Germans as *Lebensraum*. Borrowed from Ratzel and German geopolitik, the term *spazio vitale* had a different meaning for Italian geographers, as it was at times confused with other notions such as *grande spazio* (great space – the German *Grossraum*), *comunità imperiale* (imperial community), or *spazio economico autarchico* (autarkic economic space) (Antonsich 2009). According to Fascist ideologists, vital space comprehended the 'small space', that is, the physical space inhabited by Italians only, and the 'great space', the largest geographical area of the empire extended to the entire Mediterranean (the *Mare Nostrum* of imperial rhetoric) and northern Africa, from the Atlantic to the Indian Ocean.

Whereas the expansion of the Nazi vital space involved a racial engineering operation on Europe, to be carried out with the genocide of the subjugated nations, Mussolini's mission was to export the Fascist revolution beyond Europe, to 'civilize' the conquered territories and 'impose the moral and racial criteria, the law, virtus and libertas' (Rodogno 2003, 72; author's translation). This way, non-European populations, once defeated, would have been subjected to the power and protection of Rome but would have maintained their language and culture. When the fifth map was added to the Roman streetscape, Italy had already expanded its 'vital space' to include Libya in 1929 (Tripolitania and Cyrenaica were already conquered in 1912 by the Italian Kingdom) and Ethiopia in 1936, both marked in white on the map. Unlike the other colonies of the Horn of Africa, which were familiar in Italy thanks to the initiatives of explorers and merchants, there were few contacts with Libya before the military expeditions of the twentieth century (Labanca 2002). Following the annexation of Libya, the lack of direct knowledge of the country in Italy was replaced by the idea that Libya had been a part of the Roman Empire and thus, following colonial rhetoric, it was incorrect to refer to the Italian occupation as an 'invasion'. By virtue of their common past, in other words, this occupation was a paternalistic and necessary 'returning home' for Italy. In this sense, Italian control over the Mediterranean was 'both a means and an end of Italy's expansionism. The ultimate goal was to recreate the *Mare Nostrum* (Our Sea) of olden times: the Mediterranean as a Roman lake' (Jacobs 2014, no pages).

Once all the maps were installed, their iconicity spread beyond the city of Rome through frantic remediation in schoolbooks, newspapers and in other buildings, as in the murals recreated elsewhere in the empire (Follo 2013).

In 1937, in the city of Como (in Lombardy), the colonial exhibition of the empire annual was preceded by a tall tower made of pylons that displayed the five imperial walled maps, known as *tavole imperiali*. In Padua, an updated map of the Italian Empire was installed in 1939 in Piazza delle Erbe (see figure 7.1). Located at the back of Palazzo Moroni, the venue of the municipality of Padua, this map was never taken down (unlike that in Rome). Even today you can raise your head and look at the former Italian colonies such as the Dodecanese (with Rhodes), Libya, Abyssinia (Ethiopia), Somalia, Eritrea and Albania (the last was militarily occupied in 1939). This enduring and capillary cartographic appearance perpetuated 'the myth of Mussolini as the new founder of the Empire and cemented the idea that the Fascist Regime was something new, but also the continuation of a glorious past' (Follo 2013, 141). This connection to the past was also accomplished through design strategies: although the minimalist iconography utilized in the mural was influenced by the art of futurism and the avant-garde, Mussolini's use of large-scale maps was also inspired by Roman precedents, exemplified both in the world map prepared by Agrippa, and the marble plan of the Templus Pacis (Minor 1999). The choice of an austere aesthetic, far from the pompous propagandistic maps of Renaissance, was also encouraged because, according to Muñoz, Mussolini wanted such maps to be intelligible 'both to the learned and the uncultivated' and to 'evoke our pride and hope for the future'

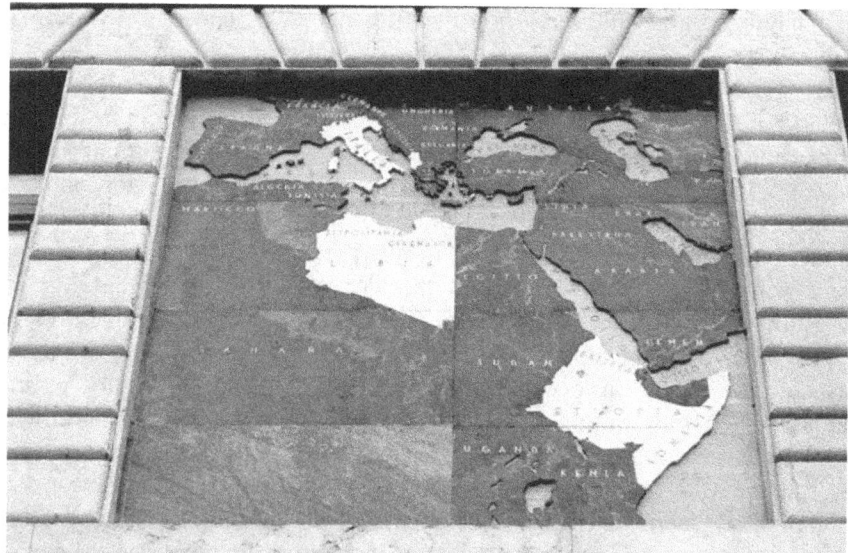

**Figure 7.1. A map of the Italian Fascism's Empire still displayed in Piazza delle Erbe, Padova (Italy). Photograph taken by Giada Peterle.**

(Minor 1999, 150). Recognizing the persuasive and informative legibility of large wall maps, political actors and geographers of that time inferred that those maps could 'talk' autonomously through their plastic materiality. This is confirmed by Kemp's celebratory comment:

> The Dictator-Geographer knows that the most ignorant native, looking first at one map and then at the other, is struck by the fact that much of Europe – most of it, indeed – once belonged to the Empire and therefore should belong to it now. Without even a caption these maps are working *every minute of the day, and every day*. When the Geographer remarks now, however casually, 'we really should have this or that territory', he does not have to argue the point. The maps have done that job for him.
>
> (1940, 140; emphasis added)

The legibility of giant public maps was also possible because of the presence of motifs familiar to the audience, usually borrowed from cartographic images published in newspapers and in schoolbooks (Brückner 2017). In considering the receptive context of wall maps, Daniels (2010, 475) makes an additional crucial point:

> How . . . did these wall maps make their impression on the people who came across them, seen from a distance, more closely inspected, or even overlooked, as people walked past, up to or back from them? How did people conduct themselves with these maps as they went about their business, as the maps variously functioned in their fields of vision, whether as background scenery or as powerful, transformational objects?

'Every minute of the day, and every day' (Kemp 1940, 140), those marble maps developed specific pragmatics of viewer's body and gaze (Della Dora 2009), that presumably engaged the eye now in a fleeting, now in more curious and enduring, attention. The actionable properties of maps, and their concrete use, would then allow for different understandings. We might suppose that the repetitive and subtle work of those maps produced imaginaries of connectivity, that is 'understandings of wider worlds,' and, at the same time, constructed the 'place' of Italian identity 'within these worlds' (Atkinson 2013, 561). Put differently, in the words of Wood (2010, 1), maps might have done 'that job' for Mussolini, that is connecting provincial Italy to the wider physical imagery of a solid and coherent empire, because that 'is what maps do: they work' by 'operating effectively' and by achieving 'the ceaseless reproduction of the culture that brings maps into being'. Still, it is problematic to conclude generally, as any viewer could have been differently affected by such maps, remaining quite indifferent to them or contesting them mightily, as we might presume in the case of an anti-fascist and anti-colonial observer of the time. In this regard, Minor (1999) remembers that until the 1970s these maps did not really disturb the post-war Italian audience, as these images were continually used as a background in the annual celebration of the Italian Republic. A video recorded in 1944, and stored in the digital archive of Istituto Luce, shows, for example, American soldiers in Rome looking curiously at the large marble tables and then discussing the meaning of the maps with an Italian soldier. Some months later, however, the *tavole imperiali* were deprived of the fifth map, which incurred a more tragic destiny. Vandalized by antifascists and removed after the liberation of Rome in November 1944, this map was rediscovered many years later in the basement of the Theatre of Marcellus. Although no choice regarding whether to destroy or reassemble the marble map has been made in the following years, time is taking its toll by corroding and eroding 'every minute of the day, and every day' (Kemp 1940, 140) the cartographic remains of the Fascist empire.

What can be learned from this residual map's story? 'Non-human agents' – says Rossetto (2019, 134) – 'may intervene in a destructive way on an object, but their intervention could be seen as productive of other indirect resources for recalling the past'. In this way, the interrogative mode of the map's decay elicits my interest in the fragility and vulnerability to which many imperial impulses appear to have been destined over time. If we considered the project of the empire as that of a work of art, we might reflect on the idea that empires merely gave an illusion of permanence and continuity: 'Despite their aspiration to the illusion of permanence, they [artworks] are only momentary aggregations of material, such as paint, bricks, glass, acrylic, cloth, steel, or canvas' (Appadurai 2006, 15). Similarly, the aggregation of different cultures, economic systems, spatialities and temporalities within one homogenous system – all forcibly mingled in the construct of the empire of Italian Fascism – was just precarious and momentary, a rush of the moment. Even Mussolini's famous slogan, 'It is the spirit which tames and bends the material' (Antonsich 2009, 268), may be now seen for what it really was: a performative, but perishable, contradiction.

## THE EMPIRE OF SMALL MAPS

The profusion of maps inaugurated under the Fascist regime was not exclusively limited to outdoor public spaces, where full-size, spectacular maps could more easily integrate the military advancement of Fascism in Africa with everyday pedestrians' urban rhythms. In truth, there was a clear interest within the regime, especially at the beginning of the 1930s, in invading every corner of daily life with the popular iconography of the dictatorship and, especially, with the powerful iconography of empire conveyed by maps. In this regard, the creation of minor and micro-sized indoor cartographies allowed a denser mass circulation of mapped images of empire which were especially targeted to offices, homes and schools. Atkinson (2013), for instance, notes that, in the late 1930s, the Fascist Education Minister Giuseppe Bottai became a great promoter of geography within Italian academic structures and society more broadly because he was aware of the role of geography as a catalyst for the dissemination of imperialist imaginations. This was also a response to the party's request for an entirely Fascist politicization (*fascistizzazione*) of the national imagery. While large and public maps acted as a hub for gathering the masses, especially during spectacular presentations and exhibitions, the cartographic reproduction of the Fascist Empire and its achievements in light, portable, or mobile artefacts transformed the regime into a popular and intimate presence in the everyday life of its citizens. 'With the creation of the Empire, newspapers and books have a specific task' – said an exponent of the Fascist political party in the mid-1930s – 'which is not only to inform people about the daily life of the great Mussolini creature, but to permeate the old and new generations with present and future needs of the Empire, to make all the Italian people live on an entirely imperial level' (Crespi 1937, no page; author's translation).

Yet, despite the desire to make 'all the Italian people live on an entirely imperial level', a real definition of the empire was never directly given by Mussolini or his intellectual circle. Like the map, the empire was self-evident, self-constructing, self-operating. According to de Grand, Mussolini 'believed that imperialism was a law of nature, just as life was struggle, conflict and conquest' (2004, 128). Through and with the diffusion of the informal cartographic visuals, but especially with the support of the broader iconographical and vocal apparatus of the regime, the materiality of the empire became largely unquestioned as it became more visible. This was particularly evident in the educational sector. At school, for instance, maps did not only rest on the accustomed surfaces of walls and did not only silently observe the *fascistizzazione* of the youth; they also started to be printed on objects which did not have any cartographic function, such as pupils' report cards. Depending on the school year, a student would have found on his report card – in addition to his marks – a map illustrating the differences between the Italian colonial possessions before the march to Rome (October 28, 1922; see figure 7.2, on the left) and those conquered with the heavy price of violence and use of toxic gases (figure 7.2, on the right).[4] In addition, many toys and gameboards began to display the iconography of imperial Italy. The gameboard for *Gioco dell'Oca* (corresponding to the game of snakes and ladders) was, for example, transformed into a map of Africa, with the goal being the progressive conquest of the colonies.

As I have underlined in the introduction, the most palpable example of the miniaturization of the empire was offered by the millions of cartographic

Figure 7.2. School report card showing the progressive imperial conquests of Fascism on the front and the back of the document. Year 1939–1940. Manieri Collection. Courtesy of Enrico Manieri.

colonial postcards published by the Istituto Geografico Militare. Those small maps became part of a wider popular culture that cultivated interest in the imperial project not only through images of heroic, romantic departures but also through depictions of colonial encounters in foreign places (figure 7.3). These imaginative cartographies presented an exciting and acceptable face of colonialism which served to enchant as well as inform the domestic audience. The contingent involved in military operations in Africa, as well as their distant families in Italy, could in fact personalize the postcards with their own dedications, touching and caressing their loved ones and the empire alike. In this way, 'ephemeral little maps became the envelopes containing the tiny and disposable records of personal experience – from the sensory to the somatic to the phatic – inflected by map interactions and map knowledge' (Brückner 2017, 276). Later on, when the Fascist regime financed topographical, architectural and infrastructural work directly in the colonies, the imperialistic narrative presented in such postcards shifted again, moving from the representation of the colonies as exotic places to homely environments. By visually presenting and materially reshaping colonies as natural and cultural *extensions* of the motherland, not only through urban mural maps, but also by means of a portable cartographic iconography, Fascism proposed a novel imaginary of connectivity, attempting to create 'a parallel but artificial Italy overseas' (de Grand 2004, 138).

However, just as it had for the marble map of Via dell'Impero, for the majority of paper map-like objects, fate soon became unavoidable. Following

Figure 7.3. Examples of colonial postcards with cartographic representations of the Empire. Author's photograph.

the 1929 global financial crisis, Italy had to face a serious collapse of the paper sector. The regime was constantly searching, both in the south of Italy and in the colonized territories, for new fibres that could replace paper; these searches often proved useless. For this reason, many paper documents started to be printed with very low-quality materials, normally wooden pulp, meaning many report cards, postcards, newspapers and maps were destined to premature death. The 'sickness' of paper was already being described in the 1930s:

> As time passes, today's paper blackens, turns to dust and, almost without touching it, it breaks into fragments. Hygroscopic and sensitive to the maximum degree of atmospheric agents, it shrinks by an oxidation process, disconnecting the felting of the sheet and causing destruction after a few decades. Well, perhaps more than 90% of today's publications are printed on paper containing pulp and these are mainly scientific and historical publications of great importance, which should have a long life.
> (Testi 1935, 20; author's translation)

The intellectual branch of Fascism was worried about the disappearance of the imperial imagery consolidated in written and graphic reports. This materialistic concern suggests that, however abstract and virtual the notion of empire was, it did not require an equally immaterial plan to operate. Indeed, what would an *incorporeal* empire look like? When we start to reflect on this question, it becomes clear that visual, sound, verbal and tactile effects, as well as objects, uniforms, architecture, jobs, infrastructures, scars – all produced in the name of empire – have to be recognized as the material cultural traces that make an empire *the Empire*.

## MAPPING AN EMPIRE IN MOTION

We have seen how maps on the streets, at school, in games and on postcards – made with different materials and circulating in different contexts of everyday life – attempted, day by day, to externalize and make intelligible the propaganda machine of the Italian Empire. We should not, however, overlook the fact that one of the spheres in which maps best emphasized their own movement and temporality – their being a mapping, and thus their behaviour as a material becoming of the empire – was at work in the audio-visual industry. Radio programmes, movies and documentaries performed an endless profusion of maps, especially in the 1930s. In 1935, when Italy undertook the invasion of Ethiopia, radio transmissions were increasingly interrupted by radio commentary informing the population of the imperial war. In February 1938, the minister of National Education made the installation of centralized radio mandatory in middle schools. In this way, the culture of the regime entered the ears of its subjects in a capillary way, allowing the students to listen to Mussolini's conferences and speeches. During the colonial conquests, it was not rare for a speaker on the radio (which, across Italy, generally hung on the school wall) to ask pupils to both activate the silent African map and to act on it: indeed, students were required to go in front of a map and trace the birth of the 'New Italy' by marking battles and conquests. Filippuzzi, a member of the Fascist and colonialist journal, *L'Italia Coloniale*, developed a radio competition that involved local youths drawing the political frontiers, major cities and the two military fronts upon maps of East Africa as the invasion progressed (Atkinson 2013). This strategy once more reveals the desire of the intellectuals working behind the Fascist machine to use disciplinary, routinized and repetitive mapping experiences to construct an informed and governed audience. In these aural and visual activities, maps were not only prosthetic devices that stretched human sensorial perception, especially concerning the optical sensorium, but also touchable surfaces that materialized the sonant and vocal itineraries narrated by the radio speaker. Such ritual multisensorial experiences of imperial conquests established, once more, imaginative connections to remote others. Specifically, they made children live the experience of being on the front line to conquer the empire.

Visual contemplation of the progress of empire was evident in multisensory interactions with the cartographic objects occurring at school, but also became increasingly noticeable in the use of cinematic images in newsreels and documentaries produced by Istituto Luce. The movie industry emerging during the imperial era in Italy was one that explicitly presented maps in multifarious roles and with varied purposes. 'Cinemaps,' defined as 'maps in motion developed specifically in cinema for narrative purposes' (Caquard 2013, 46) were already used throughout Europe before the 1930s, for instance in the docudramas appearing between 1910–1920, and they manifested some innovative features that would only be found decades later in the best advancement of digital cartography (Caquard 2013). In the case of Fascist cinema in Italy, one of the most vivid examples of the cartographicization of cinematographic images is *Sulle orme dei nostri pionieri* (In the footsteps of our pioneers), a documentary directed by Luciano de Feo in 1936, following the proclamation of the birth of the Empire of *Africa Orientale Italiana* by Mussolini.[5] Here, the cartographic image becomes the real protagonist of the whole narrative.

The documentary opens with a huge rotating globe that stops when the Mediterranean basin catches the camera eye. By zooming in, the director approaches the cartographic silhouette of the Mediterranean, whose design resembles the marble tables of Via dell'Impero. Thanks to the possibilities of cinematography, the map is animated, kinaesthetically showing how the Roman Empire – that 'today spiritually guides its prole towards East Africa's conquest' (voice-over; author's translation) – is gradually expanding due to the contribution of Fascism. As the white advances to replace the static dark grey of the map, the frame moves again on the rotating globe, this time emphasizing the ecumenical contribution that Italian explorers, navigators and intellectuals have provided in the creation of the *Imperium* (which, in this context, does not specifically refer to the Italian empire). In fact, in the cartographic-centred narration of the voice-over, the speaker explains that all the other European imperial powers could not have existed without 'the sacrifice and the genius of Italians'.

The style of the documentary looks avant-garde, the font of the lettering recalling the visual language of advertisements. For instance, a logo displaying of the names of the explorers who, between the thirteenth and fifteenth centuries, brought 'the light of civilization to the darkness of Africa' is frantically shown: the cartographic silhouette of Africa appears again as a dark territory, a semantic void, a *horror vacui*, that is progressively crossed – filled of meaning – by a progression of white lines that serve different purposes in the various scenes of the documentary (see figure 7.4). Animated lines trace the movements of the Italian troops, increasing the tension regarding the destiny of the military contingent in Africa, or represent the transport and communication systems built in the colonies under Fascism, thereby underlining 'the Italians' ability to impose a vision of modernity in sync with Fascist social and military aims, one founded on the regimentation of bodies and the

192                              Chapter 7

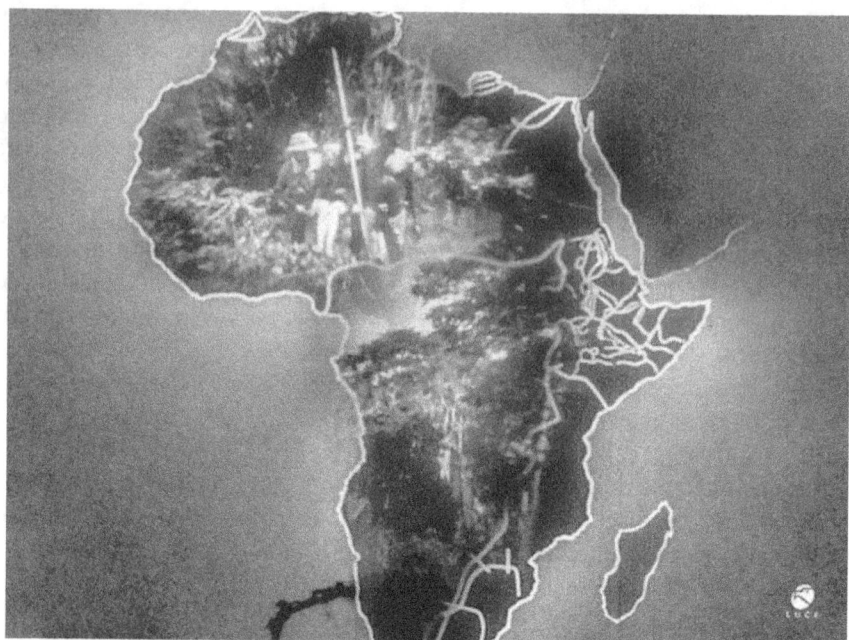

Figure 7.4.  Video still from 'Sulle orme dei nostri pionieri' (De Feo, 1936). Copyrights: Istituto Luce. The documentary represents several transformations and uses of the map in the cinematographic narrative of the empire.

mastery and transformation of terrain' (Ben Ghiat 2015, xvi). On the naked body of the African country, progressively 'humanized' and 'civilized' by Western forces, spectators also attend to the overlay footage of daily moments, guerrilla warfare, air flights and landscapes projected on the map. In the cinematic narrative of the empire, the unfolding map thus changes, performing various aspects and functions. In some scenes, for instance, the map is flat, becoming a game table where imperial powers parcel the world, leaving Italy alone, weak, and without any space to colonize. In other scenes, the map inflates and acquires volume, transforming itself into a globe that connects the local discourse to a wider, geopolitical scale. The map is also deployed for its mimetic function, as a secure and unquestioned representation of the territory; or its surface is bombarded with lettering, images, landscapes and recordings that transform the virtual map into a hybrid trans-medial image, both geometric and photographic, both real and visionary (figure 7.4).

Because 'cinematic cartography combines the documentary side of cartography with the fictional side of cinema' (Caquard and Fraser Taylor 2009, 7), the animated maps of the documentary inform the audience about the progressive advance of the troops in external territories, the role of the

Italian pioneers, and more broadly, about the inevitable Italian influence over the Mediterranean. In the movie industry in Italy at this time, the cartographic imaginary was in fact largely mobilized for both its pedagogic and entertaining role. As Atkinson remarks, 'the regime's efforts to encourage public interest in Italy's colonial possessions and in further expansionism similarly required Italians to comprehend the world at wider, international scales' (2013, 562).

The act of exploration, therefore, was not only practical but – on an imagery level – produced connectivity effects on the audience. To this end, exploration, wayfinding, encounters and conquests were often reproduced and aesthetically reinterpreted in contexts different from real surveys and military expeditions, like movies and documentaries, to bring the empire at the heart of the citizens' experience. Being *in*-corporeal, the image of the empire ordinarily re-emerged, intact, from the interaction between practice and abstraction, between timely discoveries and general reflection on the globe. In this sense, geographical knowledge became an indispensable epistemological and aesthetic tool to imagine, represent and rewrite the empire.

Acquiring knowledge of foreign places and having the potential to reorganize them according to one's own cultural, political and perceptual perspective were the essential aspects for the establishment of a widespread, powerful, authoritative *cartographic* cultural politics. The speaker (and the director) looks to be fully aware of this, confirming the authority of maps: 'the Italian character of Africa was indicated by the names themselves and consecrated by worldwide cartographies' (voice-over; author's translation). Geographer Emanuela Casti (1995) has also noted that the cartographic efforts of the Italian imperial machine were not only driven by the desire of more detailed and exact maps, but to create a tool able to affirm the colonizing presence. Within 'the militarization of the cinematic apparatus' (Ben-Ghiat 2013, 254) the transfiguration, manipulation and the frenetic filming of the map were perfectly at ease with the project of imperial affirmation. The cartographic, route-oriented narration of the 'elsewhere' was particularly welcomed in its ability to connect, rationally and emphatically, the domestic audience with the outside world.

## CONCLUSION

In this chapter, I engaged with a much more material and multisensorial embodiment of imperial life; this is an embodiment that it is possible to revive through the re-enactment of past cartographic performances and practices. Taking as a specific case the 'beggar' imperialism of Italy (Maione 1979), I concurred with historiographic claims that Mussolini hardly created and imposed order in the face of national disorder. By amplifying and strengthening the political and cultural machine of propaganda, he (and the intellectual class supporting him) did however aim to ameliorate this weakness in the eyes of the Italians and other external powers. In this regard, the historian Nicola Labanca has recently recognized that feelings of excitement, pride – and even conviction that the Italian Empire could last for a long time in history – made in many cases large sections of the Italian population 'enthusiastically imperialist' (2018, 131). However, Mussolini eventually realized the excess and effects of living on *an entirely imperial level*: 'The empire is swallowing Italy,' he commented to Guarneri in 1937 (de Grand 2004, 138). Indeed, the empire was not just a rational, no less propagandistic, construct: at a certain point, it became ordinary through practice; it was concrete, it had material effects. Because of this, it had limits, it was a precarious and perishable organism. The exploration of the material and narrative temporalities that different maps of empire and their messages were encountered and decoded during everyday life speaks about this uneven transformation, as well as the different contexts of the receptions it received. The spatialities, bodily practices, protocols and pragmatics officiated by maps, although placed in contexts different from surveys, colonial explorations and conquests, allowed mapping and the making of the empire to bleed into one another. The empire performed through such cartographic vulgarization gave a sense of an unfolding, desired and perfect order that, however, never materialized beyond the imagination of a politicized audience.

By following the cartographic lives of the Italian Fascism's Empire, my effort has been to retrace the imprint of the creation of an imperial consciousness and sensitivity in Italy. This has been done not exclusively by looking at the intentions of the cartographers and policy-makers who produced and discussed the design and information of maps, but also by shedding light on the various ways that the becoming of empire, and the domestic connectivity to far-flung territorial imaginations, were conceivable, by letting a wider audience engage performatively and sensorially with those cartographic imperial formations. The communicative (that is, other than navigational) role played by popular cartography opened two sets of reflections. The first one is methodological: the scarcity of direct sources that discuss the relationship different observers had with the empire and with its cartographic representations may lead to a primary conclusion, that configurations of past cartographic performances often resolve in 'an exploration of how our map *asked to be* used, rather than of how it actually *was* used' (Hornsey 2012, 168). By imagining how not only political actors but also pedestrians, students, readers and other spectators interacted with cartographic representations and the materialities of the empire, I perhaps ran the risk of speculating about maps' and people's lives. I have nevertheless made this attempt by keeping in mind two methodological enquiries. One is focused on rewriting the object biographies (Hoskins 1998; Harding 2016) of the empire, wherein the observer attempts to speculate about how certain objects are perceived by the persons that they are closely connected to. The other, perhaps more consistently undertaken in this chapter, attempts to interrogate objects themselves (Harding 2016), by placing them 'in a historical context,' thus considering the 'environmental contingencies' and 'historical particularities' (Hornsey 2012) wherein they are framed while interlacing them with vocal, verbal and visual sources found during the research. Under this framework, it seems productive to begin to practice *multisensory* historical geographical research as a fresh entryway to gathering knowledge about historical moments and phenomena (Hacke and Musselwhite 2018).

The second line of reflections brings out the multifaceted connective effects enacted by kinaesthetic representations of maps in the imperial machine. Highlighting the visual and material dynamic performances of maps of empires in many contexts of everyday life, I stress the idea that connectivity to the empire can be experienced at different levels: by giving attention to the many sites, devices and materials through which maps of empires migrated and infiltrated, connectivity translated into the enduring sensory circulation of the colonial and imperial cartography; by focussing on the map as a multisensorial experience – a touchable, observable, audible medium – connectivity transformed into a multisensorial ritual, where the imaginal empire of fascism took on flesh and became understandable by larger strata of the population; by addressing the temporal narrative plotted in the granite of large maps or in the celluloid of newsreels, connectivity further emerged as a chronomobile frame, superimposing the glories of the Old Roman Empire on the Fascist present in order to manipulate imperial future claims. Overall, emphasis on the processual becoming of maps allows us to see geography not as 'something already possessed by the earth but an active writing of the earth by an expanding centralizing imperial state' (Ó Tuathail 1996, 1). Ó Tuathail (1996, 2) concluded that geography 'was not a noun but a verb, a geo-graphing, an earth-writing by ambitious and colonizing and ex-colonizing states who sought to seize space and organize it to fit their own cultural vision and material interests'.

Yet, even though mapping is the most concrete output of the geo-graphing activity, the bond between mapping and empire is never a straightforward causal relationship, but one muddied and muddled by all sorts of contingencies, circuits and loose ends. To trace the everyday use of mapping *and*, *in* and *with* empire is not only a methodological challenge but an attempt to capture something (un)common and fleeting about those modes of thinking – often taken for granted – and practicing the relationship between space and identity. In this sense, I had the feeling that the particular design of such maps, as much as their contingent circulation and use in several contexts of everyday life, could truly hint at the experiences and impressions of viewers at the time, though I cannot overestimate 'the troubling and exhilarating feeling that things could be different, or at least that they could still fail' (Latour 2005, 89). Even if I ended up emphasizing some contexts in which banal maps manifested a kind of operational power, eventually disregarded, for the construction of spatial orders, an entire space in the scholarship opens for events in which maps *could still fail*: where maps are useless, do not do their job, or are impotent, or work differently than expected, as has been demonstrated my many chapters in this volume. Considering also the many failures and constraints that Italian Fascism encountered, Labanca further argued that: 'Given an empire that was so little loved or wanted, it was easier to bring it to an end' (2018, 130). In this way, not only a sensory history of the mapping and making of empire, but also of mapping the *un*making of empire, is to be written.

## NOTES

1. At the end of the nineteenth century, the Geographical Society of Rome stated its support for African expansionism, followed by many newly founded associations such as the African Club of Naples, the Society of Geographical and Colonial Studies of Florence, the Exploration Commercial Society in Milan and, finally, the Italian Colonial Institute, founded in 1906.

2. In this regard, the historical role played by official cartography in surveying, patrolling, producing and disseminating the knowledge of empire has assumed centre stage in books and publications, both in Italy (Cerreti 1987, 1995; Casti 1995; Boria 2007) and abroad (Driver 1992; Edney 1997; Harley 2001; Akerman 2009; Branch 2014). On the theme of mapping and the making of the empire, Italian scholarship has been particularly fertile with studies that illustrate how Africa was cartographically constructed by colonizers (Cerreti 1987, 1995); research that examines the cognitive short-circuits of surveyors and map-makers when they attempted to codify the experiences of unknown places, such as the desert, in Western maps (Casti 1995); works that discuss the relationship between geography, publishing and fascism (Carazzi 1972; Monina 1992; Boria 2007; Atkinson 2013); and macro-structurally analyses of the geographies of Italian imperialism (Gambi 1992).

3. Part of the inauguration of the fifth map is also accessible on YouTube: https://www.youtube.com/watch?v=32txTQNnT7k.

4. Italy was indeed the first country of the world to use asphyxiating gas and mustard gas against colonies (see Del Boca 2007 and Labanca 2002).

5. The whole documentary can be watched at the following link: https://patrimonio.archivioluce.com/luce-web/detail/IL3000096344/1/sulle-orme-nostri-pionieri.html?startPage=0&jsonVal={%22jsonVal%22:{%22query%22:[%22*:*%22],%22fieldDate%22:%22dataNormal%22,%22_perPage%22:20,%22temi%22:[%22\%22Dubat\%22%22]}}

## REFERENCES

Akerman, James R. 2009. *The Imperial Map: Cartography and the Mastery of Empire*. The Kenneth Nebenzahl, Jr., Lectures in the History of Cartography. Chicago: University of Chicago Press.

Antonsich, Marco. 2009. 'Geopolitica: The "Geographical and Imperial Consciousness" of Fascist Italy'. *Geopolitics* 14 (2): 256–77.

Appadurai, Arjun. 2006. 'The Thing Itself'. *Public Culture* 18 (1): 15–22.

Atkinson, David. 2013. 'Geographical Imaginations, Public Education and the Everyday Worlds of Fascist Italy'. *Journal of Modern Italian Studies* 18 (5): 561–79.

Batuman, Bülent. 2010. 'The Shape of the Nation: Visual Production of Nationalism through Maps in Turkey'. *Political Geography* 29 (4): 220–34.

Ben-Ghiat, Ruth. 2013. 'Narrating War in Italian Fascist Cinema'. In *Narrating War. Perspectives from the XVI – XX centuries*, edited by M. Mondini and M. Rospocher, 249–68. Berlin and Bologna: Duncker & Humblot/Il Mulino.

———. 2015. *Italian Fascism's Empire Cinema: New Directions in National Cinemas*. Bloomington: Indiana University Press.

Ben-Ghiat, Ruth, and Mia Fuller. 2005. *Italian Colonialism*. 1st ed. Italian and Italian American Studies. New York: Palgrave Macmillan.

Boria, Edoardo. 2007. *Cartografia e Potere*. Torino: Utet.

Branch, Jordan. 2015. *The Cartographic State: Maps, Territory and the Origins of Sovereignty*. Cambridge: Cambridge University Press.

Brückner Martin. 2017. *The Social Life of Maps in America, 1750–1860*. Williamsburg, Virginia: Omohundro Institute of Early American History and Culture.

Buisseret, David. 1992. *Monarchs, Ministers, and Maps: The Emergence of Cartography As a Tool of Government in Early Modern Europe*. The Kenneth Nebenzahl, Jr. Lectures in the History of Cartography. Chicago: University of Chicago Press.

———. 2003. *The Mapmakers' Quest: Depicting New Worlds in Renaissance Europe*. Oxford: Oxford University Press.

Caquard, Sébastien. 2013. 'Foreshadowing Contemporary Digital Cartography: A Historical Review of Cinematic Maps in Films'. *The Cartographic Journal* 46 (1): 46–55.

Caquard, Sébastien, and D. R. Fraser Taylor. 2009. 'What Is Cinematic Cartography?' *The Cartographic Journal* 46 (1): 5–8.

Carazzi, Maria. 1972. *La Società Geografica Italiana e l'esplorazione coloniale in Africa (1867–1900)*. Firenze: La Nuova Italia.

Casti, Emanuela. 1995. 'La Libia nella cartografia coloniale italiana: Tripoli e Cufra'. In *Colonie africane e cultura italiana fra Ottocento e Novecento. Le esplorazioni e la geografia (Roma, 20 maggio 1994)*, edited by Cerreti Claudio, 99–110. Roma: CISU.

Cerreti, Claudio. 1987. *La raccolta cartografica dell'Istituto Italo-africano, presentazione del fondo e guida alla consultazione*, Roma: Tipografia G. Pioda.

———, ed. 1995. *Colonie africane e cultura italiana fra Ottocento e Novecento. Le esplorazioni e la geografia*. Roma: CISU.

Crespi, Mario. 1937. *Alcuni problemi vitali del giornalismo fascista*. Roma: Tipografia del Senato, Available online at https://cronologia.leonardo.it/storia/a1937d.htm.

Daniels, Stephen. 2010. 'Putting Maps in Place'. *Journal of Historical Geography* 36: 473–80.
De Grand, Alexander. 2004. 'Mussolini's Follies: Fascism in Its Imperial and Racist Phase, 1935–1940'. *Contemporary European History* 13: 127–47.
Del Boca, Angelo. 2007. *A un passo dalla forca*. Milano: Baldini Castoldi Dalai.
Della Dora, Veronica. 2009. 'Performative Atlases: Memory, Materiality and (Co-)authorship'. *Cartographica* 44 (4): 240–55.
Dodge, Martin, Rob Kitchin, and Chris Perkins. 2009. *'Rethinking Maps: New Frontiers in Cartographic Theory*. Routledge Studies in Human Geography, 28. London: Routledge.
Driver, Felix. 1992. 'Geography's Empire: Histories of Geographical Knowledge'. *Environment & Planning D: Society and Space* 10 (1): 23–40.
Edney, Matthew H. 1997. *Mapping an Empire: The Geographical Construction of British India, 1765–1843*. Chicago: University of Chicago Press.
———. 2009. 'The Irony of Imperial Mapping'. In *The Imperial Map: Cartography and the Mastery of Empire*, edited by James R. Akerman, 11–45. Chicago: University of Chicago Press, 2009.
Follo, Valentina. 2013. *The Power of Images in the Age of Mussolini, PhD thesis, Publicly Accessible Penn Dissertations*.
Gambi, Lucio. 1992. *Geografia e imperialismo in Italia*. Bologna: Patròn.
Hacke, Daniela, and Paul Musselwhite, eds. 2018. *Empire of the Senses: Sensory Practices of Colonialism in Early America*. Early American History Series: The American Colonies, 1500–1830, Volume 8. Leiden: Brill.
Harding, Anthony. 2016. 'Introduction: Biographies of Things'. *Distant Worlds Journal* 1 (7): 5–10.
Harley, J. Brian. 2001. *The New Nature of Maps, Essays in the History of Cartography,* Baltimore: The Johns Hopkins University Press.
Hornsey, Richard. 2012. 'Listening to the Tube Map: Rhythm and the Historiography of Urban Map Use'. *Environment and Planning D: Society and Space* 30: 675–93.
Hoskins, Janet. 1998. *Biographical Objects: How Things Tell the Stories of People's Lives*. London: Routledge.
Jacob, Christian. 2006. *The Sovereign Map: Theoretical Approaches in Cartography throughout History*. Chicago: University of Chicago Press.
Jacobs, Frank. 2014. 'Making Italy Great Again: A Map of Mussolini's Mediterranean Ambitions'. https://bigthink.com/strange-maps/italy-embiggened-and-encircled.
Kemp, Harold. 1940. 'Mussolini: Italy's Geographer-In-Chief'. *Journal of Geography* 39 (4): 133–41.
Kim, Yong Woo. 2009. 'From "Consensus Studies" to History of Subjectivity: Some Considerations on Recent Historiography on Italian Fascism'. *Totalitarian Movements and Political Religions* 10 (3–4): 327–37.
Kitchin, Rob, Justin Gleeson, and Martin Dodge. 2013. 'Unfolding Mapping Practices: A New Epistemology for Cartography'. *Transactions of the Institute of British Geographers* 38 (3): 480–96.
Kosonen, Katarlina. 2008. 'Making Maps and Mental Images: Finnish Press Cartography in Nation-Building, 1899–1942'. *National Identities* 10 (1): 21–47.

Labanca, Nicola. 2002. *Oltremare. Storia dell'espansione coloniale italiana.* Bologna: Il Mulino.
———. 2018. 'Exceptional Italy? The Many Ends of the Italian Colonial Empire'. In *The Oxford Handbook of the Ends of Empire*, edited by Martin Thomas and Andrew S. Thompson, 124–42. Oxford: Oxford University Press, 2018.
Latour, Bruno. 2005. *Reassembling the Social: An Introduction to Actor-Network-Theory.* Clarendon Lectures in Management Studies. Oxford: Oxford University Press.
*L'Azione coloniale.* 1935. 'Attività Radiofonica – Vita delle sezione'. 14 (November): 4.
Lenin, Vladimir I. 1917 (2000). *Imperialism, the Highest Stage of Capitalism.* New Delhi: LeftWord Books.
Lobo-Guerrero, Luis, Suvi Alt, and Maarten Meijer, eds. 2019. *Imaginaries of Connectivity: The Creation of Novel Spaces of Governance.* Global Epistemics Series. London: Rowman & Littlefield International.
Lo Presti, Laura. 2019. *Cartografie (in)esauste. Rappresentazioni, visualità, estetiche nella teoria critica delle cartografie contemporanee.* Milano: Franco Angeli.
Maione, Giuseppe. 1979. *L'imperialismo straccione. classi sociali e finanza di guerra dall'impresa etiopica al conflitto mondiale (1935–1943).* Bologna: Il Mulino.
Minor, Heather Hyde. 1999. 'Mapping Mussolini: Ritual and Cartography in Public Art during the Second Roman Empire'. *Imago Mundi* 51 (1): 147–62.
Monina, Giancarlo. 2002. *Il consenso coloniale. Le società geografiche e l'Istituto coloniale italiano (1896–1914).* Roma: Carocci.
Oliver, Jeff. 2011. 'On Mapping and Its Afterlife: Unfolding Landscapes in Northwestern North America'. *World Archaeology* 43 (1): 66–85.
Ó Tuathail Gearóid. 1996. *Critical Geopolitics: The Politics of Writing Global Space.* London: Routledge.
Palma, Silvana. 1999. *L'Italia Coloniale*, Roma: Editori Riuniti.
Pitts, Martin, and Versluys Miguel John. 2015. *Globalisation and the Roman World: World History, Connectivity and Material.* Cambridge: Cambridge University Press.
Proudfoot, Lindsay J., and Michael M. Roche. 2005. *(Dis)Placing Empire: Renegotiating British Colonial Geographies. Heritage, Culture, and Identity.* Aldershot: Ashgate Pub.
Rodogno, Davide. 2003. *Il nuovo ordine mediterraneo: le politiche di occupazione dell'Italia fascista in Europa (1940–1943)*, Torino: Bollati Boringhieri.
Romano, Sergio. 2005. *La quarta sponda.* Milano: Longanesi.
Rossetto, Tania. 2019. *Object-Oriented Cartography: Maps as Things.* London/New York: Routledge.
Segrè, Claudio G. 1979. Beggar's Empire: Ideology and the Colonialist Movement in Liberal Italy. *Proceedings of the Meeting of the French Colonial Historical Society* 4: 174–83.
Testi, Giulio. 1935. 'Appunti tecnici sulla carta e sugli inchiostri'. *La Chimica nell'industria, nell'agricoltura, nella biologia e nelle altre applicazioni* 13 (2): 18–35.
Wilmott, Clancy. 2020. *Mobile Mapping: Space, Cartography and the Digital*, Amsterdam: Amsterdam University Press.
Wood, Denis. 2010. *Rethinking The Power of Maps.* New York: Guilford Press.

# Index

absolutism, in Denmark, 70–71
Abyssinia, 184
actor-network-theory (ANT), 111
*Adam of Bremen,* 62
Africa: as blank space, 116–19; construction of, by cartography, 196n2; early maps of, 118; German expansion into, 116–26; German Inner-Africa Expedition, 120–26, *122, 125–26*; Italian Fascism Empire in, 183, 186; Scramble for Africa, 175, 196n1; Wadai Empire, 120–21, 124
African Club of Naples, 196n1
age of reconnaissance, in Greenland, 62
Albania, 184
Albuquerque, Alfonso de, 37–38
Alexander VI (Pope), 25, 28
Alfonso VIII of Castile, 25
Alfonso X (King), 31
Algeria, 161
Allday, Jacob, 61
'already encoded eye,' xvi
Álvarez Cabral, Pedro, 26
American colonies, in North America: Carolina Provinces, 97–98; Connecticut, 89, 95, *96,* 97; Conojocular War, 98–99; establishment of borders for, 14, 83–85, 93–94, 98–100; imperial cartography for, 80–83; Iroquois Confederacy, 99; land control in, 77–78; landowner settlers in, 78–79; linearization of territoriality in, 92–95, 97–100; mapping of, 77–80; maps of, 77, *78;* Maryland, 84, 98–99; Mason-Dixon line, 84, 99–100, *101;* Massachusetts, 89, 93–94; Native American land in, dispossession of, 14, 78–79, 85–86; New Jersey, 77, *78;* New York, 95; under Paris Treaty (1783), 85; Pennsylvania, 77, *78,* 98–99; *Plat of the Seven Ranges of Townships, 91,* 100–101; private property in, 79; surveying of land in, 14, 85; under Treaty of St. Germain, 94; Virginia, 89, 92, 97–98; War of Independence and, 92
*Annales géographiques,* 154
ANT. *See* actor-network-theory
d'Anville, Jean Baptiste Bourguignon, 118
Arctic Ocean region, *128–29;* Open Polar Sea theory, 106–7, 117, 127–32. *See also* North Pole expeditions; North-West Passage

Arianism and, conversion from Catholicism, in Spain, 25
Aristotle, 19
Armitage, David, 11
Arnoldi, Ernst-Wilhelm, 113
*The Art of Surveying* (Wing), 87
assemblages, 3
*The Athenaeum*, 106–7
d'Aulnay, Charles, 94
Austro-Hungarian Empire: dissolution of, 15; German Reich and, 108
Austro-Hungarian North-Pole Expedition, 132
autonomy, of maps, 6
Aztec Empire, 31–32. See also Moctezuma

barbarians, mapping and, xvi
Barents, Willem, 107
Barth, Heinrich, 116, 120, 121
beggar imperialism, of Italy, 175, 193–94
Benoist, Charles, 151–52
Berghaus, Heinrich, 116
Bernard, Augustin, 141, *153*, 157, 159, 168; on Peace Conference, 151–52, 154–56
Bielke, Jens, 70
Bisgaard, Lars, 73n13
blank spaces, 6, 108; Africa as, 116–19; pseudo-topography and, 118
Bolzé, René, 141, *146*; *France du Levant*, 145, 147–49, 151, 159, *160*, 161–62, 169
borders and boundaries: for American colonies, establishment of, 14, 83–85, 93–94, 98–100; of Germany, 84; of Italy, 84; of New Spain, French-Spanish border, 99
Borges, Jorge Luis, 1
Bottai, Giuseppe, 187
Bowen, Clarence, *96*
Brahe, Tyco, xx, 60
Branch, Jordan, 3, 81–82
Brendecke, Arndt, 35, 39

Briand, Aristide, 154
British Mandate, proclamation of, 169n3
Byrd, William, II, 97–98

Cabot, John, 28, 66–67
Caix, Robert de, 152, 167–68
Carolina Provinces, in American colonies, 97–98
*Carta de Juan de la Cosa*, 13, 23, 26, *27*
*Carte du Liban*, 143
cartography: centers of calculation and, 109–16; colonial Africa constructed by, 196n2; colonialism and, 2; criticism of, 80; definition of, 2; domestication of, xvii; as epistemic community, xvii–xx; geometric, 59, 68–70, 72n2; Gotha school of, 114; Humboldtian tradition, 108; imperial, 80–83; International Relations and, xvii; in Italy, as propaganda, 177; jurisdictional boundaries through, 2; materialization of power through, 1; materiality of, 5; of Middle East, 142; modes of writing, 169n7; naming and, 69; as privileged instrument, 3; as propaganda, in Italy, 177; property rights and, legitimacy of, 2; Ptolemaic, 83–85; as representation of space, 59; representations through, homologies enabled by, 83–85; scientific management of, 109–16; as set of practices, 57–58; sovereignty through, 2; specialization of material, 113–14; of Syria, 142–44; territorial boundaries through, 2; Western imperialism and, 2. See also specific topics
*Casa de Contratación de Sevilla*, 34–35, 37, 40–41
*Casa de India*, 35, 109
Casti, Emanuela, 193
Catholic Empire, in Spain, 23, 25–30; Arianism and, conversion from,

25; conceptualization of, goals and purposes of, 25–26; Council of Toledo, 25; papal legitimization of, 25–26; Reconquista and, 25; Spanish Inquisition, 26
Cavafy, Constantine, xv
celestial navigation, 39
centers of calculation: cartography and, 109–16; Latour on, 107, 109–16
ceremonies of possession, maps as, 52
Charlemagne, 31
Charles I (King): abdication of, 39; *Casa de Contratación de Sevilla*, 34–35, 37; *Casa de India*, 35; Council of Castile, 34; Council of the Indies, 34; in Holy Roman Empire (as Charles V), 30–39; *Junta de Pilotos*, 38; *Padrón Real* and, 32–33, 37; *Piloto Mayor*, 35–37; during Spanish Empire, 23, 25, 30–39; Treaty of Zaragoza, 38; Universal Monarchy, 31
Charles II (King), 98
Charles V (Emperor), 112
Charlotte of Mecklenburg-Streilitz, 92
Christian II (King), 60
Christianity. *See* global Christian space
Christian IV (King), 63–65
Ciunet, Vital, 152
Claudius Clavus. *See* Swart, Claudius Claussøn
cold maps, 58–60
colonialism: cartography and, 2; in Greenland, 52, 72; imaginaries of space and, 12; invention and, 21; by Italy, 175–76; private property and, 79; Scramble for Africa, 175, 196n1; in West Indies, 73n14. *See also* American colonies; Middle East; North America; South America; Syria
colonial networks, in France, 14
colonial postcards, *189*
Columbus, Ferdinand, 38
Congress of Vienna, 112

Connecticut, as American colony, 89, 95, *96*, 97
connective spaces, Greenland as, 55–58
connectivity effects: composite methodologies, 7–9; homology and, 7, 79; imaginary of, 188; levels of, 8; map-making and, 7–9; in Spanish Empire, 9
Conojocular War, 98–99
conquest: mapping and, 175; navigation and, 175
Conrad, Sebastian, 112–13
Cortés, Hernán, 31
*Cosmographiae Introductio*, 41
cosmography: imperialism and, 13; knowledge through, 36–37
Council of Castile, 34
Council of the Indies, 34
Council of Toledo, 25
Cressaty, Salim, 148, 156
cultural syncretism, imperialism and, 10
Cunningham, John, 65, 68
Cusanus, Nicolaus, 58

da Gama, Vasco, 37
Dante Alighieri, 31
de Feo, Luciano, 191, *192*
de la Cosa, Juan, 13, 26, 35
de la Tour, Charles, 94
deconstruction, 3
Deleuze, Gilles, 3
Denmark: absolutism in, 70–71; constitutional change in, 70–71; empire-building by, 14; European Renaissance and, 60; Frederick II and, xx; genealogy of kings in, 60; in Kalmar Union, 72n3; mapping of Greenland by, 8; Norway and, reconnection to, 60–64; sovereignty over Greenland, 51–52; Sweden and, 70–71; as tax dependency, 72; unicorns in, meaning of, 73n13; in West Indies, colonization of, 73n14
Deraa-Damas-Aleppo line, in Syria, 163
Derrida, Jacques, 3, 21

Desai, Guarav, 21
Diaz, Bartolomeu, 26
Díaz de Solís, Juan, 35
Dubois, Marcel, 155
Dutch West India Company, 94–95
dynamic stabilization processes, in empires, 10

Edney, Matthew, 54, 110, 118; on imperial mapping, 2
Egede, Hans, 72
Egypt, Napoleon invasion of, 143
Elizabeth I (Queen), 51
Elizabeth of Valois, 40, 42
empire, as concept: actor-network-theory and, 111; cartography and, foundations of, 13–15; connectivity in, 9; dynamic stabilization processes and, 10; European discovery and, 11; geography and, 59; hierarchization processes in, 10; International Relations and, 9–12; as language game, 111–12; mapless, 13, 54; ordering processes and, 10; problematization of, 23; space-making in, 24–25, 178; spaceness of, 12; space-sensing in, 178. *See also* American colonies; colonialism; Italian Fascism Empire; Spanish Empire
empirical navigation, 57
enclosure movement, in England, 86
England: enclosure movement in, 86; imperial expansionism by, 108; land ceded to U.S., 89; land ownership rights in, 86; Royal Geographic Society, 106, 115–16, 120. *See also* American colonies
episteme: definition of, 21; spatial, 176
epistemic community, xvii–xx
epistemic formations: maps and, 21; Spanish Empire as, 43–44
epistemological novelty, maps and, 38–39
*Erebus* (ship), 105–6, 127, 133n1

Eric the Red. *See* Thorvaldsson, Erik
Eritrea, 184
Ernst II (Duke), 113, 121
Ethiopia, 183, 190; Second Ethiopian War, 177
Europe: cartography of Syria, 142–44; in Scramble for Africa, 175, 196n1. *See also specific countries*
European imperialism: discovery as element of, 11; Indigenous peoples and, identity of, 11
European Renaissance, 60
Evans, Lewis, 77
Exploration Commercial Society, 196n1
extra-territoriality, 176–77
*Eye of Power* (Foucault), 12

Ferdinand (King), 25, 44n1
fjords, 69–70
Foucault, Michel, 3, 12; 'already encoded eye,' xvi; on epistemes, definition of, 21; on reflexive knowledge, xvi
Fraccaro, Plinio, 182
France: Algeria and, 161; geographical imaginary of, 141; imperial expansionism by, 108; maps in, municipal uses of, 82; Marseilles Congress, in Syria, 147–49, 154; Middle East treaty with United Kingdom, 139; in Ottoman Empire, 140–41; private colonial networks in, 14; Syria controlled by, 139–40, 144–45, 156–57, 165. *See also* Syria
*France du Levant,* 145, 147–49, 151, 159, *160,* 161–62, 169
Franco-Prussian War, 132
Franklin, David, 169n4
Franklin, John: North-West Passage expedition, 105–6, 119, 127; Royal Geographic Society and, 106
Frederick II (King), xx
Frederik II (King), 51, 60–61, 114
French Empire: circulating maps for, 167–69; graphic networks of,

156–57; imperial space-making and, 167; material networks of, 156–57; Syria in, 139–40, 144–45, 156–57, 165
Frobisher, Martinus: Greenland and, 51, 64–65; Muscovy Company and, 51; North-West passage and, 51, 64–65
Froidevaux, Henri, 145–46, 148–49, 151, 155, 162, 167–68

Galli, Carlo, 11
García Redondo, José María, 32, 35–36
Gattinara, Mercurino, 31
geo-bodies, in Middle East: man-made territorial definition, 143; of Syria, 142–44
*Geodaesia* (Love), 87–88, *88*, 97
geography: of knowledge, 114; materialization of power through, 1
*Geography* (Ptolemy), 62
geometric cartography, 59, 72n2; for agriculture and farming, 85–86; enclosure movement, 86; Greenland and, 68–70; as new form of literacy, 87; property claims as result of, 88; for public commons, 86; quantitative measures of, 86; rhetoric of, 85–92; surveying and, 87
George, Lloyd, 139
Georges-Picot, François, 139–41; Sykes-Picot Agreement, 140–41, 163
German Confederation, 112–13, 123; division of, 113; fragmentation of, 128; Franco-Prussian War and, 132; German-German War, 130
Germandom, Germanness and, xvii–xviii, 134n4
German-German War, 130
*Germania* (ship), 130–32, *131*
German Inner-Africa Expedition, 133; Heuglin and, 121, 123–24; map of, *122*, 122–23, *125*, 125–26, *125–26*; patriotic purpose of, 125; scientific value of, 125; Wadai Empire, 120–21, 124

German North Pole Expeditions, 109, 127–33; Franklin Expedition and, 127; *Germania,* 130–32, *131*; Open Polar Sea theory, 127–32; Royal Geographic Society and, 127
German Reich, 108
Germany: borders of, 84; expansion into Africa, 116–26; far-right groups in, 134n4; German Inner-Africa Expedition, 120–26, *122*, *125*, 133; German North Pole Expeditions, 109, 127–33, *131*; imperial aspirations of, 116–19; *Lebensraum* in, 109; unification of, 108; *Weltpolitik* in, 109
Ghanim, Shukri, 151
global Christian space, 13
globality, emergence of, 116
Gotha school, of cartography, 114
Greek mythology, xv–xvi
Greenland: age of reconnaissance in, 62; as cartographic space, 54; changing conceptions of, 52–53; colonization of, 52, 72; as connective space, 55–58; Danish sovereignty over, 51–52; as dependent colony, 52; early geographic knowledge of, 62; European imperial ambitions for, 72n1; fjords, 69–70; geometric cartography and, 68–70; *Groenlandia* Treaty, 71; Hall expeditions to, 52, 65–70; *Hauksbogen,* 57; in historical texts, 53–54; Inuit natives, 68; lost settlements in, reconnection to, 61; mapless empires and, 54; mapping of, 8, 14, 63, 68–71; maps of, *53–54*; Muscovy Company and, 61; networked polity and, 54; reconnection of travel routes to, 64–68; as *terra nullius,* 66–67; as territory, 52–53; Thorvaldsson in, 55–56; *Trost,* 69–70; during Viking Age, settlements during, 51, 56
Greer, Allan, 86
Gregory, Derek, 169n5

*Groenlandia* Treaty, 71
Grotius, Hugo, 40
Guattari, Félix, 3
Gutierrez, Diego, 13, 23–24; map of New World, 40–41, *41*, 43

Hachette (publishing house), 109, 114
Hall, James, 13; Greenland expeditions by, 52, 65–70; map of Greenland, *53–54*
Harley, Brian, 2, 7, 54, 59, 80, 108, 117–18, 140
*Hauksbogen,* 57
Heuglin, Theodor von, 121, 123–24, 130
hierarchization processes, in empires, 10
History of Cartography Project, 169n7
*History of the Dividing Line* (Byrd), 97–98
Holy Land, rediscovery of, 143
Holy Roman Empire, 82; Charles V in, 30–39; German Confederation as replacement of, 112; Italian Fascism Empire influenced by, 181; mural maps in, 181–82; Punic Wars, 181
homogenization, homology and, 84
homology concept: connectivity effects and, 7, 79; enabler of, cartographic representation of, 83–85; homogenization and, 84
House of Bourbon, in Spain, 44n1
Huitfeldt, Christopher, 59
*The Human Condition* (Magritte), 3–5, *4*
Humboldtian tradition, of cartography, 108
Huré, Georges, 155, 167
Huvelin, Paul, 148

Iceland, 56–57; *Hauksbogen,* 57; travel routes to Greenland, 60
identity creation: imperialism and, 10; space and, relationship between, 195–96
*Imaginaries of Connectivity,* 7
imaginaries of space: colonialism and, 12; territory and, 3

imaginary of discovery, 19–20
immutable mobiles: Latour on, 110; maps as, 8, 110–11
imperial cartography, 80–83
imperialism: beggar, 175, 193–94; cosmography and, 13; cultural syncretism and, 10; definition of, 11; identity creation and, 10; mapping of, 9–12; maps as weapons of, 108; Western, 2. *See also* colonialism; *specific topics*
imperial mapping, 2, 9–12
imperial space-making, by French Empire, 167
India, geography and empire in, 59
Indigenous peoples: European imperialism and, lack of identity for, 11; Inuit natives, on Greenland, 68. *See also* Native Americans
Ingold, Tim, 156
International Relations: cartography and, xvii; empire and, 9–12; methodological nationalism and, 9; as territorial trap, 10; in Westphalian tradition, 10
invention: colonization and, 21; of Spanish Empire, 21–23
*The Invention of Africa* (Mudimbe), 21
Iroquois Confederacy, 99
Isabel (Queen), 25, 44n1
Isidore of Seville, 29
Islamic State in the Levant (ISIL), 139
Istituto Geografico Militare, 177, 188
Italian Colonial Institute, 196n1
Italian Fascism Empire, *184*; in Africa, 183, 186; cartographic senses of, 179–81; colonial postcards, *189*; colonies of, 184; cultural politics of, 179, 193; Ethiopia, 183, 190; expansion of, *188*; export of, 183; Holy Roman Empire and, 181; imaginary of connectivity, 188; as incorporeal, 189–90; intellectual branch of, 189–90; Istituto Geografico Militare, 177, 188; Libya, 183; mapmakers in, point

of view of, 180; mapping and, 177, 195; maps in, 9, 181–86; *Mare Nostrum*, 183; miniaturization of, 187–88; multisensory interactions in, 190–91, 193, 195; mural maps in, 179, 181–86; murals as propaganda in, 179, 181–86; newsreel images of, 190–91, *192*; object biographies of, 195; regimentation of bodies, 191–92; sensory milieu of, 178, 180–81; small maps in, 186–90; space-making and, 178; space-sensing and, 178; in urban streetscape, 181–86

Italy: beggar imperialism of, 175, 193–94; borders of, 84; cartographic products in, 177; cartography as propaganda, 177; colonialism and, 175–76; in Scramble for Africa, 175, 196n1; in Second Ethiopian War, 177. *See also* Old Roman Empire

James I (King), 65
Jefferson, Thomas, 87
John (King), 38
Johnson, Alexander Keith, 115
*Journal of Geography,* 179
*Junta de Pilotos,* 38
Justus Perthes (German publishing house), xvii, 14, 107–9, 112–16; Petermann and, 109, 113; *Stielers Hand-Atlas,* 114–15

Kalmar Union, 72n3
Kaufman, Asher, 143
knowledge: cosmographical, 36–37; through cosmography, 36–37; geographies of, 114; of Greenland, 62; reflexive, xvi; of seafaring, 51
Koldewey, Karl, 130
*Kosmos* (Humboldt), 116

Labanca, Nicola, 194, 196
Lammens, Henri, 143, 157, 171n28
*landnam* (land-taking), 56, 58
Land Ordinance of 1785, U.S., 89–90
land-taking. *See landnam*

Latour, Bruno, 57, 70, 107; on immutable mobiles, 110
Law, John, 110
League of Nations, 169n3
Lebanon, 169, 169n3
*Lebensraum* (living space), 109, 183
Levant region, geographical imaginary of, 141
Libya, 183, 184
Lindenov, Godske, 65
linearization of territoriality, 92–95, 97–100
living space. *See Lebensraum*
Livingstone, David, 116
Louis XIV (King), 81
Love, John, 87–88, *88*, 97
Lower Mesopotamia region, 140, *158*
Luhmann, Niklas, 33
Lyschander, Claus, 70

MacKenzie, Donald, 134n3
Magrethe I (Queen), 72n3
Magritte, René, 3–5, *4*
Manuel I (King), 45n3
map-interpreters, xvi
mapless empire, 13; Greenland and, 54
map-making, map-makers and, xvi; connectivity effects of, 7–9; increase in, 81; Italian Fascism Empire and, point of view as factor for, 180; as process, 5; spatial imaginaries and, 7–9
*Map of Western Palestine,* 143
mapping, as practice: of American colonies, 77–80; of barbarians, xvi; conceptualization of, 58–59; definition of, 22–23; epistemological novelty in, 19–20; as experimental sites, xvi; goals and purposes of, 84; graphic modes of, 5; of Greenland, 8, 14, 63, 68–71; imperial, 2, 9–12, 22; Italian Fascism Empire and, 177, 195; navigation and, 175; for New World, 13; as performative, 5; political elements of, 80; post-representational approach to, 5–6;

private agencies, 114; problematizing representation in, 3–7; as rhetorical, 81; societal elements of, 80; for taxation uses, 82; training for, lack of, 176. *See also specific regions*
maps: of American colonies, 77, *78*; autonomous life of, 6; as ceremonies of possession, 52; circulating, for French Empire, 167–69; cold, 58–60; as element of material culture, 6; epistemic formations through deconstruction of, 21; epistemological novelty and, 38–39; in France, municipal uses of, 82; of German Inner-Africa Expedition, *122*, 122–23, 125–26, *125–26*; as graphic representations, 59; of Greenland, *53–54*; as immutable mobiles, 8, 110–10; in Italian Fascism Empire, 9, 181–86; of Lower Mesopotamia region, *158*; Mercator, *64*; in murals, 179, 181–86; as mutable mobiles, 8, 110–11; political use of, 81; pseudotopographic, of Syria, 147; for representation of spatial ideas, 2; as sources of historical fact, 1–2; of Syria, *150*, *153*, *158*, *166*; as weapons of imperialism, 108
map-users, xvi
*Mare Clausus*, 40
*Mare Liberum*, 40
*Mare Nostrum*, 183
*Mar Oceanum*, 28
Maronites, 165
Marseilles Congress, in Syria, 147–49, 154
Martonne, Emmanuel de, 152, 154, 155
Maryland, as colony, 84, 98–99
Mason-Dixon line, 84, 99–100, *101*
Massachusetts, as colony, 89, 93–94
materiality: of cartography, 1; of maps, 6
Medici, Lorenzo Pietri di, 19
Meier, H. H., 130

Mercator maps, *64*
methodological nationalism, 9–10
Middle East: cartography of, 142; geo-bodies in, 142; Holy Land, rediscovery of, 143; Lower Mesopotamia region, 140, *158*; Peace Conference and, 141, 144–45, 151–52, 154–56; Suez Canal, 159; Sykes-Picot Agreement, 140; treaty between France and United Kingdom, 139; Zionist nationalist movements in, 140. *See also specific countries*
mobiles. *See* immutable mobiles; mutable mobiles
Moctezuma, 31–32
modern cartography. *See* geometric cartography
Mol, Annemarie, 110
*Monarchia* (Alighieri), 31
Mudimbe, V. Y., 21
multisensory interactions, in Italian Fascism Empire, 190–91, 193, 195
*Mundus Novus* (Manuel I), 45n3
Munk, Jens, 70
Muñoz, Antonio, 181
Munzinger, Werner, 124
mural maps: in Holy Roman Empire, 181–82; in Italian Fascism Empire, 179, 181–86; legibility of, 185; purpose of, 182; receptive context of, 185; semantic of colour, 182–83
Murray (publishing house), 109, 114
Muscovy Company, 51, 61
Mussolini, Benito, 177, 183. *See also* Italian Fascism Empire
mutable mobiles, maps as, 8, 110–11

naming, power of, 69
Nanatianus, Rutilius, 11
Nansen, Fridtjof, 132
Napoleon (Emperor), 143
Napoleonic Wars, 112
narwhals, as unicorns, 69
nationalism, methodological, 9–10

Native Americans: conversion of lands from, through delegitimization of ownership, 14; dispossession of land, 14, 78–79, 85–86; Iroquois Confederacy, 99
navigation: celestial, 39; conquest and, 175; empirical, 57; mapping and, 175; of oceans, 37. *See also* seafaring
Neocleous, Mark, 2, 108
Netherlands: Second Anglo Dutch War, 95. *See also* New Netherlands
New France, 94–95, 100
New Jersey, as colony, 77, *78*
New Netherlands, 100
New Spain, 32; French-Spanish border, 99
New World: Gutierrez map of, 40–41, *41*, 43; imaginary of discovery and, 19–20; mapping of, 13, 19–20; Spanish Empire in, 20–21. *See also* New Spain; North America; South America
New York, as colony, 95
Nietzsche, Friedrich, xviii
Nordby, Søren, 60–61
North America: Dutch West India Company, 94–95; English colonies in, boundaries of, 14, 83–85, 93–94, 98–100; geography and empire in, 59; New France, 94–95, 100; New Netherlands, 100; New Spain, 32, 99; Second Anglo Dutch War, 95. *See also* American colonies; New Spain
North Pole expeditions: Arctic Ocean region, 106–7, *128–29*; Austro-Hungarian North-Pole Expedition, 132; *Erebus,* 105–6, 127, 133n1; by Germany, 109, 127–33; *Terror,* 105–6, 127, 133n1. *See also* North-West Passage
North Sea Empire, 55
North-West Passage: Arctic Ocean region, 106–7, *128–29*; center of calculation and, 107; *Erebus,* 105–6, 127, 133n1; Franklin Expedition, 105–6, 119, 127; Frobisher and, 51, 64–65; Munk and, 70; Open Polar Sea theory, 106–7, 117, 127–32; *Terror,* 105–6, 127, 133n1
Norway: Denmark and, reconnection to, 60–64; in Kalmar Union, 72n3; mapping of Greenland by, 8; travel routes to Greenland, 60; in West Indies, colonization of, 73n14

oceans: mapping of, in Spanish Empire, 28–29; navigation of, 37. *See also* Arctic Ocean; seafaring
O'Gorman, Edmundo, 20–21
Old Roman Empire, 9
Olesen, Simon Mølholm, 68, 73n14
*On Exactitude in Science* (Borges), 1
Open Polar Sea theory, 106–7, 117, 127–32
ordering processes, in empires, 10
Ottoman Empire: dissolution of, 14–15; expansion of, 31; France in, 140–41; public debt administration, 170n11
Overweg, Adolf, 120
Owens, Patricia, 7, 79
ownership of land: in American colonies, 14; for Native Americans, delegitimization of, 14

Padrón, Ricardo, 20
*Padrón Real,* 13, 23, 32–33, 37
Pagden, Anthony, 24–25
Palestine, 169; *Carte du Liban,* 143; international administration of, 140; *Map of Western Palestine,* 143; Napoleon invasion of, 143
Palestine Exploration Fund, 143
Pan-Islamism, 164
Pan-Syrian nationalism, 169
Pan-Syrian nationalist narratives, 169
papacy, legitimization of Catholic Empire, in Spain, 25–26
Paris Treaty (1783), 85
passive space, 6, 108

Payer, Julius, 132
Peace Conference: Bernard on, 151–52, 154–56; for Middle East, 141, 144–45
Pennsylvania, as colony, 77, *78*, 98–99
Perthes, Johann George Justus, 113
Petermann, August, 14, 109, 113, 119, 132–33; Open Polar Sea theory, 106–7, 117, 127–32; Royal Geographic Society and, 115. *See also* Justus Perthes
*Petermann's Geographical Messages* (Petermann), 115
Philip II (King): accession to throne for, geopolitical circumstances of, 39; *Casa de Contratación de Sevilla*, 40–41; *Piloto Mayor,* 40–41; Spanish Empire and, 23, 25, 31, 39–43; Treaty of Cateau-Cambresis, 39–40, 42; Treaty of Tordesillas and, 40, 42
*Physical Atlas* (Berghaus), 116
*Piloto Mayor,* 35–37, 40–41
*Plat of the Seven Ranges of Townships, 91*, 100–101
Portugal, imperial expansionism by, 108
Portuondo, Maria, 34
*Poseidonians* (Cavafy), xv
possibilities, stratified conditions of, xvi
post-representational approach, to mapping, 5–6
power: through cartography, 1; through geography, 1
private property: in American colonies, 79. *See also* property rights
problematization: of empire, 23; Foucault on, 3; of representation, in mapping, 3–7
property rights: cartography and, 2; in England, 86
pseudotopographic maps, of Syria, 147
Ptolemy, 37, 62; cartography and, 83–85
publishing houses. *See specific publishing houses*
Punic Wars, 181

Rantzau, Breide, 69
Reclus, Élisée, 157, 162, 164
Reclus, Onésime, 148–49
Reconquista, 25
*De Reditu Suo* (Nanatianus), 11
reflexive knowledge, xvi
representation, 1; through cartography, homologies enabled by, 83–85; cartography as, 59; homologies enabled by, 83–85; post-representational approach, to mapping, 5; as space, 59
Resen, Peder Hansen, 71
Ribeiro, Diego, 13, 23, 37, *37*
Richardson, James, 120
Rittenhouse, David, 84
Rodriguez de Fonseca, Juan, 26
Romania, 152, 154
Royal Geographic Society, 106, 115–16, 120, 169n4

Sacrobosco, 37
Saletta, Tancredi, 175–76
Sánchez Martínez, Antonio, 32
Sanna, George, 151
scientific management, of cartography, 109–16; *tertium non datur*, 118
Scramble for Africa, 175, 196n1
seafaring: Frobisher's knowledge of, 51; Muscovy Company, 51; for North-West Passage, 51
Second Anglo Dutch War, 95
Second Ethiopian War, 177
*A Secret Atlas,* 58
Seed, Patricia, 52
Siam (Thailand), 142
Sixtus IV (Pope), 29
Society of Geographical and Colonial Studies of Florence, 196n1
Somalia, 184
Sound Dues, xxiin1
Sound of Toll Registers, xxiin1
South America: geography and empire in, 59. *See also* New Spain

sovereignty: through cartography, 2; over Greenland, by Denmark, 51–52
space: blank, 6, 108, 116–19; cartography as representation of, 59; global Christian, 13; identity and, relationship between, 195–96; imaginaries of, 3; invention of, 5; materialization of power in, 1; passive, 6, 108; political sensorial economy of, 15; world, 38
space-making, in empires: Italian Fascism Empire, 178; in Spanish Empire, 24–25
space-sensing, in Italian Fascism Empire, 178
Spain: Arianism in, conversion from Catholicism, 25; nation-building in, 25
Spanish Empire: artistic expression in, new forms of, 22; Catholic Empire in, 23, 25–30; under Charles I (Charles V), 23, 25, 30–39; conception of, 23–24, 44n1; connectivity in, 9; cultural genres in, creation of, 22; as epistemological formation, 43–44; in global trading circuit, establishment of, 44; House of Bourbon in, 44n1; imperial expansionism by, 108; imperial space-making in, 24–25; invention of, 21–23; mapping of New World, 20–21; mapping of ocean, 28–29; Moctezuma and, 31–32; *Padrón Real,* 13, 23, 32–33, 37; under Philip II, 23, 25, 31, 39–43; recognition of power of, 39; territorial claims of, in New World, 31; Tordesillas Line, 28–29; trade and exchange in, new terms of, 22; Treaty of Tordesillas, 28, 35, 40, 42, 44. *See also* New Spain; New World
Spanish Inquisition, 26
spatial epistemics, 176; communicative, 179
spatial imaginaries, xvi; map-making and, 7–9

spatiality: maps as representation of, 2; politics of, 1; from social practices, 169n6
Steudner, Hermann, 124
Stieler, Adolf, 114
*Stielers Hand-Atlas,* 114–15
Strandsbjerg, Jeppe, 108
stratified conditions of possibilities, xvi
surveying: in American colonies, 14, 79, 85; purpose of, 79
Swart, Claudius Claussøn (Claudius Clavus), 62–63, *63*
Sweden: Denmark and, 70–71; in Kalmar Union, 72n3
Sykes, Mark, 139–41, 163
Sykes-Picot Agreement, 140–41, 163
syncretism. *See* cultural syncretism
Syria: authoritative map of, 144; under British Mandate, 169n3; campaign for, 155–56, 168; cartographic strategies, 144–45; colonial networks in, 144–45; Deraa-Damas-Aleppo line, 163; economic development in, primacy of, 163; European cartography of, 142–44; fragmentation of, 163–64; in *France du Levant,* 145, 147–49, 151, 159, *160,* 161–62, 169; French control of, 139–40, 144–45, 156–57, 165; geo-bodies of, 142–44; geographical definition of, 161–62; as global rail hub, 157, 159; map of, *150, 153, 158, 166;* Maronites in, 165; Marseilles Congress in, 147–49, 154; Pan-Syrian nationalist narratives, 169; Peace Conference and, 141, 144–45, 151–52, 154–56; pseudotopographic maps of, 147; true boundary of, 162; unification of, 162–65, 167

*Terra Laboratories,* 63
*terra nullius,* Greenland as, 66–67
territories: boundaries for, through cartography, 2; Greenland, 52–53; imaginaries of space and, 3;

International Relations and, 10;
linearization of, 92–95, 97–100;
Spanish Empire claims of, in New
World, 31
*Terror* (ship), 105–6, 127, 133n1
Thirty Years War, 40
Thomeh, Abdullah, 156, 161–62
Thorlacius, Gudbrand, 70
Thorvaldsson, Erik (Eric the Red),
55–56
*Thus Spake Zarathustra* (Nietzsche),
xviii
Tinné, Alexine, 124
trading, global, by Spanish Empire,
establishment of, 44
Transjordan, 169
Treaty of Cateau-Cambresis, 39–40, 42
Treaty of St. Germain, 94
Treaty of Tordesillas, 28, 35, 40, 42, 44
Treaty of Zaragoza, 38
*Trost* (ship), 69–70
Turkey, 169
Turnbull, David, 110

U.K. *See* United Kingdom
unicorns: meaning of, in Denmark,
73n13; narwhals as, 69
United Kingdom (U.K.): British
Mandate, 169n3; Middle East treaty
with France, 139. *See also* England
United States (U.S.): Conojocular War,
98–99; early land sales, free market
for, 90; land ceded to, by England,
89; Land Ordinance of 1785, 89–90;
land speculation in, 90; *Plat of
the Seven Ranges of Townships,
91*, 100–101; U.S. Congress in,
land surveys and, 89–90, 92; War
of Independence and, 92. *See
also* American colonies; Native
Americans
Universal Monarchy, 31
urban streetscapes, in Italian Fascism
Empire, 181–86
U.S. *See* United States

Vespucci, Americo, 19–20, 35,
42, 45n3
Vidal de la Blache, Paul, 152–53
Vikings, Age of: empirical navigation
during, 57; expansion of, 56;
geographical connection during,
55; during Greenland, settlements
during, 51, 56; *Hauksbogen*, 57;
Iceland and, 56; *landnam* and,
56, 58; mapless empires and, 13;
North Sea Empire during, 55; oral
traditions, 57; uninhabited lands, 58
Virginia, as colony, 89, 92, 97–98
Vogel, Eduard, 116, 120, 123
von Bismarck, Otto, 128, 131
von Humboldt, Alexander,
116, 119
von Roon, Albrecht, 128
von Wrangel, Ferdinand, 107

Wadai Empire, 120–21, 124
Waldseemüller, Martin, 41, 63
Walkendorf, Erik, 60
War of Independence, 92
Washington, George, 87, 90
*Weltpolitik* (world politics), 109
Western imperialism, 2
West Indies, colonization of,
73n14
Westphalian tradition, International
Relations and, 10
Wilhelm I (Emperor), 132
Wing, John, 87
Winichakul, Thongchai, 142
Wood, Denis, 5
Woodward, David, 54, 59
*World Map* (Ribeiro), *37*
world politics. *See Weltpolitik*
world-space, 38

Yanez Pinzón, Vicente,
26, 35

Zionist nationalist movements, in
Middle East, 140

# About the Editors and Contributors

**Filipe dos Reis** is Assistant Professor of Geopolitics and Connectivity at the Department of International Relations and International Organization, University of Groningen. He completed his PhD in International Relations at the University of Erfurt, where he also held a position as research associate (*Wissenschaftlicher Mitarbeiter*) and has been a member at the Interdisciplinary Center of Political Practices and Orders. His current research focuses on the history and politics of international law, Imperial Germany and maps. He is co-editor (with Zeynep Gülşah Çapan and Maj Grasten) of *The Politics of Translation in International Relations* (Palgrave Macmillan, 2021).

**Kerry Goettlich** is Lecturer in International Security at the University of Reading. He previously completed his PhD in International Relations at the London School of Economics, where he was an editor of *Millennium: Journal of International Studies*. His current project examines the historical emergence of scientific practices underlying modern territoriality, such as border surveying, as they emerged in seventeenth-century colonial North America and were globalized in the late nineteenth century. His work has appeared in the *European Journal of International Relations* and the *Oxford Research Encyclopedia of International Studies*.

**Louis Le Douarin** is a geographer who is completing his doctoral dissertation at the European University Institute in Florence (Department of History and Civilization). His research focuses on the production and circulation of geographical and cartographical knowledge in Syria and Lebanon before and during the French Mandate, and on the role this knowledge played in the transformation of the region's political geography. He is currently research and teaching assistant in geography at the University of Aix-en-Provence Marseille.

**Luis Lobo-Guerrero** is Professor of History and Theory of International Relations at the University of Groningen where he chairs the department under this name. He is also director of the Centre for International Relations Research. His current work explores the invention of globality in the early modern period. As part of the trilogy of books of which this volume is part, he was co-editor of *Imaginaries of Connectivity: The Creation of Novel Spaces of Governance* together with Suvi Alt and Maarten Meijer (Rowman & Littlefield, 2020). His monographs include *Insuring Security: Biopolitics, Security and Risk* (Routledge, 2011), *Insuring War: Sovereignty, Security and Risk* (2012) and *Insuring Life: Value, Security and Risk* (2016).

**Laura Lo Presti** is Postdoctoral Researcher at the Centre for Advanced Studies in Mobility and the Humanities, hosted at the University of Padova. She is also Visiting Research Fellow at The Groningen University Research Institute for the Study of Culture (ICOG). Her current research focuses on the cultural ecologies and the technological and political conditions that allow maps and mapping to elicit a plethora of discourses, actions and feelings about the European migrant crisis and its forms of hierarchized mobilities. Her publications include a book, *Cartografie (In)esauste* (FrancoAngeli, 2019) and several articles published in international journals such as *Political Geography*, *Dialogues in Human Geography*, *Mobilities* and *Acme*.

**Jeppe Strandsbjerg** is Editor-in-Chief at Djøf Publishing, Senior Researcher at the Danish Institute for International Studies and Visiting Research Fellow at the Groningen Research Institute for the Study of Culture (ICOG). He holds a doctorate degree in International Relations from the University of Sussex. He has mostly written on the concept of space in international relations with a particular focus on cartography. He is the author of *Territory, Globalization and International Relations: The Cartographic Reality of Space* (Palgrave 2010) and co-editor (with Lars Bo Kaspersen) of *Does War Make States? Investigations of Charles Tilly's Historical Sociology* (Cambridge University Press, 2017) and (with Ulrik Pram Gad) of *The Politics of Sustainability in the Arctic: Reconfiguring Identity, Space, and Time* (Routledge, 2019).

www.ingramcontent.com/pod-product-compliance
Lightning Source LLC
Chambersburg PA
CBHW052037300426
44117CB00012B/1855